DANTE ALIGHIERI

Dante Alighieri

CITIZEN OF CHRISTENDOM

GERALD G. WALSH, S.J.

THE BRUCE PUBLISHING COMPANY
MILWAUKEE

Imprimi potest: F. A. McQuade, S.J., Praep. Prov. (N. Y.)
Nihil obstat: John A. Schulien, Censor librorum
Imprimatur: ✠ Moyses E. Kiley, Archiepiscopus Milwaukiensis
July 31, 1946

SORORI DILECTAE
A. E. F.

Contents

DANTE ALIGHIERI

Prologue

If I should prove a timid friend to truth,
I fear to lose my fame among the folk
Whose age will call this present epoch "ancient."[1]

DANTE ALIGHIERI was born in Florence, toward the end of May, in the year of our Lord, 1265. In 1274, before he was nine, he fell passionately in love with a little girl called Beatrice. By 1283, this "glorious mistress of my mind" had lifted him to what he calls the "very limits of beatitude." Seven years later, in 1290, when Beatrice went to heaven, the poet soared, in "thought" and "sorrowing heart," above the stars and there remained, "spiritually, like a pilgrim beyond the frontiers of his native land."[2]

Ten years after that, in 1300, Dante was elected to the highest political office in the fiercely competitive democracy of Florence. He became, so to speak, the mayor of medieval New York. In that same year he went on a pilgrimage to Rome, the capital of Christendom, and wrote, it would seem, the first cantos of the *Divine Comedy*. Between 1300 and the date of his death, he wrote a number of songs (*Rime*[3]), a "banquet" (*Convivio*[4]) of philosophical essays in Italian prose, a work in Latin on artistic language (*De vulgari eloquentia*[5]), another on the government of "one world" (*Monarchia*[6]), and a third on "global hydrography" (*Quaestio de aqua et terra*[7]). Besides these we have from his pen thirteen letters (*Epistole*[8]), and two poems

[1] *Paradiso*, xvii, 118–120.
[2] *Vita Nuova*, ii, 1; iii, 1; xli, 5. The references to all works of Dante are to *Le Opere di Dante*, Testo critico della Società Dantesca Italiana, Firenze, 1921.
[3] *Op. cit.*, 57–139.   [5] *Op. cit.*, 319–352.   [7] *Op. cit.*, 467–480.
[4] *Op. cit.*, 147–315.   [6] *Op. cit.*, 355–412.   [8] *Op. cit.*, 415–446.

(*Egloghe*[9]) written in rather remarkable Virgilian hexameters. He died in 1321.

Taken separately, these dates may seem without significance. Taken together, they mean that Dante was born in antiquity, died in the modern age, and commuted, for most of his life, between this world and the world to come. It was a relatively short life of fifty-six years, but between its beginning and its end there yawns a chasm that cuts in two the whole history of Western man.

To measure the chasm it is enough to recall two names: St. Thomas Aquinas (1225–1274), the "angelic doctor," the clearest head and most authentic voice of the thirteenth century; and Francesco Petrarca (1304–1374), the "first modern man," the tender and tormented heart that heralds the world in which we live.

In 1265, the year of Dante's birth, St. Thomas began his series of Commentaries on the *Physics, Metaphysics,* and *Ethics* of Aristotle. Between the pagan philosopher, writing in ancient Athens, and the Dominican friar, lecturing in the convent of Santa Sabina in medieval Rome, lay sixteen fateful centuries, filled with private passions and public wars, the rise and fall of the Roman Empire, the birth and unbounded expansion of the Church of Jesus Christ. To read the Commentaries you would never guess it. They are a calm profession of cultural continuity. The philosopher and saint are citizens of "one world." Their central convictions are identical. Both men acknowledged the same objective, universal laws of being, thought, and action. They were both quite certain that seventeen times twenty-three made, had made, and always would make 391. That same calculation, they knew, could be made by anyone who would use his head or hands, and the conclusion would apply with equal validity to all kinds of things, from clods of clay to kings. Aristotle and St. Thomas shared identical definitions of one and many, true and false, good and bad, right and wrong, fair and foul, thought and thing, "form" and "matter," "act" and "potency," liberty and law, man and nature. The ideas of these things seemed to them clear, distinct, unchanging. Both men were equally aware that some things, like moods and manners, languages and customs, climate and clouds, change with time and place and circumstance. They were equally convinced that other realities, like the essential dignity, duty, and rights of rational human beings, are always and everywhere the same.

[9] *Op. cit.,* 456–463.

Both men believed in the validity of knowledge and the primacy of reason — and that both in private and political life. Conscience and law for them were other names for reason; the one produced order in the soul, the other order in society. Both men recognized an innate power in the human spirit to find and follow the path of reason in a wood of passion. This power makes men free, and makes them persons. No less innate, it seemed to them, was the urgency in human nature to seek happiness and perfection in ordered institutions.

This ancient age of reason may seem to us to have been a closed-in world. If you dashed down the dark corridors of lust, looking for escape, there at the door stood conscience, adamantine, flail in hand, demanding that you thresh the wheat of rational choice from the chaff of irrational desire. At the end of every avenue of social, economic, political life, justice stood at the gate, scale in hand, insisting that you weigh the greed of your prices, profits, rents, or foreign policy against the gold of her untarnishable reason. It was the same at the skylights, giving on to the stars, and at the windows high above the mud-filled moat. There stood common sense challenging pride with: "Better try the wings of reason before you leap or soar."

Things were different in 1321 when Dante died. The doors, gates, windows, skylights, and even the drawbridge stood wide open. The heart was more than the head, the eyes more seeing than the soul, the part more important than the whole. The new age of romanticism, nominalism, nationalism, individualism called for new norms. The tyranny of reason was over.

In 1321, the "first modern man" was in the full flush of his eighteenth year. He was studying, very much against his will, Aristotle and Roman law at the university of Montpellier in the south of France. His father, made rich by politics, had been banished from Florence along with Dante in 1302. The boy had been made to study Latin, logic, and law, not for the sake of intelligence, conscience, or community service, but as a means to the practical purpose of prosperous living.

Francesco at seventeen was not yet a "pragmatist"; he would not have called himself a "nominalist" in philosophy, or a "nationalist" in politics, or even an "individualist." He thought of himself as a poet, a man of feeling and fancy. But primacy had shifted from the head to the heart. He hated logic, metaphysics, and law. He hated the name of Aristotle. He loved language and learning, art and nature. Later he would love Laura and Italy, his native land. At all times he loved himself. He was too confused in mind or too cowardly in will to cast off altogether the rags and tatters of the Middle Ages. He would write — as though he were still an "ancient" rather than a "modern man" — on "contempt for the world" and "monastic life" and the "true wisdom" of faith. Nevertheless, the key to his life was ardor; not, as in the case of St. Thomas and Aristotle, order. Will, not reason, was his sovereign ruler. He loved what his heart liked, not what his head thought good.

Between the ancient age of reason, into which Dante was born, and the modern age of revolt, in which he died, falls the *Divine Comedy*. It fills the chasm between these two worlds. It is a bridge between the age of the head and the age of the heart. Even before the *Divine Comedy* was conceived, the young Dante had begun to build for himself such a bridge. "Love," he says on the first page of his first book, "was the lord of my soul." He immediately adds: "Never did love rule me without the faithful counsel of reason."[10]

It is this sublime contradiction, this seemingly double allegiance to the "lordship of love" and the "rule of reason," that makes Dante so important today.

We have now seen more of the age of revolt than Petrarca, Ockham, or the contemporary kings of France could ever have imagined to be possible. We have begun to wonder whether the heart is not in need of the head; whether "names" and "things" and "science" can dispense with conceptions, ideas, and invisible values; whether efficiency and political power can be trusted with sovereign control over human persons. Our statesmen, economists, and even our scientists are clamoring for "one world." Our educators answer: A chimera, a leviathan, unless it can be peopled with "whole men." *One, whole, man, world* — all four words are, as it were, reeking with metaphysics — and not only with metaphysics, but with religion as well.

In calling Dante a "citizen of Christendom," I am here suggesting that he may be the kind of "whole man" that our educators are looking for, the kind of man the age of tomorrow will need as a citizen of its "one world." I am also venturing to hint that the only kind of a world that can long remain "one" may prove to be a world that has its roots deep in Christendom.

[10] *Vita Nuova*, ii, 7, 9.

The first three lectures are unconscionably dull. There is a preliminary distinction between the "Dante" of the Poem and the Dante of history which may prove annoying to the expert and boring to the average reader. Lectures two and three are written in the flat style of narrative history. They should be skipped by those who are impatient of humdrum facts. In one sense, however, they seem to me important. They reveal Dante as a "common" man of Christendom in the lowly sense of a man who needed a home where he could love his father and mother, a school where he could learn the wisdom of the past, a wife who could take care of his children, a city in which he could see men and women striving, however falteringly, to achieve some kind of common good, a Church to illumine human dignity by faith in immortal destiny. Only such a "common" man, it may be, can be trusted to become a "community" man, a man fitted to be a citizen of a world community. Some among us who talk most loudly of "one world" have been quite unsuccessful in running one home — or even in running one person.

And now a word to those readers who were kind enough to listen to the lectures when they were first delivered in the public library, Copley Square, Boston, between November 9 and December 4, 1945.

You may miss, I fear, the music of those Italian lines that sound so lovely to the ear but which would clutter a page that is printed for the eye. And, second, you may miss the salt of those improvised *obiter dicta* that seemed to help you swallow the lectures, but which would be out of place in a book. One of these I may be allowed to recall, since it has some relevance to the main point of this Prologue. It was about Beatrice, Descartes, and the chasm between the medieval and the modern worlds.

I was saying that what happens in an artist's eye, head, heart, and hand may help us glimpse, however faintly, something of what theologians like Dante mean by the "mysteries" of the Trinity and Creation. The artist looks at a sunset; God looks at Himself. The artist sees a vision. It is passing as thought, indelible as memory. God sees a Vision of His infinite Being. It is not merely indelible. It is permanent, subsistent, incommunicable, living — a Person, the Word, the Logos, the Son. The artist falls in love with his vision. His passion is fleeting as emotion but potent as energy. It imperatively demands expression. God falls in love with His Vision. This love, like the Logos, is an eternal Person — the Holy Spirit. The artist with a passionate vision is driven, as we now say, to "create" — a painting, a poem, a song. The word "create" (like that most indispensable of all words in modern democratic political theory — a "person") is taken straight (seldom with acknowledgment) from the lexicon of those old fogeys, the theologians. God, the supreme Artist, creates. The energy of His Vision of Infinite Perfection passes, with the irrepressible urgency of divine Love, into the void. It does so, as Beatrice reminds us, "not for any good He could get in return, for that is impossible, but merely that the echo of His splendor may become a living voice that can say: 'I am,'" *subsisto*.[11]

God thinks; therefore, I am. That was the deepest wisdom of the Middle Ages. *I* think; therefore, I am. That was the wisdom of Descartes. And out of his wisdom our modern world has evolved its various forms of idealism, its unsubstantialities, its mental and moral vacuum, and all those things, like totalitarian tyranny and world wars, that fit so nicely into such a vacuum. Between "God thinks" and "Descartes thinks" lies the chasm that separates two worlds.

I put all that more happily when I spoke to you in Boston; but for what it is worth it must serve as a token of all the other odds and ends that are here omitted. I shall only add that if Ralph Lowell had not asked me — with a little prodding, I suspect, from the late, lamented Mr. Rand and my friend, Msgr. John Wright — to deliver the lectures, this book would not have been written. It would not have been published so soon but for the kindness of another friend, Mr. Joseph White.

[11] *Par.*, xxix, 15.

I

When Love Lectures in the Heart

. . . I am a man who, when
Love lectures in the heart, takes notes, and then
Retells the lessons to the rest of men.[1]

I

"DANTE"

IT IS sometimes said that the *Divine Comedy* is hard to understand. It is, in fact, no more difficult than opening a door. It is difficult only if one has lost the key or if one tries to use a wrong one.

So, too, with Dante Alighieri, the author of the Poem. It is often assumed that he was a person of harsh, abnormal, complicated character, a person hard to understand and impossible to like. That is because the "Dante" of the Poem is presumed to be the person who wrote it.

It is well to take a look at this "Dante" before turning to the Dante of history. In the opening scene of the *Inferno*, he is a man "half way through the pilgrimage of human life,"[2] that is to say, a man of thirty-five. He has lost his way in a "dark wood." But this is not a real wood. The "dark wood" is a symbol of ignorance and sin, of darkness in the mind and wanderings in the will. "Dante" is assailed by three beasts; not real beasts, but symbols of human passions, of pride and greed and lust. Then the poet Virgil comes to the rescue. He says that he was a Mantuan; that he was born in the days of Julius Caesar; that he lived at Rome under the "good Augustus, at the time of the false and lying gods"; that he was a poet who

[1] *Purgatorio*, xxiv, 52–54.
[2] *Inferno*, i, 1.

7

sang of the "just son of Anchises." And yet, as the Poem proceeds, this "Virgil" turns out to be quite unlike the historical Virgil. He has Boethius and St. Thomas Aquinas and all kinds of medieval learning at his finger tips. He is, in fact, a symbol — a symbol of the authority of reason in the guidance of human life.

In the presence of this Virgil, "Dante" becomes a different "Dante." The victim of pride and lust becomes the humble admirer of "the honor and light of all the other poets."[3] His new passions are those of the scholar and artist — for truth and beauty. But not for long. In the next canto another "Dante" appears. He is a Hamlet-like creature who cannot make up his mind whether to follow "Virgil" or not. His resolution is "sicklied o'er with the pale cast of thought."[4] He becomes, in fact, a plain coward — like the man in canto III "who made the great refusal."[5] Then "Dante" is told that Beatrice and the court of heaven have taken pity on his plight. At once, the coward is filled with courage and chivalrous ardor.[6]

Perhaps in canto IV we may feel we have the real Dante. We meet in limbo the great poets of antiquity, Homer and Horace, Ovid and Lucan; and these four along with Virgil nominate Dante to the sixth place in the "society of supreme song." Dante takes the honor handsomely with a kind of austere and classic nobility, without the complaints of a false humility or the complacency of pride. But then in canto V, the canto of Paolo and Francesca, we have a different "Dante." From the classicism of the "noble castle" we are plunged into the torments of romanticism. In all literature there is, perhaps, no more poignant song of romantic passion than Dante's tragic tale of Paolo and Francesca. To the lost lovers, tossed and tormented by the eternal tempest of their passion, without hope of respite, without hope even of lesser pain, our "Dante" seems a "living creature gracious and benign."[7] For all the stern unbending theology in his head, he has such a tender and understanding heart! He understands what sweet thoughts, what tremendous passion brought the lovers to their "dolorous pass." He breaks down and sobs. And when Francesca has told her story to the bitter end, the

[3] *Inf.*, i, 82.
[4] *Pensando consumai la 'mpresa. Inf.*, ii, 41.
[5] . . . *che fece per viltà il gran rifiuto.* Cf. *Inf.*, ii, 45, with *Inf.*, iii, 60.
[6] *Inf.*, ii, 131.
[7] . . . *animal grazioso e benigno. Inf.*, iv, 88.

romantic "Dante" collapses completely. He fell "as a dead body falls."[8]

We turn the page and find ourselves half in tears, half in laughter, in the company of a great fat lubber of a politician, Ciacco, the glutton of Florence and a friend of Dante. We wonder whether our hero has not turned into a tavern-haunting rollicker with a boon companion. With canto VII we turn a somersault. "Dante" is now deep in philosophy, discussing with Virgil the strange revolutions of the wheel of fortune, the mysterious vicissitudes of men and nations.

For all I know, it may be possible to make a single person out of all these "Dantes"; and that person, in fact, may be the author of the *Divine Comedy*. But it is difficult if not impossible to fit into this picture the monster of brutality who appears in canto VIII. Safe in a boat with Virgil, "Dante" is crossing a marsh of black water and unmentionable filth. A poor devil of a damned soul emerges from the filth. "See," he says, "I am a man who moans."[9] "Dante" shoots back: "Remain, damned spirit, in your grief and groans, because for all your filth, I know you." The poor wretch then stretches out both his hands toward the boat. By what seems a horribly mean trick, "Dante" makes Virgil utter the words that were on his own lips: "Get thee gone with the other dogs."[10] Then says "Dante": "Master I should like to see him soused in this broth before we leave the lake." And sure enough the whole fellowship of filth shouted: "Let's get Filippo Argenti." "Dante" saw such a rending of the wretch that — so he says, with revolting smugness — years later he praised and thanked God for the sight!

You can find a dozen more and different "Dantes" in the remaining cantos of the *Inferno*. One of the most interesting is the archaristocrat of canto X. Another is the highly serious moral philosopher of canto XI. One of the most appealing is the affectionately grateful scholar of canto XV. "Dante" becomes, seemingly, more heartless as he descends deeper into hell. For all his "reverence for the papal keys,"[11] he is merciless in reproaching the tortured shade of the Orsini Pope, Nicholas III. But a little later the bold-tongued "Dante" turns into a rather weak-kneed victim of fright and nervous imaginings. "Master," he whines, "if you do not quickly

[8] *Inf.*, v, 142.
[9] *Inf.*, viii, 36.
[10] *Inf.*, viii, 42.
[11] . . . *la reverenza de le somme chiavi. Inf.*, xix, 101.

hide yourself and me, I fear the Malebranche. We have them right behind us. In my imagination I can feel that they are already on us."[12] In canto xxiv he sinks down fainthearted and fatigued and pleads that he can go no farther; it takes a long speech of Virgil to "unpoltroon" him. In the deepest pit of hell, "Dante" is as cold and relentless as the ice of the Lake of Cocytus.

Taken all together these "Dantes" add up to a problem rather than to a person. They make an all but impossible combination of pride and humility, envy and charity, anger and meekness, sloth and energy. To assume that the historical Dante Alighieri was a compound of such contradictory passions and virtues is to try to open the door of understanding with the wrong key.

There is no difficulty if we take the "Dante" of the *Inferno* as a symbol of mature human nature, as "Everyman" in the prime of life, alert like Faust in the vigor of all his powers and passions.

A notable change comes over this symbolic Dante after he has emerged from hell and finds himself on the shores of the hill of purgatory. He seems to be at least ten years older, as though he had passed from the second period of life to the third, from the "youth" (*giovanezza*) that ends at forty-five to the senescence (*senettute*) that, according to Dante's *Convivio* lasts from forty-five to seventy.[13] Like most men in this third period of life he is moved by the changing aspects of physical nature. He takes delight in the "sweet color of oriental sapphire."[14] When the sun is about to rise he notices the "trembling of the sea."[15] His movements are slower. He is now more willing to "go in heart and in his body linger."[16] Along with his love of nature is a love of art. When he meets an old friend, Casella, he is delighted to listen to him sing. He has to be scolded for his sloth by the old man, Cato. Dante's whole life now becomes more interior. He is less interested in action than in observation and reflection; he takes delight in describing minutely the slow, short, lazy words and movements of Belacqua, who seemed to him the very brother of sloth herself. In the early cantos of the *Purgatory* there are magnificent stories of Manfred and Buonconte da Montefeltro, but they are tales of men's pious deaths rather than of their active lives. In canto vi there is a tremendous invective on divided Italy, but it is the invective not of a man engaged in the battle, but of one whose battling days are

[12] *Inf.*, xxiii, 24.   [14] *Purg.*, i, 13.   [16] *Purg.*, ii, 12.
[13] *Convivio*, IV, xxiv, 4.   [15] *Purg.*, ii, 17.

over.[17] When Sordello leads Dante to the valley of the negligent kings, he merely listens and makes no comment. "He" is now like the noble Judge Nino de' Visconti who when he spoke was "stamped with the righteous zeal that glows with due measure in the heart."[18] When at last Dante passes up the three steps of contrition, confession, and satisfaction, he becomes a plain, humble Christian who throws himself at the feet of the angel of God to ask for mercy and pardon.

In canto x and the following cantos of the *Purgatory* the symbolic Dante comes close to the real Dante. He shows an artist's delight in the marvelous carvings that seemed to him like "visible speech," *visibile parlare*.[19] He is ready to discuss the relative merits of Cimabue and Giotto in painting, of Guido Guinizelli, Guido Cavalcanti, and Dante Alighieri in poetry.[20] The Dante of canto xii admires the exquisite shading effects in the carvings below his feet, shadings that "would make a subtle genius marvel."[21] The sculptured dead seemed really dead and the sculptured living really living so that, says Dante, no one looking at reality could have seen better than he could see.[22]

In canto xvi the artist turns into a political philosopher; he agrees completely with the ideas of Marco Lombardo on the separation of Church and State and on the proper relations of liberty and law. In the next two cantos he appears in the role of moral philosopher, as he listens with approval to Virgil's great exposition of the ethical basis of human responsibility.

Toward the end of canto xx an earthquake seems to shake the whole mount of purgatory. It was a signal for the liberation from purgatorial pain of the soul of Statius, the Latin poet and teacher, who, according to Dante in the *Convivio,* was a great exponent of the virtues of early adolescence in the home and the school. The "Dante" of cantos xxi to xxv is curiously like a symbol of youth at school. His main enemy is now ignorance.[23] His predominant passion is now thirst for knowledge.[24] He listens eagerly to Statius' highly academic lecture on the supernatural seismology and meteorology of the mount.[25] He listens, too, with bursting interest when Statius speaks of his literary devotion to Virgil and, still more, when he learns that the reading of Virgil was the occasion of his conversion to Christianity.

In canto xxiii this symbol of adolescent human nature, of *puerizia,*

[17] *Purg.,* vi, 76–151.
[18] *Purg.,* viii, 83, 4.
[19] *Purg.,* x, 95.
[20] *Purg.,* xi, 94 ff.
[21] *Purg.,* xii, 66.
[22] *Ibid.,* 68.
[23] *Purg.,* xx, 145, 6.
[24] *Purg.,* xxi, 1, 6.
[25] *Purg.,* xxi, 40–72.

again seems to come close to the real Dante, to Dante as he was known to his wife and children, to his relatives and friends. Canto XXIII is devoted to the least poetical of all the human failings, to the venial sin of eating not wisely but too well. The poor sinners, with dark hollow eyes, were reduced to unrecognizable bags of skin and bone. Among these sinners Dante meets his dear friend, Forese Donati, over whose dead face he had wept bitter tears.[26] Forese has a tender word for his widow Nella, whose devout prayers and pious grief had been heard by God and had lessened his pains in purgatory. In contrast, he has a harsh word for the *sfacciate donne fiorentine,* the "shameless dames who strut about with neck and breasts all bare." In the following canto he makes an unforgettable allusion to his sister, Piccarda, who was "so good and so fair" he didn't know which to call her first.[27] Then he points out some of his fellow sinners. Among them is an old-fashioned poet of Lucca, Bonagiunta Orbicciani degli Overardi. Bonagiunta, seeing Dante, asks if he has before him the poet of the "sweet new style," the *dolce stil novo,* the author of the canzone, *Donne ch' avete intelletto d'amore.* Dante answers with what seems to me the most perfect of all pictures of himself. "I am a man," he says, "who when love lectures in my heart takes notes, and then retells the lessons to the rest of men,"

> . . . *I mi son un, che quando*
> *Amor mi spira noto, e a quel modo*
> *ch'ei ditta dentro vo significando.*[28]

II

DANTE ALIGHIERI

It is with this Dante — Dante, the lover, listening to the lectures in his heart and Dante the artist, retelling the lessons to the rest of men — that I intend to deal in these eight lectures.

One lecture, of course, will be about Beatrice. The love that lectured in Dante's heart was, at least in the beginning, a romantic love. It was this love that dictated the first of the sonnets that appear in his romantic autobiography, the *Vita Nuova.* It begins: "To every gentle heart and soul in love," *A ciascun alma presa e gentil core.* It is a

---

[26] *Purg.,* xxiii, 55, 56.   [27] *Purg.,* xxiv, 13, 14.   [28] *Purg.,* xxiv, 52, 53.

musical little song, with something that may seem to a modern taste rather primitive or, at any rate, "precious." In the last six lines, Love is pictured holding Dante's flaming heart in one hand while in his arms he carries the lightly veiled and sleeping Beatrice. Beatrice is awakened; she begins, bashfully, to feed on the flaming heart, as in a kind of holy communion of romantic love. A rough rendering of these lines might run something like this:

> At first, the lord of love seemed gladsome, keeping
>   My heart within his hand and, on his arm,
> My lady, covered with a veil and sleeping.
>
> Then, wakened, of my heart with flames upleaping
>   She ate in lowliness and much alarm.
> Then, Love I saw go on his way aweeping.[29]

That is, obviously, the dream of a very young man deep in romantic love, put into a song that has few if any overtones of allegory or of supernatural sublimation.

Nevertheless, at the time when Dante came to write his romantic autobiography, love seems to have meant more than his first sonnet indicates. You get a hint of this on the very first page of the *Vita Nuova.* Where you would expect Beatrice to be called "the lady of my heart," she is called, in fact, the "glorious mistress of my mind," *la gloriosa donna della mia mente.* That word *gloriosa* suggests more than our vague word "glorious." There is a hint in it of that heavenly glory which is higher than supernatural grace on earth and, therefore, much higher than any kind of merely natural grace or feminine beauty. And the word *mente,* "mind," is a reminder that Dante was in love not merely with beauty but with truth.

One has only to read a few pages of Dante's *Convivio* to realize how sincerely and how deeply its author was in love with truth. He took the word "philosophy" in its literal Greek sense of a love of wisdom, but he meant by love an emotion as passionate as romantic feeling. Take, for example, an outburst like this: "O dear and indescribable glances, when the demonstrations of philosophy ravish of a

---

[29] It sounds, of course, more musical than that in the original:
> *Allegro mi sembrava Amor tenendo*
>   *meo core in mano, e ne le braccia avea*
>   *madonna involta in un drappo dormendo.*
>   *Poi la svegliava, e d'esto core ardendo*
>   *lei paventosa umilmente pascea;*
>   *appresso gir lo ne vedea piangendo* (Vita Nuova, iii).

sudden the mind of a man like the eyes of a lady flashing upon her lovers. What can I call it but a sort of salvation, a species of beatific vision, when the lovers of wisdom, basking in a light like this, are redeemed from the death of ignorance and sin."[30]

A third love that lectured in Dante's heart was the love not of beauty or of truth but of goodness, the love of rectitude, the love of personal righteousness and of political justice. He says quite plainly in his Latin work, *De vulgari eloquentia,* that he considered himself not a poet of love or of chivalry but a singer of moral virtue. In one of his letters he defines himself "a man at home in philosophy . . . a man preaching justice."[31] One of the most remarkable of his *canzoni* is a song on righteousness, *Tre donne intorno al cor mi son venute.*[32] It deals with conscience, law, and grace. It is the crowning triumph of Virgil in the Poem that he leads the symbolic Dante to a point where conscience becomes the undisputed sovereign and master of his moral life. "I have brought you to this point with genius and with art. Now take conscience for your guide. . . . Your will is free, up-right, and sound and it would be an error not to follow where it leads. And so I give you a crown and a doctor's cap," that is, authority to rule and teach yourself.[33]

Dante loved not merely the inner kingship of conscience, but also, the outer lordship of public law. As conscience is the key to inner freedom from passion, so is law the guarantor of external, political liberty. This is the meaning of the conclusion of Marco Lombardo's discourse on personal and political freedom in the sixteenth canto of the *Purgatory*: "We take the wrong road . . . unless our love is led or bridled. Hence law is needed to serve as a bridle; we need as king one who can discern at least the towers of the true city."[34] We shall understand little of the passion that produced the beauty of the *Divine Comedy,* if we forget Dante's love of righteousness in both public and in private life.

Beyond this human goodness of moral and political peace, Dante fell in love with ultimate goodness, that is to say, with God. This is what Beatrice means when she tells Dante that she has led him "to love the good beyond which there is nothing for the heart to long for."[35] The *Paradiso* from its opening line, *La gloria di colui che*

[30] *Conv.* II, xv, 4.
[31] *Epist.,* xii, 6, 7. *Absit a viro phylosophie domestico . . . a viro predicante iustitiam.*
[32] *Rime,* civ.   [34] *Purg.,* xvi, 92–96.
[33] *Purg.,* xxvii, 121–142.   [35] *Purg.,* xxxi, 23.

. *tutto move,* to its last line, *L'amor che move il sole e l'altre stelle,* is
an eloquent witness of a soul passionately in love with the truth and
beauty and goodness of God. So it is that we shall need to know something of Dante not only as a philosopher but also as a theologian.

There may be a still higher level of Dante's love and art. Beyond
his love for the mysteries of faith as revealed by Scripture and the
Church, he seems to feel a passion for a beauty that distills its joy
only in a special kind of personal, religious experience. There is a
hint of this in such lines as these in the twenty-seventh canto of the
Paradiso:

> I heard such songs, and saw such things, and after
>   Was so inebriated with delight,
> The very universe seemed one long laughter.
>
> O life of love and unperturbèd peace,
>   O unimaginable plenitude
> Of blessedness's infinite increase.[36]

Long after Beatrice in the Poem has bidden Dante her last fare-
well, and has taken up her place as a petal in the "sempiternal rose,"
Dante goes on listening to Love lecturing in his heart. Only, they are
lectures that can no longer be taken down in notes; still less, can the
lessons be retold to the rest of men. When, in his last blinding vision,
he sees "the scattered leaves of all the universe, bound by love in a
single book," he seems conscious of an apparently ineffable contact
with an ultimate and undifferentiated light, *un semplice lume;* his
spirit, "fixed, immobile, attentive" and on fire, is purely passive. Love
then speaks to him love's last word. And all Dante can say is: "Oh
but how short is song, how weak to utter thought, and thought, to
what I saw, how less it is than little."[37] The fact that Dante's art could
keep pace — or nearly so — with these high flights of metaphysical (if
not mystical) love is proof that the *dolce stil novo* means, in the concrete, more than mere romantic poetry.

On the other hand, the "sweet new style" means something less. It
was used to tell in song the simpler lessons that Dante learned from
life and books. The Poem is full of wide and varied scholarship. The
erudition is inextricably bound up with some of the poet's loveliest
music and his most important meaning. To try to cut it out is to

---

[36] *Par.,* xxvii, 4–9.
[37] *Par.,* xxxiii, 121–123.

inflict a grievous wound on the living tissue of the Poem as a whole. For that reason we must know something of Dante's education.

Dante the lover, artist, philosopher, and theologian was a Florentine, an Italian, and a citizen of Christendom. He was a passionate publicist. His vision of his city, his country, and his world can only be separated from his "poetry" by an act of aesthetic abdication. If we are not to renounce an immense inheritance of enjoyment we must grasp at least the outlines of his world and the general character of his personality and life.

III

BLOOD AND BONES

There is, finally, a still more lowly Dante about which something should be said. There is the little mass of blood and bones that came into the world when Dante, as he puts it, "first felt the Tuscan air."[38] From those bones we can learn much that is important for us to know. They have had a somewhat exciting history. When Dante died in 1321, they were buried with honor in a classical sarcophagus in Ravenna. Later on, Florence made many attempts to recover them. Finally, in 1519, there was a command from the pope that the bones be returned to Florence. Jealous of their great treasure, the Franciscan friars of Ravenna stole the bones from the sarcophagus and put them into hiding. Eventually the secret of the hiding place was lost. Only in 1865, when the world was preparing to celebrate the sixth centenary of Dante's birth, were they discovered by the sheerest of accidents. They had been hidden in a walled-up door. On May 27 of that year this door was broken open. A stonemason struck the wood of a small box. On the box were found the words, *Ossa Dantis*. The bones of Dante had been found. Some of the bones had been lost or stolen. Those that remained were subjected to a scientific examination by Giovanni Puglioli and Claudio Bertuzzi. They weighed, measured, photographed, and catalogued the bones and wrote a book about them.

In 1921, on the occasion of the celebration of the sixth centenary of Dante's death, Professor Fabio Frassetto of Bologna was allowed to

[38] *Par.*, xxii, 117.

subject the bones to a second and more careful scientific examination. In a book, *Ossa Dantis,* Professor Frassetto has set forth his findings. Dante's cranial capacity was found to be exceptionally large; the calculated weight of the brains is enormously in excess of the average; a good deal in excess of the average of recognized world geniuses. An attempt was made to arrive at an index of Dante's mental capacity. Representing average mental capacity by an index of 2.7, Dante's was found to be 3.25.

His stature was small. As he walked about the streets of Ravenna stooping somewhat by reason of his arthritis he could not have been more than five foot, three inches. The most interesting part of Professor Frassetto's work was the preparation of a series of cranial outlines corresponding in size and position to all the more important representations of Dante in art. The outlines were then compared. Under this test the painting of Dante attributed to Giotto comes out with triumphant exactitude in regard to the sweep of the forehead, the moderate aquilinity of the nose, the prominence of the zygomatic arches, the ample and vertical orbit of the eye, the position of the lips and the slightly protruding chin. The so-called "death masks" were found definitely defective in one or more points. The Kirkup mask, while generally correct, is at fault in the slope of the forehead. The same must be said of the Torrigiani mask in the Bargello, in Florence. Equally incorrect, especially in the narrowness and slope of the forehead, is the bust preserved in the National Museum at Naples.

Professor Frassetto's final preference, in the light of the criteria of science, art, and spiritual interpretation, is for the bust by Vincenzo Vela in the Turin Museum of Modern Art. It appears as the frontispiece of this book. The defect of a slightly exaggerated massiveness of the forehead is accepted as artistic license to interpret the impression of spiritual greatness. The rest of the profile is in rigorous conformity with the scientific findings made available by Professor Frassetto.

We have a tendency to imagine that Dante must have had a "Dantesque" appearance; that he must have looked like one or other of the fierce or brooding creations of his imagination; that he must have had the sort of beetling brow and tremendous nose and protruding chin that Raphael imagined him to have. The facts are quite otherwise. Dante was a rather serious, but pleasant, mild-featured, normal-looking human being.

From the bones we pass to Dante's blood. And here even Dante himself had some illusions. It had never entered his head that his skull (and, therefore, his blood) was Etruscan. He insisted on believing that he was one "in whom there lived again the blessed fruit of those Romans who remained when Florence became a nest of [Tuscan] wickedness."[39] That was a common enough theory among Florentines of those days. A chronicler like Giovanni Villani explains the feuds and wranglings in Florence by saying that "the noble, virtuous Romans" were bound to be at war with uncouth and tough Fiesolans.[40] Mixing blood in the body politic, says Dante, is the source of civic sickness.[41] His own blood, he felt, was old and noble. Even in his poetical paradise, where feeling could not be marred by passion, he gloried in his ancient lineage. "O meager nobleness of ancient blood! If thou dost make folk glory in thee here, where our desires are sickly, it shall never seem a marvel to me more, for there, even in heaven, where appetite swerves not aside, I boasted of my blood."[42] Not that he believed in blue blood as such. Aristocracy, to Dante, was a kind of knight errantry where each bachelor must win his spurs. This can be seen very well in the long *canzone* which he sets down and analyzes in the fourth book of his *Convivio*. Convention, he says, is never more perverse than when public opinion calls a man a gentleman merely because he can say: "I am the scion or the son of such and such a worthy gentleman" — being, in fact, a nincompoop.[43] Still less did Dante believe in bankers' blood. Not even imperial authority (which in its proper sphere he idolized) could persuade him, "that (as many do believe) wealth which, of itself, is vile can give or take away nobility."[44]

Nor did he like the idea that a *villano* — as we should say, a peasant — might not become a gentleman. His root idea was this: "Wherever there is worth there is your gentleman."[45] He also held that "blood is a mantle that shrinks up all too soon; for if, from day to day, new patches be not added, time goes about it with the shears."[46]

All this theory had its application to the Alighieri stock. In the course of the poetic pilgrimage described in the *Paradiso,* Dante passes beyond the moon and Mercury, Venus and the sun to Mars. Here there appeared to him the souls of those who on earth had

[39] *Inf.*, xv, 76–78.   [41] *Par.*, xvi, 67–69.   [43] *Rime*, lxxxii, 35–37.
[40] *Cronaca fiorentina*, I, 38.   [42] *Par.*, xv, 1–6.   [44] *Ibid.*, 49–51.
[45] *E gentilezza dovunqu' è vertute, ibid.*, 101.
[46] *Par.*, xvi, 6–8.

fought with fortitude for the Kingdom of God. Among these souls was that of Dante's great-great-grandfather. Dante calls him Cacciaguida. A document dated April 28, 1131, mentions a Cacciaguida, son of Adamo of Florence, in connection with some property close by the church of San Martino which is just across the street from the traditional site of Dante's home. Hence the historians have agreed to take Dante at his word. Thus they have been able to reconstruct Dante's family tree, and, to some extent, his family history.

Cacciaguida was made a Christian in the venerable Battistero in Florence, on Holy Saturday, in the year 1100.[47] In 1147, it would seem, he took the Crusader's oath. "Then followed I the Emperor Conrad, and he girt me with the sword and made a knight of me; for so my deeds delighted him."[48] Cacciaguida did not return. Far from Florence, "by the foul folk, he was untangled from the meshes of the world's deceit, and from the love that stains so many souls and from martyrdom came to this peace."[49]

He left at least two sons behind him, Preitnitto and Alaghiero. Of their mother we merely know, if we may trust Dante, that she came from the valley of the Po. She may thus have brought to Dante's stock some strain of Lombard or of Celtic blood. Alaghiero, Cacciaguida's son, appears twice in extant documents, once in 1189, and again in 1201. He married into the very high Florentine family of Bellincione Berti dei Ravignani. Alaghiero's wife, the daughter of Bellincione had two other sisters highly married, one into the family of the Donati, and one into that of the Adimari. Two sons of Alaghiero appear in the documents, Gabriello (Bello, for short) and Bellincione (Cione, for short). Bello must have been recognized as a noble or at least as a learned man, for they gave him the honorable title of *dominus*. Of his sons, the eldest, Geri del Bello, left a name for himself. He was one of those powerful Guelfs who in 1269, after return from political exile, managed to get compensation for damaged property. Our poet, his cousin, puts him in the ninth "pocket" of the eighth "circle" of hell among the sowers of discord. The story is that he met violent death, stabbed in a family feud, by Brodaio dei Sacchetti. That is why, in hell, Geri points angrily and scornfully at

[47] This date is determined by *Par.*, xvi, 34–39. The commentators reach various conclusions from the data provided by Dante. I have followed the computation of Nicola Zingarelli, *La Vita, i Tempi e le Opere di Dante*, Vol. I, p. 57.
[48] *Par.*, xv, 139–141.
[49] *Ibid.*, 145–148.

Dante, as though to remind him of the debt of family honor that could be paid only in Sacchetti blood.

The second son of Alaghiero was Bellincione. He appears to have played an honorable, prominent, and, as far as we know, peaceful part in the history of Florence during the great decade that preceded the disaster of Montaperti in 1260. Four of his sons are known, Drudolo, Brunetto, Gherardo, and Alaghiero. This last was Dante's father.

IV

Father and Mother

About Alaghiero, Dante's father, very little is known. He could hardly have been in exile, as his brothers were, in 1265, since Dante was born in that year in Florence. Dante must have had in mind his uncles and his cousins when he introduced into the *Inferno* the famous episode in which he meets the haughty spirit of the Ghibelline, Farinata degli Uberti. Farinata was so scornful in his ways "that even hell he seemed to hold in high contempt," *com'avesse l'inferno in gran dispitto*.[50] He looks Dante over for a moment. Then he asks disdainfully: "And who were your ancestors?" Dante told him all, concealing nothing. Whereupon Farinata, raising his eyebrows somewhat, said: "fiercely, they were opposed to me and to my sires, and to my party; so that twice I routed them."[51] He had in mind the scattering of the Guelfs in 1248 and again in 1260. Dante quietly but quickly answered: "If they were routed, they returned, the first time and the second, and from everywhere; but yours learned ill that art."

In all this epic rivalry of Guelf and Ghibelline, Dante's father had little part. He makes no clatter at all in crossing the stage of history. It is as though divine Providence had assigned him no other task than that of fathering and fostering the sublime poet of Christendom. When he appears in the documents of the time he is not styled *dominus,* like his uncle Bello, nor even *ser* or *messer*. In 1257, eight years before the birth of his immortal son, plain Alaghiero appears in the humble capacity of a moneylender. It was a matter of a small sum; nominally about $100 of our money, twenty *librae* and eight *solidi*. It was lent to a widow who was called Bencisia. No interest

[50] *Inf.,* x, 36.   [51] *Inf.,* x, 45–48.

was mentioned; for interest, as such, in those days was "a breed of barren metal," and was condemned by holy Church. However, Alaghiero stipulated, with every precaution that legal technicality could invent, that failure to return the money within one year would involve the penalty of paying twice the sum, or of owing it, in the form of a mortgage on the widow's property.

Moneylender may seem a harsh name for Alaghiero di Bellincione da Firenze. No doubt, banker would better express the social standing of Dante's father. There is no evidence that he was a successful banker. To judge by the inheritance that fell to his family, he was an unambitious man of small means and, in the matter of money, of modest ability.

His first wife — for he married twice — was Donna Gabriella (Bella, for short), the daughter, so it seems, of Durante (Dante, for short) who was son to Scolaio degli Abati, and the mother of our poet. Dante never mentions her openly, by name, in any of his works; as he never mentions his father — except, of course, indirectly, by his tender allusions to parents in general. Of the Abati family he mentions Bocca degli Abati, the Florentine traitor, who betrayed the Guelf cause at the battle of Montaperti. He is punished in the lowest part of hell, frozen in the ice, and barking like one "made doggish by the cold." It was he of whom Dante relates that "whether it were my fault, or destiny, or chance, I know not; but walking among the heads, strongly I dashed my foot against the face of one of them; who screamed to me in tears: Why tramplest thou on me? Unless it be to punish me the more for Montaperti, why dost thou molest me?"[52] Dante with all the ruthlessness befitting the loveless and lightless lake of Cocytus demanded Bocca's name. But the traitor obstinately went on "barking and keeping down his eyes"; until another denizen of Antenora cried out: "Bocca, what ails thee? Is not jittering with thy jaws enough, without this barking? What sort of devil prods thee?" "Now, accursed traitor [said Dante, having heard the name] I do not want thy words; for, to thy shame, I shall tell true tidings of thee."[53]

So did Dante hate all treason, even though the traitors were of his kith or kin. After Donna Bella's death Alaghiero tried to find another mother for his children. He married Lapa di Chiarissimo Cialuffi. She is mentioned in a document of May 16, 1332, as the wife of Alaghiero deceased and mother of his son Francesco. There is no known

[52] *Inf.*, xxxii, 76–81.   [53] *Inf.*, xxxii, 106–111.

reason for imagining that the stepmother was cruel to the little Dante, unless we can argue something from the fact that more than once "stepmother," *matrigna,* is used by the poet in its conventional connotation.

Altogether there were two boys and two girls in the home of Dante's childhood. Of one of the girls Boccaccio tells us: "Dante had a sister who was married to one of our citizens called Leone Poggi, and became the mother of several children, among whom the eldest was called Andrea; he was extraordinarily like Dante in the lines of his face, and even in his size and general appearance, so that he walked with a bend in the back as Dante is said to have done, and though he was a man with no particular education, he had much good sense and was remarkable for his conversation and general behavior."[54]

It is possible to speculate that this sister is the "sweet young woman" who is mentioned in the *Vita Nuova* as being of his nearest kin. She nursed Dante in one of his sicknesses, when he was deep in his mysterious love — passionate, poetical, rational, and religious — for Beatrice Portinari.

What happened inside the Alighieri home during the childhood days of Dante few written records have survived to tell. His father Alaghiero died before Dante reached the age of twelve; his mother, so it seems, before he reached the age of reason.

Much has been written about this orphanhood. It has been assumed that the little lad, as he grew older, never recovered from an unappeased nostalgia for his dead mother's arms. It has been supposed that he was too young to remember much about his living mother and that somehow his imagination went on making compensation for the lack of memory. It has even been suggested that, like certain dreams in Freudian theory, the *Commedia* was a sort of psychological sublimation, an inevitable, imaginary peopling of the solitudes in the poet's soul, which had been laid waste by loss and sorrow. Dante was forever making mothers and fathers for himself — a father out of God, out of Adam, out of Cacciaguida, out of his teacher, Brunetto Latini, out of Statius, and most of all out of Virgil, the faithful "leader, lord, and teacher" in Dante's hell and on the hill of purgatory; a mother out of the Blessed Virgin Mary, but also out of Beatrice.

[54] *Commento,* Inf., viii.

In a special sense, he makes a mother out of the mysterious lady, Matelda, who guides him in the "earthly paradise." As soon as Dante meets her he exclaims: "Thou dost make me call to mind the tale of Proserpina, where she was, and what she was, what time she lost her girlhood, and her *mother,* her."[55] Something about this "lovely lady," *bella donna,* made Dante think of the separation of a mother and her child. A moment later the *bella donna* lifts her eyes to look at Dante; and the poet says: "I do not believe that so much light of love shone out from Venus' eye what time the arrow of her *son* pierced her heart so strangely."[56] Again the mysterious lady made Dante think of a mother and her child. Throughout the cantos that follow, the relations between Dante and Matelda remind one of those of a mother and her child. "I went along with her [Dante says], my tiny steps in pace with hers," *picciol passo con picciol seguitando.*[57] And when the time came for symbolic baptism in the waters of Lethe, "the lovely lady opened her arms, and took my head in them, and dipped me where I had to swallow of the water; then took me out, all washed, and led me where the virtues danced."[58] And when Dante falls asleep, the "lovely lady" says to him, just like a mother to her child: "Get up, what ails thee," *Surgi; che fai?*[59] And when he saw her leaning over him tenderly, as mothers do, he remembered that she was the "motherly one who first led my steps along the stream."[60] Five times this "motherly one" is called *bella donna.* It is difficult not to recall that Dante's mother was Donna Bella.

On one occasion Dante's mother appears in the *Commedia* without the veil of symbolism. In the eighth canto of the *Inferno,* as was mentioned earlier, the poet imagines himself passing in a boat across a filthy marsh which is meant as a symbol for the punishment of the sin of angry hate. The sin, as usual, is personified. In this case, the person is a certain Filippo Argenti. He is represented as the completest contradiction of motherly love, a monster as eager to do evil as a mother to do good, a brute whose life "produced no thread of good to fringe his memory."[61] When Filippo stretched up his hands, trying to drag Dante from the boat, Virgil "the wary master, thrust him off, saying: 'Get thee gone with the other dogs!' " Then turning to Dante, "He [Virgil] put his arms about my neck, and kissed me on

---

[55] *Purg.,* xxviii, 49–51. [58] *Purg.,* xxxi, 100–104. [61] *Inf.,* viii, 47.
[56] *Ibid.,* 64–66. [59] *Purg.,* xxxii, 72.
[57] *Purg.,* xxix, 8–9. [60] *Ibid.,* 83.

the face, and said: 'O lofty soul! Blessed is she whose womb it was that bore thee.' "[62]

The contrast is complete between the "damned spirit," the *maledetto,* and the "blessed lady," the *benedetta,* between the monster and the mother, the symbol of hate and the symbol of love. There is something further to be noticed. Virgil's words, "Blessed is she whose womb it was that bore thee," are meant to recall the words once spoken of a still more lovely mother: "Blessed is the womb that bore Thee!"[63] It was this same association between Mary and Donna Bella that the poet had in mind in singing of Matelda. When the *bella donna* leads Dante toward the "mystic procession" in the "earthly paradise," the elders in the procession hail her with the words: "*Benedicta* art thou among the daughters of Adam, and blessed be thy beauties everlastingly."[64] The Angel Gabriel had said to Mary: *Benedicta tu in mulieribus.*[65] Dante's use of the Latin *benedicta* seems to me a hint that he meant Matelda to symbolize, by sublimation, the perfect mother, Our Lady, the very mirror of maternal love. It is possible (though we have no proof) that Dante meant the name Matelda to suggest both *Mater Dei* and *Mater Dantis.*[66]

In this connection it is well to recall that there are in Dante's works many reminiscences of early childhood. Take, for example, the picture: "As children stand, when caught and conscience-struck, shamefaced and dumb, with eyes to earth, penitently listening, so did I stand."[67] Or take this hint, in the *Convivio,* of delicacy of conscience being helped by parental guidance: "It is a very good sign, indeed, of better breeding when children not yet grown up blush with shame, when they have acted ill."[68] This sounds less like a piece of copybook deportment than a living lesson from a mother's lips. Take, again, this picture: "And of a sudden my leader grasped me, as a mother, awakened by the noise, and seeing the kindled flames about her, grasps her child, and flees, and thinking more of him than of herself, delays not even to put a robe about her."[69] Or this: "Just as a mother to a child seems stern, so did she seem to me; for bitter is the taste of pity when 'tis harsh."[70] Or, finally, this: "Like a child who turns un-

[62] *Ibid.,* 45.
[63] Luke 11:27.
[64] *Purg.,* xxix, 85–87.
[65] Luke 2:2.
[66] See Gerald G. Walsh, "Dante's Matelda," in *Thought,* xii (March, 1937), pp. 78–106.
[67] *Purg.,* xxxi, 64–67.
[68] *Conv.,* IV, xix, 10.
[69] *Inf.,* xxxiii, 37.
[70] *Purg.,* xxx, 78–80.

failingly to one he trusts completely, I turned, all puzzled, to my guide; and, like a mother prompt to succor a pale and gasping child with the familiar voice she knows will bring him comfort, she said to me: Dost thou not know . . . that what is done up here springs from righteous zeal?"[71]

It is perhaps more hazardous to speculate on Dante's memories of his father. There is, however, a ring of reminiscence in Dante's words in the *Convivio*: "The child who enters upon the puzzling wood of this life would not know how to keep to the right path were it not shown him by his parents. Yet this, without obedience to their commands, would be of no avail; hence the necessity of obedience during adolescence."[72]

The whole context is here instructive. Dante argues that as soon as a boy has reached the age of reason, he should turn as naturally to his father for correction as a baby turns to a mother's breast. The father, of course, has the correlative obligation to teach his boy; and this not merely by word but by example. "For [says Dante] every son looks, by nature, rather to the footsteps of his father than elsewhere." Hence "written reason," that is, Roman law, commands that the person of the father be held sacred by the son. "And if [continues Dante, now nearer than ever to autobiography] the father is no longer alive, then the duty of obedience is toward the person who has been left in the place of the father according to the father's will."

It is possible to be morally noble and personally well endowed, even though politically insignificant and financially unsuccessful. Some at least of his gifts Dante seems to have felt were inherited from his father. In Dante's theory of heredity, the soul as such is the gift of God; something of one's genius depends on the stars; the rest depends on the father. The father's seed, says Dante (following Aristotle in this as in so much else), carries with it the qualities of the progenitor's soul. There is, Dante continues, a not improbable opinion that should all three factors in human heredity — the father's soul, his seed, the stars — be perfectly and harmoniously disposed then so much of the divine would descend upon a soul as to constitute a "quasi-incarnation."[73]

There is no hint here that Dante was thinking about his own birth. However, in this connection, he was fond of mentioning the stars.

---

[71] *Par.*, xxii, 1–8.   [72] IV, xxiv.
[73] . . . *quasi sarebbe un altro Iddio incarnato. Conv.*, IV, xxi, 10.

The sun, he tells us, was in the constellation of the twins when he was born. That, he felt, had something to do with his poetical genius. "O glorious stars," he sings in the *Paradiso*,[74] "O light pregnant with great power, to which I owe whatever genius I have! With you the father of all mortal life [that is, the sun] was rising and setting when first I felt the Tuscan air." So, too, Brunetto Latini is made to say to Dante: "If you but steer by your star you cannot miss the port of greatness."[75] This means that Dante's birthday fell within the last ten days of May or the first twenty days of June. A notary who talked with Dante on his deathbed assured Boccaccio that Dante was born in May. The German Dantist, Karl Witte, picked out May 30. Another guess would be May 27. It was on May 27, 1865, that Dante's long-lost bones were rediscovered in Ravenna. It was on another May 27, in 1483, that Pietro Lombardo dated the bas-relief of Dante that still adorns his sepulcher. May 27, in 1265, the year of Dante's birth, was the Wednesday ember day falling between the Feast of Pentecost and Trinity Sunday. Such a birthday would be more than appropriate for the austere apostle of the Father, Son, and Holy Spirit.

Some have been tempted to speculate further on Dante's horoscope. If he came into the world between three and four on the morning of May 27, he would have had directly overhead a garland of stars formed by the three constellations, the Cross, the Eagle, and the Lyre. There in the zenith they seemed to remain until the first flush of a new day creeping up the eastern sky put them out. It was to be the triumph and tragedy of Dante's age that the Cross, the Eagle, and the Lyre — symbols of the Church, the Empire, and medieval culture, the *Sacerdotium, Imperium* and *Studium* — should reach their zenith and then be dimmed by the dawn of a new day of secularism, nationalism, and nominalism. His lyre was to make a last effort to hold together the dissolving harmony of the Eagle and the Cross, of Caesar and Christ, of law and grace, of the arguments of reason and the mysteries of faith. He was to be the last great citizen of Christendom.

[74] xxii, 112–117.
[75] *Inf.*, xv, 55–57.

II

Long Study and Great Love

Vagliami il lungo studio e 'l grande amore.[1]

I

ELEMENTARY EDUCATION

THE first words uttered by the "Dante" of the *Divine Comedy* were a plea for pity. *Miserere di me,* he cries out to the apparition that appears to him in the "great desert" of the "dark wood."[2] And when the shade declares himself to be the poet who wrote the *Aeneid,* "Dante" exclaims: "Are you really Virgil? Are you the spring from which there flowed so wide a stream of language? O glory and light of other poets! May my long study and the great love that led me to your song be now rewarded. You are my master and my model. From you, and you alone, I learned the lovely style that brought me fame."[3]

That is the voice of the real Dante, not only the symbol. The mask, for the moment, is dropped; Dante's heart speaks out. It is a heart obviously in love with the life of the spirit, with beauty and truth, with language and learning, with all that paves the way to art and wisdom.

One of the earliest loves that lectured in Dante's heart was the love for the Tuscan language. It was in that language, he reminds us in the *Convivio,* that his father and mother first made love — without which, he adds, he himself had not been born. Language, in a real sense, was a cause of his physical life. It was more. It was a cause of his intellectual life. It put him on the road to learning, and learning, for Dante as for Aristotle, was not merely a second, but a better kind

[1] *Inf.,* i, 83.　　　　[2] *Ibid.,* 65.　　　　[3] *Ibid.,* 82–87.

27

of, living. Tuscan made possible the learning of Latin; Latin opened the door to all further knowledge and wisdom; and this, he says, led the way to the very heights of human perfection and happiness. And besides, he adds, he and his native Tuscan have continued the best of friends. His songs helped the language and the language helped him. And so for all these reasons he concludes: "I shall not say love, but the most perfect love is that which I ought to have for it and have."[4]

The life of learning began for Dante as a boy and continued throughout his life. It has left a deep trace on almost everything he wrote. We can, of course, enjoy Dante without trying to learn all that he knew. We need not follow him in his "long study." But we must, I think, make some effort to understand his "great love," his passionate pursuit of every kind of truth.

Take, for example, canto xv of the *Inferno*. Here Dante meets his old teacher, Brunetto Latini. He meets him in the last place in hell where one would expect to find an instructor of youth. He meets him in a waste of sand where fire, like flakes of livid snow, falls relentlessly on the bare backs of men and women guilty of unnatural lust. Brunetto's face was burned beyond recognition, but there was something in the affectionate and pathetic upstretching of his arms that made him known directly to Dante's soul. Dante leaned down and with his hand tried to feel the features of his master's face. Then he exclaimed: "Are *you . . . here . . .* Ser Brunetto," *Siete voi qui, ser Brunetto?*[5] I do not know any line in all literature more pathetic than that. There is pathos, too, and poetry in the lines: "For in my memory your face is ever fixed and now my heart is bursting with the thought of the dear, good father who in life, hour after hour, taught me how a man becomes immortal."

> *Chè 'n la mente m' è fitta, e or m' accora*
> *la cara e buona imagine paterna*
> *di voi quando nel mondo ad ora ad ora*
> *m'insegnavate come l'uom s'etterna.*[6]

Long before Brunetto Latini guided Dante's first steps in the grammar, syntax, poetry, and rhetoric of the Latin classics, Dante had made his way through the elementary manuals of medieval schoolboys. He seems to have been taught by a certain Romano, a friend of the Alighieri family and a man described with the official title

---

[4] *Conv.,* I, xiii, 10.   [5] *Inf.,* xv, 30.   [6] *Ibid.,* 82–85.

of *doctor puerorum*. The young Dante first learned by heart the Latin psalter. Then he had to master the moral lessons of the so-called Distichs of Cato *(Disticha Catonis)* and the Fables of Aesop. Then there were summaries of the teachings of St. Augustine, Prosper and Boethius, and the manuals known from their opening words as *Eva columba, Tres leo naturas,* and *Aethiopum terras.*

No reader of the *Inferno* can ever forget the reference to the Fables of Aesop. Cantos xxi and xxii describe with a kind of hellish humor the dark thoughts and crooked feelings of the ghoulish guardians of a lake of boiling pitch. In this pitch notorious political grafters are immersed. They keep bobbing up and down like bits of fat in a pot of stew. Evil Tail *(Malacoda)* was the captain of the crew of devils. Big Tough *(Scarmiglione)* was one of the most rowdy. He was armed with a barbed hook, and had the hardest time keeping himself from giving Dante "a nick on the rump." Limp Wing *(Alichino)* and Trample Frost *(Calcabrina)* are old established mutual enemies. When one of the sinners in the pitch stuck his nose out, like a frog on the edge of a pond, Dogscratcher *(Graffiacane)* swooped down and with his hook twisted in the sinner's tar-clotted hair dragged him up, dripping like an otter. You can almost feel the tar in your own hair when you read the line, *gli arruncigliò le 'mpegolate chiome.*[1] The devils with their bawling and mauling and clawing give him what, in this context, can only be called "a hell of a time." But they forget that Ciampolo was a politician. By a trick worthy of his reputation at the court of King Thibaut of Navarre, Ciampolo gets the devils off guard and jumps from the bank into the pitch. Alichino flaps his wings and swoops after him. Calcabrina swoops, too, secretly hoping that the sinner will escape, and delighted to have a claw at Alichino. The batlike devils seize each other and fall with a flop into the sticky pitch. Alichino had wanted to flay Ciampolo, and Calcabrina wanted to "get" Alichino. The boiling pitch got both of them.

By a curious association of ideas, Dante, who watched the scuffle, thought of a fable he had learned as a child. He calls it a fable of Aesop. It was in fact the fable of the mouse and the frog as told by Phaedrus. It had been edited and re-edited in prose or verse by one after another of the unnamed schoolmasters of the Middle Ages. In the original fable the mouse asks the frog to help him across a pond.

[1] *Inf.,* xxii, 35.

The frog agrees, but when he has the mouse secure on his back he dives in the hope of drowning the mouse. There is a struggle in midstream. An eagle swoops down and devours both the mouse and the frog. The moral which the little Dante had learned was that those who plot against others come to an evil end. By the time he came to write the *Commedia* he may no longer have remembered the fable by heart, but he never forgot the meaning and the moral. That was precisely what a medieval teacher most wanted a boy to remember.

"In the training of boys from seven to fourteen," writes Aegidius Colonna in his *Education of Princes*, "our main purpose must be to develop the will in rectitude and moderation; although we should also make them learn Latin and logic, which are avenues to other branches of learning. The final result will be that when in time they have learned the other sciences, they will lack neither a good mind nor good morals."

Besides the moral implications in the matter which he taught, the medieval schoolmaster used to insist on other levels of significance. In a famous scene in the second canto of the *Purgatory* Dante has in mind, I think, the lessons he was taught when he learned the psalter. In that scene Dante is standing at the antipodes of Jerusalem, on the beach at the foot of the hill of purgation and watching an angel of God piloting a ship without oars or sails. It was speeding across the ocean from the mouth of the river Tiber carrying souls to purgatory. Dante counted more than a hundred spirits in the boat, and he noted that they "sang, all together, with one voice, *In exitu Israel de Aegypto,* with the rest of the psalm that follows after."[8] It is implied that the spirits knew the psalm by heart. They had learned it as a part of their elementary education. They were singing that particular psalm because they had learned not only its literal meaning, but also its various "mystical" meanings — allegorical, moral, and anagogic. Those joyous spirits on their way to purgatory were thinking particularly, of the "anagogic" meaning. And this meaning, which Dante had learned as a boy he explains thus:

The fourth sense of a psalm is called "anagogic," which is to say the sense above; and this is when a text, which is true in the literal sense, is expounded in a spiritual sense so that it points to the supernal things

[8] *Purg.,* ii, 46-48.

of eternal glory. And this may be seen in that song of the prophet which says that, in the going out of the people of Israel from Egypt, Judaea was made holy and free. This is manifestly true according to the letter. It is no less true in its spiritual meaning, namely, that in the escape of the soul from sin, it is made holy and free to use its power.[9]

The souls on the way to Dante's purgatory were also, no doubt, thinking of the other meanings of the psalm. All four interpretations are enumerated in one of Dante's letters:

For if we look only to the *letter* it means for us the going out of the sons of Israel from Egypt in the time of Moses; if to the *allegory*, it means for us our redemption wrought by Christ; if to the *moral sense*, it means the turning of the soul from the grief and misery of sin to a state of grace; if to the *anagogic* it means the going forth of a holy soul from the slavery of this corruption to the liberty of eternal glory.[10]

The spirits in the angel's boat were thinking of all those meanings. They were recalling a piece of Bible *history* which had been linked in their minds with the *dogma* of redemption, with the *experience* of conversion, and with the theological *virtue* of hope. Dante himself had been taught in this way to use his memory, understanding, will, and faith on the matter, meaning, moral, and mystery of all he read and saw and did and suffered. His head and heart were filled by his teachers with a rich tradition of pictures, ideas, maxims, and metaphors which he never forgot.

Take the case of what we may call the moral geography of Dante's hell and the mental topography of his paradise. Much erudition has been dedicated to the sources of the punishments assigned in the various regions of Dante's hell. What suggested to his imagination all these types of torture? It suffices to open some such popular school manual as "The Bower of Flowers" (*Floretus*) to see how many of these pains had been put into hexameters very easy for a youngster to learn by heart. Take the lines:

> Vermes cum tenebr*is*, et verbera, frigus et ign*is*,
> Demonis aspect*us*, scelerum confusio, luct*us*,
> Fetor, serpent*es*, languor sine fineque perp*es*
> Pravos torque*bant* semperque quiete care*bant*,
> Esurient, siti*ent*, deformes corpore fi*ent*
> In terre cent*ro* percussi turbine te*tro*.
> Non est oran*dum* pro damnatis neque dan*dum*
> Nam support*ari* non possunt sive iuv*ari*.

[9] *Conv.*, II, i, 6–7.
[10] *Epist.*, xiii, 21.

A rough rendering might run something like this:

> Vile worms and darkness, blows and cold and fire,
> The devil's glare, the damned confounded, dire
> Grief and the stench, snakes and the endless sense
> Of sickness serve for peaceless penitence,
> While thirst and hunger gnaw their shapeless forms
> Wind-tossed by blasts of subterranean storms.
> Vain all our prayers, bootless our tears and grief,
> Useless our aid where aid brings no relief.

Or take this account of the ten spheres of the heavens:

> Deni sunt ce*li* referendi cordi fide*li*
> Luna stat in pri*mo*, mercurio estque secun*do*
> Ac venus in ter*no*, sol vult lucescere quar*to*
> Mars nitet in quin*to* sed jupiter ordine sex*to*
> Saturnus ce*lo* septimo sistitur al*to*
> Octavo ce*lo* tibi stellas esse reve*lo*
> Stat cristalli*num* super istos luce sere*num*
> Fulget in empire*o* summo paradisus olim*po*
> In quo sunt iunc*ta* sine defectu bona cunc*ta*
> Hic deitas tri*na* regnat super omnia dig*na*
> Astat regi*na* sibi mater virgo benig*na*
> Inde ierarchia triplici sunt agmine nona
> Dat seraphim cherubimque thronos distinctio summa
> In medio dominans, princeps simul atque potestas
> Virtutes sistunt archangelus angelus atque.
> Hic homines gra*ti* domino sunt associa*ti*
> Iuxta pro meri*ta* presente data sibi vi*ta*
> Letum laudan*tes* dominum semper speculan*tes*
> Cernit amatque de*um* sanctis fruitur, tenet ips*um*
> Sic gaudet psall*it* laudat sine fine quiesc*it*
> Dives, honora*tus*, tutus, liber, satia*tus*,
> Clarus, agilis, subtilis, non passibilis fit.

In a rough rendering the lines run:

> Ten heavens may the Christian mind retrace:
> The moon; then Mercury in the second place;
> Venus is third; the sun shines fourth; and then
> Mars; next comes Jupiter; the seventh to ken
> Is Saturn; number eight, the stars; and nine,
> Serene and lucent is the crystalline.
> Above all else (but not for human eyes)
> The empyrean, where is paradise.
> Here, all good things, in endless harmony;
> Here, over all, one God in Trinity.
> Nigh to His throne, the Virgin, mother, queen
> Benign; below, the hierarchy (I mean
> The triple order of the ninefold tones)

> Seraphim and cherubim and thrones,
> Lordship and principality and power,
> Virtues and angels (twice, the higher and lower),
> Here, too, companions in beatitude,
> Men, for their merits and their gratitude
> Have won the vision and eternal bliss;
> Each sees and loves and holds to God, and is
> Joyous and sings in everlasting peace,
> Rich and rewarded, safe and free; release
> He feels, and lightness and agility,
> And heavenly impassibility.

Another illustration. Few things strike a reader of the *Commedia* more than the poet's practice, especially in the *Purgatory*, of bringing together in the focus of his imagination pairs of pictures, one of them borrowed from classical literature, the other from Holy Scripture. The parallelism may seem at times a little forced. Yet the habit is of the very essence of Dante's art. He is ever trying to see (and sing) whatever is true and good and fair and one (or the reverse — false and bad and foul and chaotic), as it were, in four dimensions. He sees first the thing of sense — the surface, shape, and color. Then he explores with his mind, taking off the lid, so to speak, to see what the thing is, and how it works, and what it is for. Next, he weighs the thing to find its worth, its relation to other things, its place in a cosmic whole. Finally he opens the eyes of his soul with another and more mysterious wonder. He tries by intuition to see with the eyes of God. His art is multidimensional. He paints with the eyes of a scientist, the memory of a historian, the imagination of a poet, the mind of a philosopher, the conscience of a moralist, the faith of a theologian and, perhaps in some degree, the vision of a mystic.

Think of his way of dealing with the sin of envy in *Purgatory* XIV. He calls to mind the story he had read as a boy at school in Ovid's *Metamorphoses* XIV, of Aglauros, daughter of Cecrops, King of Athens, and how Aglauros was changed into stone by Mercury because she was jealous of the god's love for her sister, Hersë. Dante pictures the scene to himself and he feels the pathos as any poet would. But something else in Dante seizes, at the same time and with the same passionate perception, the meaning and the moral of the story. On these levels he asks himself: How does the story of Aglauros and Hersë differ from that of Cain and Abel? Is there not behind the punishment revealed in Scripture[11] and the punishment related in the song of Ovid, the same mysterious voice of eternal justice? Both stories seem to Dante pregnant with poetry and meaning, with a moral and a hint of supernatural mystery. They are linked in his mind. And so he sings:

> As soon as we were left to go our way alone,
> a voice that cleared the air like lightning seemed
> to strike us in the face, and say:
>
> "Every man that findeth me, shall slay me" —
> and fled as fast as does the thunderclap
> when with a sudden snap it cracks a cloud.
>
> No sooner was there truce betwixt that voice
> and our stunned ears when lo! a second, with a clap
> like thunder, followed on its heels:
>
> "I am Aglauros who was turned to stone."
> And I, to nestle nearer to the poet,
> moved me to the right instead of going forward.
>
> And he to me, so soon as the air on every side was still:
> "That was the hard bit that ought to hold
> a man to the right track.
>
> But you mortals bite at the ancient adversary's bait,
> and with his hook he draws you to him,
> and nought avails you, either lure or bridle.
>
> High heaven calls to you, and wheels about you showing
> its eternal splendors, but your eye is fixed to the earth.
> No wonder He who is all-seeing buffets you."[12]

This parallel between Cain and Aglauros was first suggested to Dante by the schoolbook, *Aethiopum terras*. This little book was a great favorite. It tells how the sweet shepherdess Alithia (which is Greek, of course, for *truth*) is tending her sheep and playing her harp by the side of a brook, when up comes a shepherd on the other side clothed in a panther's fell and playing a pipe with a thousand stops. His name was Pseustis (Greek for *liar* or *deceiver*). He was of Athens, as Alithia was a daughter of Jerusalem. Pseustis calls to Alithia and proposes a competition. They are to expose the beauties and wonders of their respective cultures, of revelation and mythology; and Fronesis (Greek for *wisdom*) is to be the judge. Of course, Jerusalem

---

[11] Gen. 4.   [12] *Purg.*, xiv, 130–151.

wins and Athens acknowledges handsomely a complete defeat —
although, to tell the truth, there is more magic and music in the
quatrains of Pseustis than in those of Alithia. Pseustis begins with
the story of the "golden age." Alithia counters with the story of
Adam and Eve in the Garden of Eden. Pseustis then tells of the
fall from the golden to the silver age; Alithia tells of the fall from
grace to unaided nature. And so the parallels continue: Aglauros and
Cain; Deucalion and Noe; the giants and the tower of Babel;
Hippolytus and Joseph; and many more.

II

Liberal Arts

Much as Dante may have owed to Romano, the *doctor puerorum*,
and later to Brunetto Latini, most of his learning came from his
own omnivorous reading. He confesses, in a well-known passage in
the *Convivio*:[13] "By overtaxing the eyes in my passion for books I
so weakened my sight that the stars seemed blurred in a kind of
mist." If we may believe one of the many legends about him, Dante
was so attentive a reader that he could pore over a book the whole
day long and pay no heed whatever to the hubbub of a noisy *piazza*
where he was sitting.

According to his own account his serious reading began with the
death of Beatrice in 1290. He sought consolation, he says, in the
words of Boethius and Cicero. The *Consolation of Philosophy* of
Boethius was written at the end of the first quarter of the sixth
century and the *Friendship* of Cicero two generations before the
Incarnation. They are two of the books out of which was woven the
fabric of the medieval mind. The *De amicitia* is pitched on as high
a note as Latin paganism ever reached. Laelius (as Cicero likes to
think of him) tries to believe that the soul of his dead friend Scipio
is still alive. At any rate, high-mindedness is immortal, and the
living memory of a dear friend's virtue is motive enough for drying
the warmest tears. All this is expressed in the matchless music of
Cicero's periodic prose at its very best. A book of so great beauty

[13] III, ix, 15.

and one so near in truth to revelation haunted (as it still haunts) all genuine citizens of Christendom.

So, too, the *De consolatione philosophiae*. This seemed to the Middle Ages an all but perfect synthesis of nature and grace, of reason and revelation. In Boethius, Athens, Rome, and Jerusalem seemed to meet and blend. Here was a perfect flowering from the grafting of grace onto law and learning, of religion onto civilization and culture, of Christ onto Virgil and Plato. Boethius was the sort of person the Middle Ages most admired, the combination of poet, philosopher, and man of God. He had achieved, so men felt, the right equilibrium of mind and will and spirit, of knowledge, virtue, and wisdom, of action, contemplation, and creative inspiration. Having ransacked the libraries of Athens and brought back to Rome a passion for the letters and philosophy of Greece, he put it at the service of Theodoric, who in the early sixth century was ruling Rome with Ostrogothic vigor. When at last the king's barbarism broke through the crust of his culture, Boethius was robbed of his earthly possessions, put into jail, and subjected to torture. Before he died he set down in prose and verse nearly all that Christian humanism likes to think, feel, say, and sing about the world and man and God, about good and evil, pleasure and pain, joy and sadness, providence and fate.

Later on, Dante would put Boethius in paradise, along with St. Thomas Aquinas and Albertus Magnus, Gratian and Peter Lombard, Orosius and Isidore, Bede and Richard of St. Victor, and Siger of Brabant, as one of the great teachers of Christendom. He is the "holy soul who shows to all who care to heed the world and its deceits."[14] Cicero, too, was to find a place in Dante's limbo, the "paradise of pagans," along with Aristotle, "the master of those who know," *il maestro di color che sanno,* and Socrates and Plato and the rest of the "philosophic family" from Democritus and Diogenes through Seneca to Averroes, "who made the great Commentary" on Aristotle.[15]

There are at least three dozen allusions to the *Consolation of Philosophy* and all but sixty to Cicero in the works of Dante. And yet Boethius and Cicero represent but a tiny fraction of Dante's reading. Like those earlier medieval humanists of the twelfth century, before the invasion of Aristotelian science and metaphysics

[14] *Par.*, x, 125–126.   [15] *Inf.*, iv, 144.

threatened to drive out the passion for classical Latin poetry, Dante read and reread Virgil until he knew the *Aeneid* almost by heart. There are endless citations and allusions to show that he knew his Virgil as he knew his Bible and his Aristotle. Of course, he had read Virgil, as he had read Lucan and Statius and Ovid and Horace, as a boy at school. But he must have gone on reading Virgil all his life. His boyish affection grew into a passionate love for his guide and teacher, as you can see, for example, in the words he puts on the lips of Beatrice when she comes down from heaven to seek Virgil in the dim light of limbo: "O Mantuan, O gracious spirit whose fame is still alive, and destined to outlast the world."[16] You can feel the affection in Dante's words, when Virgil has responded to the bidding of Beatrice and has offered to guide Dante out of the "dark wood" and up the side of the "mount" to the portals of paradise: "Let's go! One will now moves us both; thou art my leader, lord, and master."[17]

Virgil, for many reasons, meant more to the whole medieval world than we can now readily imagine. He was more than the "wielder of the stateliest measure ever molded by the lips of man." For example, almost everyone then believed that Virgil's fourth *Eclogue*, singing of the Consul Pollio and his newborn son, and alluding to the "last age" and the "new order" and the "virgin" and above all to the "new progeny come down from heaven," was an unconscious inspiration and a prophecy. Men of those days were never tired of meditating on the haunting lines:

> Ultima Cumaei venit iam carminis aetas;
> magnus ab integro saeclorum nascitur ordo.
> iam redit et virgo, redeunt Saturnia regna;
> iam nova progenies caelo demittitur alto.[18]

Above all, men read and reread the sixth book of the *Aeneid* with its strange story of the golden bough brought by a dove and giving Aeneas admission, under the guidance of the Sibyl, to the shades of the dead in the underworld. Dante more than the rest of men read all these things. He takes his Charon and Cerberus from Virgil. His accounts of the souls of suicides and guilty lovers recall the *Aeneid*. Virgil's Elysian fields give many a hint for Dante's "terrestrial

[16] *Inf.*, ii, 58–60.
[17] *Or va, ch' un sol volere è d' ambedue:*
   tu duca, tu segnore, e tu maestro. Inf., ii, 139–140.
[18] *Ecloga*, iv, 4–7.

paradise." By the banks of the river Lethe Dante meets *la bella donna*, Matelda, just as Aeneas had met his father, Anchises. Dante had been moved by the splendid prophecy of the Roman Empire which had been put into the mouth of Anchises, with its concluding idea that in ruling the world and in the arts of imposing peace Rome must ever be supreme:

> *Tu regere imperio populos, Romane, memento,*
> *hae tibi erunt artes, pacique imponere morem,*
> *parcere subiectis et debellare superbos.*[19]

Dante learned from reading Virgil the sense that Rome is the trunk of the tree of Western tradition. He understood that Athens, summed up in Aristotle, had given us our philosophy, the pattern of thought and the hierarchy of values that make up Western culture; that Jerusalem had given us the creed and the cross; that Rome, with its civilization, its ordered code of laws, its system of central government, its sense of practical justice, had made possible, humanly speaking, both the spread of culture and the triumph of the Christian religion.

Besides Virgil, Dante had read much else of Latin classical poetry. Of Horace, for example, he certainly knew the *Ars Poetica*, of Juvenal the *Satires*, and of Ovid the *Metamorphoses*. To Lucan's *Pharsalia* can be traced more than forty allusions in Dante's works.

There is one use of the classical poets which calls for special notice. In the *Convivio* Dante explains that he was taught to see in the fourth, fifth, and sixth books of the *Aeneid* an allegory of the second period of human life, the period of vigorous manhood from twenty-five to forty-five, *giovanezza*, as Dante calls it.[20] In the same way in the seventh book of Ovid's *Metamorphoses* Dante was taught to find illustrations of the virtues proper to *senettute*, to the senescent years from forty-five to seventy. The virtues in question were prudence, justice, generosity, and affability.[21] Similarly, in the poems of Statius, Dante had been taught to find illustrations of the virtues of adolescence, *puerizia*.[22] The virtues proper to a boy in his home and at school include, first, obedience to parents or guardians; second, courtesy in speech, service, and ways of acting; third, a delicate conscience (*vergogna*), and this in the triple sense of docility to one's teachers (*stupore*), modesty (*pudore*), and a sense of shame

[19] *Aen.*, vi, 847–853.
[20] *Conv.*, IV, xxvi.
[21] *Ibid.*, xxvii.
[22] *Ibid.*, xxv.

(*verecundia*) when one has sinned. It was of these three virtues, *stupore, pudore,* and *verecundia,* that Statius seemed to Dante the perfect teacher.

I have already offered the suggestion that the cantos of the *Purgatory*[23] in which Statius and Matelda serve as guides may be meant by Dante to symbolize human nature in the years when it is developing in the home and at school. In canto xx Statius is released from his pains endured for his prodigality and his spiritual sloth in delaying his conversion to Christianity. The whole mount seemed to shake as with an earthquake and the souls broke out into the exclamation, *Gloria in excelsis.* From that point until Beatrice appears in canto xxx there are no indications in the Poem of Dante's political and ecclesiastical passions. His interests are wholly domestic, academic, literary, and artistic. A new note is struck by the exclamation: "No ignorance, with such insistence, has ever made me so desirous to learn."[24] *Disideroso di sapere* is the expression Dante uses in the *Convivio*[25] when explaining the meaning of *stupore,* the reverent wonder proper to adolescence. Canto xxi opens with the words: "The natural thirst for knowledge, which is never sated except by the water of which the Samaritan woman begged the grace, was tormenting me." Statius overtook Dante and Virgil "just as Luke tells us that Christ, risen from the tomb, appeared to the two who were on their way" to Emmaus. If we accept the hypothesis that Statius is the symbol of authority in the school as Virgil is of authority in the State and Beatrice of authority in the Church and Matelda in the home, then we have a hint here that, in the "anagogic" sense, Statius stands for Christ the supreme teacher. Be that as it may, Statius is thoroughly professorial in his lecture on the supernatural physiography of the hill of purgatory, and especially in his use of the technical language of the second book of Aristotle's *Metaphysics.*

Statius' account in the next canto of how he became "both a poet and a Christian" expresses the argument of medieval educators in favor of using pagan authors. Virgil, says Statius, "led him to Parnassus . . . and then lighted his way to God, like a man carrying a light behind him, useless to himself but helpful to those who follow him."[26]

[23] xxi–xxix.
[24] *Purg.,* xx, 145, 146.
[25] *Conv.,* IV, xxv, 4.
[26] *Purg.,* xxii, 67–69.

When Virgil and Statius continued to converse, Dante (walking like a learner reverently behind them) listened because, he says, they "gave me understanding in the art of poetry."[27]

In canto xxv Statius gives a second academic lecture. His subject is human generation and the beginning of the life of the human soul, which "lives and feels and turns upon itself," *che vive e sente e sè in sè rigira.*[28] Finally, he describes the aerial bodies belonging to the spirits that are visible in the course of Dante's pilgrimage. It is a lecture depending partly on Aristotle, partly on St. Thomas Aquinas and partly on Dante's poetic imagination. It marks Statius as a teacher, and suggests his symbolic role in the Poem.

Along with the ancient classics Dante also read, of course, the modern and contemporary poets. In the generation before his own there were flourishing centers of song in Sicily and Tuscany and, especially, in the south of France. Just when Dante learned to read and write Provençal he never tells us, but in canto xxvi of the *Purgatorio* he manages to put into the mouth of Arnaut Daniel, the famous troubadour of Ribeyrac in Perigord, nine Provençal lines of striking beauty. Arnaut Daniel, Dante felt, had been the greatest of the Provençal poets of love, just as Bertran de Born, Lord of Hautefort, had been the supreme poet of war, and Giraut de Borneil, the outstanding poet of righteousness. From these and other Provençal poets, as from Virgil and Statius, Dante learned lessons "in the understanding of poetry," as he explains at some length in his Latin work on vernacular rhetoric, *De vulgari eloquentia.*

Of the singers of the Tuscan school Dante seems to have known personally Guittone d' Arezzo, when Guittone, now an old man, had turned from the world to the cloister. Guittone's contemporary, Bonagiunta Orbicciani degli Overardi, is made by Dante in *Purgatory* xxiv to blame a fellow notary and poet, Jacopo da Lentino, a Sicilian, for the fault of artificiality common to nearly all the Italian imitators of the Provençaux. It was immediacy of experience, Bonagiunta realized, that made all the difference between the older poets and those of the "sweet new style" of Dante and his circle.

Of these intimate friends of Dante, the best known are Guido Cavalcanti, Cino da Pistoia and Lapo Gianni. From them also Dante was willing to learn; although he was not unconscious that just as Guido Cavalcanti surpassed an earlier model, Guido Guinizelli, so

---

[27] *Ibid.,* 129.   [28] *Purg.,* xxv, 75.

would Dante himself "chase the one and the other from the nest."[29]
Guido Guinizelli was in some sense the most important of the immediate predecessors of Dante. He had become the leader of a regular
school, including such university men of Bologna as Fabruzzo de'
Lambertazzi, Guido Ghislieri, and Onesto Bolognese. From them
Dante had learned a subtle metaphysics of love which is implicit in
a very great deal of what he wrote. Guinizelli had applied to love a
philosophical analysis somewhat like that applied by the Scholastics
to knowledge. Just as the mind in the presence of objective truth
passes from possible to actual and abstract knowledge, so the "noble
heart" (cor gentile), in the presence of beauty, passes from possible
to actual and ideal love. If the beauty in question has a high spiritual
quality and if the heart has a peculiarly fine sensibility, then the love
that arises will be far removed from vulgar and sordid passion.

III

ARISTOTLE

In his reading of books Dante ranged far beyond the limits of
poetry. He tells us that after the death of Beatrice in 1290, and especially after the reading of Boethius and Cicero had fired him with
a love for wisdom, he began to frequent the schools of the religious
and the disputations of the philosophers. By 1290, St. Thomas
Aquinas and St. Bonaventure had been dead more than fifteen years.
In the meantime both Dominicans and Franciscans were lecturing
on Aristotle in all the great intellectual centers of Christendom. Just
when Dante's passion for Aristotle began is not certain; but Peripa-
teticism became to him as much a passion as poetry and politics.
Already in the *Vita Nuova,* finished it may be supposed about 1292,
there are two allusions to Aristotle as "the philosopher," *lo Filosofo.*
In the *Convivio,* which may be dated about 1307, Aristotle is mentioned by name at least fifty times, and as *lo Filosofo* very often. He
is given such other titles as "my master," "the master of human
reason," "the master and guide of humanity," "the glorious philosopher to whom nature opened wide her secrets," and so forth. Aristotle's genius is said to be "all but divine"; his opinion is of "the very

[29] *Purg.,* xi, 97–99.

highest authority." Aristotle, for Dante, was a symbol and center of
traditional Western culture, one of those supreme courts of appeal
which might not be in every instance infallible but which normally
served as a beacon light of truth to the individual tossed on a sea of
fallacies and falsehood. Aristotle, says Dante, was an authority "most
worthy to be believed and followed," *degnissimo di fede e
d'obbedienza.*[30]

This is the place to say a word on Dante's conception of authority.
It is not always easily understood. We have become, especially since
the Industrial Revolution, so accustomed to an order among men
based on subjection to power, and particularly to the power of the
purse, that we less easily grasp the medieval preference for an order
among minds based on obedience to an authority which, in turn,
rested on a faith in the primacy of reason and the ultimacy of revelation. Obedience, for Dante, means acceptance by the will; faith
(whether natural or supernatural) means acceptance by the intellect.
Not every one was capable of taking part in the discussions and debates which led little by little to the general acceptance of the
authority of Aristotle in matters of the mind. But the mass of men
came to believe that Aristotle had been sufficiently tested by the ex-
perts — much as we feel about certain things which have been tested
by the Bureau of Standards. It was not a question of majority vote
at any one moment. The mere counting of heads meant very little
to the medieval man. It was rather a question, if we must use
a modern expression, of the survival of the fittest. A tradition,
whether of thought or law or conduct, that could survive the criticism of many generations in Christendom seemed more likely to be
sound than a novel expression of private opinion. There was, of
course, no lack of criticism in the Middle Ages — as any one can find
out who will take the trouble to read a dozen consecutive pages taken
at random from, let us say, the *Summa contra gentiles* of St. Thomas
Aquinas. Authority was only worth the reason (or divine revelation)
on which it rested; Dante, who may seem almost idolatrous in his
devotion to Aristotle, is the first to insist that even the highest
authority has its limits and must be at times either rationally explained or reverently set aside.

Take, for instance, the question of a majority vote constituting
"public opinion." There is a phrase of Aristotle which to many in

[30] *Conv.,* IV, vi, 6.

Dante's day seemed to say that a majority opinion cannot be wholly wrong: *Quello che pare a li più, impossibile è del tutto essere falso.*[31] You must distinguish, says Dante. The whole world can go wrong on a matter of sensible appearance. For example, the sun seems to the senses hardly more than a foot in diameter. It is different with rational investigation. The majority of those who have calculated with their minds the dimensions of the sun know it to be, in diameter, many times as big as the earth. So that, in spite of Aristotle's authority, a majority vote is vain unless it is based on proof or reason.[32]

As Dante saw it, the authority of Aristotle was based on the fact that his system best resolved the questions: What is a man? What is the purpose of human life? What is most natural, and therefore right, for a man to seek? The end of life and, therefore, the secret of happiness is the pursuit of knowledge and virtue, the perfection of the mind and the will. Supernaturally there may be, unknown to the philosopher and undue to human nature, a supreme knowledge in the vision of God and an ultimate bliss in eternal beatitude. But as far as natural observation and thinking go, Aristotle seemed to Dante to be the wisest of men, the surest architect of human happiness. That wisdom, however, was not susceptible of a short and facile exposition. Its integral understanding and complete justification depend on the intense application of a disciplined mind to a great mass of dense and detailed discussion.

It can convey only the faintest impression of Dante's own patient and prolonged study of Aristotle to say that the poet alludes directly or indirectly to Aristotle's works nearly four hundred times, the citations being from twenty different works, some of which, like the *Nicomachean Ethics,* are very long. It must be added that in many cases where Dante quotes Aristotle it can be shown that he had read not merely the text of Aristotle, but had studied one or other of the major commentaries, by Albertus Magnus or Thomas Aquinas or Averroes.

[31] *Conv.,* IV, viii, 6.
[32] *Conv.,* IV, viii, 9.

IV

MISCELLANEOUS LEARNING

The mention of these three names is another illustration of the width and depth of Dante's reading. One of St. Thomas' students, Remigio Girolami, a Dominican friar, was established for a time in Florence; it is likely enough that Dante in his early manhood had ample opportunity of reading St. Thomas under able guidance. At any rate, by the time Dante came to write the *Convivio,* in the years between 1304 and 1307, he had a thorough knowledge of the *Contra gentiles* and the *Summa theologica* and of many of the Thomistic Commentaries on Aristotle, such as those on the *Ethics, Physics, Metaphysics, De anima,* and *Posterior Analytics.* And as the years went on Dante became hardly less familiar with the other Scholastics, with Anselm, Peter Lombard, Albertus Magnus, and Bonaventure.

There is another volume that Dante went on reading all his life. He seems almost to have known the Bible by heart. On the five hundred and more occasions when the Old and New Testaments are cited, the texts, taken from practically all the books from Genesis to the Apocalypse, seem to be at the beck and call of an astonishingly well-stored memory.

Besides the Scriptures Dante read the Fathers of the Church. In one of his Latin letters, written to the Italian cardinals, in conclave for the election of a pope to succeed Clement V who died in 1314, Dante complains that high ecclesiastics have given up the reading of the ancient Fathers and have taken to contemporary canonists. "Gregory," he says, "is covered with cobwebs; Ambrose lurks in the attics of the clergy; even Augustine is abandoned; so, too, are Dionysius, Damascene, and Bede; this or that *Speculum* [*Juris*] by Innocent or [the Bishop of] Ostia is all the rage. Why? For the simple reason that the former sought after God as their end and highest good, while the latter pave the way to pelf and position."[33]

---

[33] *Iacet Gregorius tuus in telis aranearum; iacet Ambrosius in neglectis clericorum latibulis; iacet Augustinus abiectus, Dionysius, Damascenus et Beda; et nescio quod "Speculum," Innocentium, et Ostiensem declamant. Cur non? Illi Deum quaerebant, ut finem et optimum; isti census et beneficia consequuntur. Epist.* XI, 16.

Before leaving this passage it must be remarked that, even in such outbursts, Dante never forgets the training he received (perhaps from Brunetto Latini) in the writing of Latin prose. He follows the medieval rules of ornate epistolary composition, the *ars dictaminis,* as it was called. He is careful of the *cursus,* that is to say, the "run" of

As for the Decretalists Dante at least knew enough about the *Speculum Judiciale* [or *Juris*] of Durandus, the *Summa ostiensis,* by Henry, Bishop of Ostia, and works of that sort to be able to pick out for refutation in his *Monarchia* the canonical arguments in defense of the superiority of papal to imperial authority.

Just how much of the Fathers here mentioned Dante himself had read is not altogether clear. Of the works of St. Augustine he alludes to the *De civitate Dei,* the *Confessions,* and the *De quantitate animae* in a way to make one feel that he knew at least the first two very well. There are a great many allusions to St. Gregory the Great and to Dionysius "the Areopagite" which make it clear that Dante had read the *Moralia,* the *Dialogues,* and some at least of the *Homilies* of St. Gregory, and had dipped deeply into the *De coelesti hierarchia* of Dionysius. Ambrose, Bede, and Damascene Dante may have known, much as many modern scholars know them, from the quotations in later writers like Peter Lombard and St. Thomas Aquinas.

Besides his skill in medieval cadenced prose, Dante had learned the art of writing verse according to the rules of classical prosody. Two Latin *Eclogues* that remain attest his powers. In a rather elegant but artificial composition in Latin hexameters, a professor of literature in Bologna, Giovanni del Virgilio, begged Dante, now a man of

---

accented syllables best calculated to please the ear — especially at the "close" (*clausula*) of a phrase or sentence.

The "run" of accents in the last "close" of the above passage, [bene] *ficia consequuntur,* was the most popular arrangement. It was called the "rapid run" (*cursus velox*). In its regular form, a word of four syllables with the accent on the last but one was preceded by a word of three or more syllables with the accent on the antepenultimate. The last unaccented syllable of this first word was "cut off" (*caesura*) from the second word by a short pause in reading. A somewhat similar effect is produced by the "run," *telis aranearum;* but this is slowed down by the *caesura* falling after a word of two syllables.

The regular "slow run" (*cursus tardus*) is illustrated by the "close," [cleri] *corum latibulis.* In this "run," a word of four syllables with the accent on the syllable third from the end is preceded by a word of two or more syllables with the accent on the last but one. Here again a *caesura* occurs after this first word. A recognized variation of this arrangement occurs in *finem et optimum.* The run of the accents remains the same, but the single word of four syllables is replaced by a monosyllable which precedes (or, in still another variation, follows) a word of three syllables.

A third general arrangement was known as the "smooth run" (*cursus planus*). It occurs in [Osti] *ensem declamant* and in [Augus] *tinus abiectus.* The "smooth run" was neither swift nor slow. In the regular arrangement, as in these two examples, a trisyllable with the accented syllable one from the end — "paroxytone," as the grammarians say — was preceded by a paroxytone polysyllable, with the *caesura* after the second of the five syllables that constitute the *clausula.* [Damas] *cenus et Beda* is a variation of the "smooth run" in which the paroxytone trisyllable is replaced by a monosyllable (*et*) followed by a paroxytone dissyllable (*Beda*).

Dante was fond of combining such "runs" into a compound "close." Thus, in *Deum quaerebant ut finem et optimum,* there is a normal "smooth run" in *Deum quaerebant,* a variation of this in [quaer]*ebant ut finem,* and a "slow run," *finem et optimum,* at the end.

fifty-five, to undertake some heroic theme in classical verse, to write a poem that would make him worthy of the poetic laurels of a great university.[34] Dante replied in a remarkably original bucolic poem modeled on the style of Virgil. He calls himself Tityrus and imagines he is talking with a poor fellow shepherd, Melibeus, about their great neighbor, Mopsus (Giovanni), and the promise of the laurel crown. His main point is that the only crown he wants is the laurel that he still hoped Florence might grant him for writing the *Commedia*. The professor of Bologna was charmed; and, in an eclogue very inferior to Dante's, replied to the "divine old man" (*A, divine senex*), repeating the invitation to Bologna. Dante replies in a second *Eclogue*. He is talking with the shepherd Alphesibeus, when up comes Melibeus and, with a tune on his flute, communicates the second invitation of Mopsus. Alphesibeus begs Tityrus not to desert the pleasant pastures where he now is. "Ah my dear life, I beg you, let not the dire delight delude you of having your illustrious head imprisoned between the rivers Reno and Savena [at Bologna]; because an immortal crown already is being fashioned from the laurel tree."

> *A, mea vita, precor, numquam tam dira voluptas*
> *te premat, ut Rhenus et Nayas illa recludat*
> *hoc illustre caput, cui iam frondator in alta*
> *virgine perpetuas festinat cernere frondes.*[35]

If one will read those lovely lines aloud, and particularly that last hexameter, it will be easy to see that Dante's long study and great love of Virgil was well rewarded.

Much else could be said of Dante's life of learning, for example, of his knowledge of the classical and Christian historians and of the medieval encyclopaedias. But, perhaps, enough has been said to remind us that if we try to dissolve Dante's integration of matter, music, and poetry in the *Divine Comedy* we are likely to lose much of its meaning and some, at least, of its beauty.

[34] *Promere gymnasiis te delectabor ovantum*
inclita Peneis redolentem tempora sertis.
[35] *Eclogue*, iv, 84–87.

III

The Great City on Fair Arno's Banks

. . . I' fui nato e cresciuto
sovra 'l bel fiume d' Arno a la gran villa.[1]

I

GOOD OLD DAYS

WE HAVE now seen something of the author of the *Divine Comedy* both at home with his father and mother and at school with his teachers and books. In both places, Love lectured in his heart. Of the lessons he learned there are many echoes in his Poem, particularly, in the cantos of Statius and Matelda, xx to xxix of the *Purgatory*.

These are not, however, among the most popular cantos of the Poem. Most readers prefer Dante when he passes from the mood of the home and the school to the grown-up passions of political and ecclesiastical life. They like the notes a little louder. They prefer the music written in a minor key. Particularly, when he sings of Florence, he seems to be bursting with bitterness and scorn.

Nevertheless, even here, the bitterness and scorn are those of a lover. Paradoxical as this may seem, there is never any doubt of Dante's real affection for Florence. For example, in the *Convivio*, written in exile when his bitterness was deepest, he speaks of Florence as "the loveliest and most famous of all the daughters of Rome." And he adds: "With her good leave, I long with all my heart to return and rest my weary spirit there."[2] So, too, in *De vulgari eloquen-*

[1] *Inf.*, xxiii, 94-95.
[2] *Conv.*, I, iii, 4.

47

tia, he writes: "There is no lovelier place in all the world than Florence."[3]

One can feel the combination of Dante's love and loneliness when he adds: "It is just because I loved Florence so much that I suffer an unjust exile." Dante, in fact, both loved and hated. What he loved was the Florence of his dreams, the Florence as it ought to be. What he hated was the pride and envy and greed of men who loved not Florence, but themselves.

This is the nature of nearly all of Dante's hate. It needs to be understood if we are to understand his Poem. He hates neither men nor institutions. He hates only the ignorance and sin that make men and women fail in their duty to the great institutions of society. He hates the immodesty of "the shameless dames of Florence" because their sin made duty to their homes impossible. He hates the sin he attaches to the name of his teacher, Brunetto Latini, because that kind of sin ruins the work of education. He hates the nationalism of the German kings, because nationalism interferes with the supranational work of the Holy Roman Empire. He hates the secular ambitions that he attaches — rightly or wrongly — to the name of Pope Boniface VIII, because secular ambition is bound to make a pope fail in his duty to Christendom. So, too, in Florence, Dante hates the factiousness of Guelfs and Ghibellines, of Blacks and Whites, because factiousness and peace simply do not go together.

In his heart Dante is as ready to pardon a sinner as he is to pursue his sins with scorn. He ends the great *canzone* on righteousness, *Tre donne intorno al cor mi son venuto,* by saying that "a wise man never closes the door of pardon, because pardon is the loveliest triumph of a war."[4] On the other hand, he ends the sequence of the Pietra poems — directed against the ingratitude and stoniness of Florentine politicians — by saying: "With an arrow pierce Pietra's heart, because revenge brings honor and is sweet,"[5]

The best illustration of Dante's feelings in regard to Florence can be found in the Cacciaguida cantos of the *Paradiso.* In the first of these cantos, the fifteenth, Dante is carried away on the wings of his dream to a golden age of Florence. He imagines his fellow citizens

---

[3] *In terris amoenior locus quam Florentia non existit* (I, vi).
[4] *camera di perdon savio uom non serra . . .*
 chè 'l perdonare è bel vincer di guerra. Rime, civ, 106, 107.
[5] *e dàlle per lo cor d' una saetta,*
 chè bell' onor s'acquista in far vendetta. Rime, ciii, 82–83.

living like brothers and sisters, in a heaven on earth of "sobriety, modesty, and peace,"

> Fiorenza dentro da la cerchia antica
> si stava in pace, sobria e pudica.[6]

He dreams of an age in which there was no tyranny of fashion among women, no extravagance of spending among men; an age when husbands wore simple leather jerkins and their wives came from their mirrors with unpainted lips. O happy wives! in days before foreign trade kept husbands from their homes, before the tricks of Sardanapalus emptied the nurseries of children! Those were the days when mothers rocked the cradle, spun, and told old tales of Troy, Fiesole, and Rome. Life in Florence was then so calm and sweet, the fellowship of its citizens was so full of trust, that the whole city seemed like one large home. Dante's feelings are revealed in the music of Cacciaguida's words:

> A così riposato, a così bello
>   viver di cittadini, a così fida
>   cittadinanza, a così dolce ostello,
> Maria mi diè.[7]

But, alas, heaven on earth was not to last, even on the banks of the Arno. Dante gives a hint of what was to come in the sharp contrast between "the love that breathes in a kindly will and the greed in a will that is wicked."[8] There is another hint in the contrast between the startling blaze of a falling star and the serene tranquillity of a cloudless sky:

> Quale per li seren tranquilli e puri
>   discorre ad ora ad or subito foco
>   movendo li occhi che stavan sicuri.[9]

In the next canto Dante passes from his dreams to the harsh realities of history. First came overcrowding within the ancient walls, so that the population grew to be five times what it used to be. Florence became a melting pot, filled with immigrants from Campi, Certaldo, and Fegghine, and from that pot arose "the stench," il puzzo, of alien politicians like the peasant, Baldo d'Aguglione. Worse than graft, baratteria, was the parochialism and isolationism that kept Florence from playing her proper role in the concert of Christendom under

[6] Par., xv, 97, 99.
[7] Ibid., 130–133.
[8] Ibid., 1–3.
[9] Par., xv, 13–15.

the leadership of the Holy Roman emperors. Added to all this were
the ups and downs of inexorable fortune. Lippo Velluti, for example,
now grown rich and powerful by trade and moneychanging, might
well have been a petty pedlar, had his grandfather only stayed in
Semifonte.[10] On the other hand, more nobles have become paupers
than beggars, millionaires. Gone is the renown of the once great
families, the Ughi and Catellini, the Filippi and Greci, the Ormanni
and Alberichi. But worst of all the ills of modern Florence is the
rivalry of the old nobles and the *nouveaux riches,* of the Blacks and
the Whites, *Neri* and *Bianchi.* Would to God, Buondelmonte dei
Buondelmonti had been drowned when crossing the river Ema on
his way to Florence! Then there might have been no Amidei vendetta in 1215, and the fires of hatred of the Guelfs and Ghibellines
might never have been lit in Florence.

As Dante in the Poem listens to Cacciaguida's analysis of civic ills,
he cannot help wondering what is to happen to himself in the midst
of so much discord and corruption. Not that he was afraid of the
future. He felt himself, he said, "foursquare to all the blows of fortune," *tetragono ai colpi di fortuna.*[11] And so Cacciaguida opens for
him the portals of the future. Like Hippolytus in ancient Athens, so
must Dante be exiled from Florence. A treacherous stepmother will
be found in Pope Boniface VIII, in the very Curia of the Father of
Christendom, in Rome itself, where, alas, "Christ himself is daily sold
for gold." Not even Dante's innocence will silence slander — although
the truth, at last, will out. In the meantime Dante must "leave behind him all that he loved most dearly; this will be only the first of
the arrows that the bow of exile shoots." He will have to learn how
full of salt is the taste of other people's bread, how hard the steps on
other people's stairs.

> *Tu lascerai ogni cosa diletta*
> *più caramente; e questo è quello strale*
> *che l'arco de lo esilio pria saetta.*
> *Tu proverai sì come sa di sale*
> *lo pane altrui, e come è duro calle*
> *lo scendere e 'l salir per l'altrui scale.*[12]

Worse than all will be the company of Dante's fellow exiles. They
will prove to be a wicked lot of "scoundrels, ungrateful, mad, and

[10] *Par.,* xvi. 61.
[11] *Par.,* xvii. 24.
[12] *Ibid.,* 55–60.

impious," so bestial in their ways that Dante had better form a "party by himself."[13]

There will, indeed, be consolations. And the first will be the courtesy and kindness of a great gentleman of Verona, Bartolommeo della Scala. He will be more ready to give than Dante to ask. And in the court of Verona Dante will find the young hero, Can Grande, on whom the best hopes of Christendom will rest. According to Cacciaguida's prophecy, he will do notable deeds even before the Gascon Pope betrays the high hopes of the Emperor Henry.

II

WIFE AND CHILDREN

On reading these cantos we tend to dwell on Dante's scorn for political wickedness and on his dreams of an ideal past and an impossible future. But there are other and deep emotions concealed by the deliberate indefiniteness of the line, "all that you have loved most dearly."[14] He meant, I think, his wife and children. About these a word must here be said.

The biography of Dante has suffered from a cock-and-bull story about Dante's wife. It was made up by Boccaccio out of his head. When he is through telling the incredible tale he has the honesty to admit; "I don't say these things really happened, because I don't know." He didn't know. There is not a shadow of evidence for the fable that Dante was hurried into a marriage by his relations because of his despair after the death of Beatrice, that the marriage turned out unhappily, and that, at the time of the exile, in 1302, Dante was delighted to get rid of his nagging Xanthippe.

The simple historical fact is that Dante was betrothed while still a boy of eleven, on February 9, 1277. The custom was common enough in those days. Dante's parents were both dead and an all but next-door neighbor, Manetto Donati, was Dante's guardian. There is nothing surprising in the fact that the young Dante was betrothed to Manetto's daughter, Gemma. And it would not be in the least surprising if the *promessi sposi* grew in affection for each other long before their marriage. It is certain that Dante was fond of some of

---

[13] *Ibid.*, 62–69.   [14] *Par.*, xvii, 55–56.

Gemma's relations. We have already seen his affection for Forese
Donati. Two cantos of the *Purgatory* are dedicated to Forese's memory. Two of the loveliest cantos of the *Paradiso* are devoted to
Forese's sister, Piccarda. It is she who is made to utter Dante's most
famous line: *E 'n la sua volontade è nostra pace,* "And in His will is
our peace."[15]

In the beginning of the *Paradiso,* Dante passes with Beatrice from
the earthly paradise, on the top of his hill of purgatory, to the moon.
Shades of redeemed souls appear to him, very faint at first and delicate, like the color of a pearl against a girl's face, and looking less like
persons than like images in a mirror or in still water. Dante was so
overcome by the heavenly beauty that his "will was too full for
words."[16] But he manages to ask the name of the shade that seemed
most eager to speak. It was Piccarda. She recalls how in the world she
was a nun, *vergine sorella,* and says that if Dante will but look he will
recognize who she is. Dante finds in her "marvelous beauty something more than human."[17] Piccarda's place is with the lowest in
paradise, but she is utterly happy because, as she says, in God's will
is our peace. She tells the story of the ruthless men who dragged her
from her peace and forced her into marriage; and she points to her
companion, Constance of Sicily, who, suffering a similar fate, became
the mother of the Emperor Frederick II. After which Piccarda began
to sing, as in her convent days, *Ave Maria,* and singing she passed
from sight softly and swiftly like something heavy sinking into a
deep pool.

> *Così parlommi, e poi cominciò Ave*
> *Maria, cantando; e cantando vanio*
> *come per acqua cupa cosa grave.*[18]

Loving Forese and Piccarda Donati so much, it is hard to see why
Dante should have loved his wife much less. But, of course, we have
no means of knowing for certain — unless, as seems probable, the
"noble lady, young and very beautiful," described in the *Vita
Nuova*[19] was Gemma Donati. She is pictured at a window, looking at
Dante after the death of Beatrice, so full of compassion that "all pity
seemed gathered within her." And Dante adds: "A lady so compassionate I could surely love with a most perfect love." It is true that
much of what Dante says of this *donna gentile* was later applied, alle-

---

[15] *Par.,* iii, 85.   [17] *Ibid.,* 59.   [19] xxxv, 2.
[16] *Ibid.,* 36.   [18] *Par.,* iii, 121-123.

gorically, to philosophy — just as much that is said of Virgil and
Beatrice can be understood, allegorically, of human reason and divine revelation. But there is, presumably, always some real person
behind each of Dante's symbols, and it is difficult to believe that
Dante was merely allegorical when he wrote: "The sight of this lady
brought me into so unwonted a condition that I often thought of her
as of one too dear to me, and I began to consider her thus: 'This lady
is young, beautiful, gentle, and wise; perhaps it was Love himself
who set her in my path, so my life might find peace.' And there were
times when I thought yet more fondly, until my heart consented to
Love's reasoning."[20]

But, whether or not the tender words for the *gentile donna* are
the echo of a real affection, we know that Gemma Donati became
Dante's wife and the mother of his children and the faithful cus-
todian of the family property in the difficult days of Dante's exile.
Of two of Gemma's sons, Pietro and Jacopo, and of a daughter,
Antonia, we have abundant information. There is evidence of a
third son, Giovanni, and some of a fourth son, Dante.

Pietro we know from his commentary on his father's *Commedia*.
It reveals a great width of interest and scholarship, and something of
Dante's own zeal for righteousness and truth. Pietro took his doc-
torate in law at the University of Bologna. He became a successful
lawyer and later a judge in Verona. He died sometime after 1360,
leaving a considerable fortune and a large family. A ten-line epitaph
says he was pious and just in youth and age, and learned in the
civil and canon law, and that he held the key that could open the
mysteries of his father's *Commedia*. Three of his daughters, Alighiera,
Gemma, and Lucia, became nuns; and of his other children the
names Dante, Jacopo, Pietro, Antonia, and Bernardo all suggest
affection for his father's memory.

Pietro's commentary is written in a clear, concise, businesslike,
fourteenth-century Latin. Its erudition is amazing for a man with so
many domestic and professional obligations. Biblical and classical
quotations abound on almost every page along with references to
legal texts from Ulpian and the *Decreta*. There are abundant citations from Fathers of the Church, Scholastic theologians, and Arabian
scholars and philosophers like Albumassar, Alfraganus, Averroes, and
Avicenna. There are about 150 references to St. Augustine, over

[20] *Vita Nuova*, xxxviii, 1.

eighty to Aristotle, sixty to Boethius, nearly fifty to St. Thomas; and there are odd allusions to writers like Anacreon, Apuleius, Flavius Josephus, Martial, Trogus Pompeius, and Vegetius.

Pietro had one purpose in his commentary, namely, to unlock what he calls "the treasury of the proper [or primary] wisdom" of the Poem. He thought of his father as "a glorious theologian, philosopher, and poet." By the wisdom of the Poem he meant the seven senses in which it may be understood, literal, historical, apologetic, metaphorical, allegorical, tropological, and anagogic. He admits, of course, that the "purpose of poetry is pleasure," but he also held, with Horace and Dante, that poetry is meant for our mental and moral good. Poetry, Pietro says, is "a part of ethics." He spends twenty pages on canto I of the *Inferno* to make clear that, whatever else it is, the *Commedia* is an allegory of man's universal longing to escape the dark lowlands of ignorance and sin in order to reach the heights of knowledge and virtue with the help of reason and revelation. What he calls "the moral speculation" interests him most. Other and purely literary matters, he says, the reader "can make out for himself."

Dante's other son, Jacopo, tried hard to make himself a poet, but never quite succeeded. He was old enough in 1315 to have his name mentioned in a Florentine decree renewing the condemnation of his exiled father. He was in Ravenna in 1321 when Dante died, and it was he who presented to Guido da Polenta the first complete copy of the *Commedia* of which there is record. Like Pietro, Jacopo was preoccupied with what he calls the "study of the high, deep vision of which Dante was the lowly artist"; but he was obviously not insensible to what he calls in a lovely phrase, "the beauties in my little sister's eyes," *le bellezze che mia sorella nel suo lume porta.* The Poem was his little sister, because both he and it had a single father. Jacopo seems to have died during the Black Death of 1348. He never got beyond the *Inferno* in his commentary.

In some sense the sincerest of all commentaries on the *Commedia* was written by Dante's daughter, Antonia. "The purpose of the poem," Dante himself had written, in a famous letter to Can Grande della Scala of Verona, "is to lead those who are living in this life from misery to a state of happiness."[21] Antonia decided, no doubt with Dante concurring, that the nearest thing to happiness in this

[21] *Epist.,* xiii, 39.

valley of tears was to be found in the cloister; so with the name of Sister Beatrice she lived in the convent of Santo Stefano dell' Uliva in Ravenna.

III

HEARTS ON FIRE

When Dante went into exile in 1302, there were, of course, other satisfactions besides family joys that he was forced to leave behind. His heart and head had been, for seven years, deeply devoted to Florentine political life. To this we must now turn.

It is characteristic of the schematism of the *Divine Comedy* that canto VI of the *Inferno* should be dedicated to the politics of Dante's native city, Florence, canto VI of the *Purgatorio* to his fatherland, Italy, and canto VI of the *Paradiso* to the supranational Holy Roman Empire. Dante loved all three. But, just because he loved them, his tongue is sharp in speaking of their failings. Citizen of Christendom as he was, he was primarily a citizen of Florence, and it is of Florence that he speaks most vehemently.

Down in the third circle of hell where "heavy, cold, accursed, unending rain . . . great lumps of hail, snow, and a murk of water drive through the black air . . . and the earth stinks," and Cerberus, the cruel beast, three-headed, red-eyed, greasy of beard, big-bellied, barks like a dog and with his claws "tears, and flays and quarters" the poor sinners who are suffering for their sins of gluttony, Dante meets his old friend, Ciacco, "the hog" of Florence. Like Dante's other friends, Brunetto Latini and Forese Donati, Ciacco was so disfigured by his punishments as to be unrecognizable. "It seems not that I ever saw you," says Dante. But, drenched and bedraggled as he was, Ciacco could talk. "Your city," he said, "is so full of envy that the sack is running over." "And what, then," asks Dante, "will become of the citizens of the divided city?" Ciacco replies: "There will be a long period of tension. Then they will come to blood. And the 'party of the woods' will drive the others out. But before two years are up, the Whites will fall and the Blacks will gain the upper hand, thanks to the man [Pope Boniface VIII] who now keeps playing one against the other. With heads held high, the Blacks will hold the others down, sad and shameful as such things sound. Of just men there are two, but no heed is paid them. Pride, envy, avarice — these are the three sparks that have set all hearts on fire."

> Superbia, invidia, e avarizia sono
> le tre faville c' hanno i cuori accesi.[22]

Dante deftly turned Ciacco's thoughts from the hell on earth to the hell where he was suffering. What, he asks, of the great heroes of Florentine political history, Farinata degli Uberti and Tegghiaio Aldobrandi, "who were so worthy," and Jacopo Rusticucci, Arrigo Mosca, and the others "who set their minds on working for the common weal? Tell me where they are, for I am dying to know. Are their lives sweetened up in heaven or poisoned here in hell?" "Down among the blackest souls," answers Ciacco, "and the worse their sin the deeper down. If you go deep enough, you will see them there."[23]

Then Ciacco, with a squint in his eyes, took one last look at Dante, bowed his head and fell full length in "the filthy scum."[24]

The canto of Brunetto Latini gives no better account of Florence and its ways. "A folk greedy, envious, and proud," Brunetto says to Dante, *gente avara, invidiosa e superba;* "from their customs see that you keep yourself clean. It will be to your honor that both parties will be hungry to have you — but the grass will be far from the goats. Let the beasts from Fiesole make fodder of themselves and leave alone the plants — growing on their dunghill — in which the holy seed still lives of those Romans who remained in Florence when it became the nest of so much wickedness."[25]

In the circle of Brunetto, Dante meets Tegghiaio Aldobrandi and Jacopo Rusticucci of whom Ciacco had spoken. Along with them was the great soldier, Guido Guerra. Of all three, Dante had often, as he tells us, "heard with affection, and retold, their names and honored deeds."[26] The three shades rushed through the flames when they recognized, by his dress, a fellow citizen of their "depraved country." "Tell us," they asked, "if chivalry and valor are still at home in Florence as of old, or have they gone clean out of it?" To which Dante, looking toward the city above, replied: "O Florence, the rapid profits of the upstart rich have given birth in thee to pride

[22] *Inf.*, vi, 4, 5.
[23] *Ibid.*, 79–87.
[24] *Ibid.*, 91–93.
[25] *Inf.*, xv, 68–78.
[26] *Di vostra terra sono, e sempre mai
l' ovra di voi e li onorati nomi
con affezion ritrassi e ascoltai*, xvi, 58–60.

and such disorder that thou already ruest it." And the three, who took this for the answer, "looked one at the other as one looks at truth." And then, as fast as you can say Amen, they rushed away.

Even in canto VI of the *Purgatory*, which is dedicated to Italy, Dante manages to give another dark picture of his fellow Florentines. This time he resorts to irony. In Florence, he says mockingly, the bow of justice is stretched to the very utmost! Others may shirk their civic duties, but in Florence one and all cry out: "I bend me to the burden!" *I' mi sobbarco!* Then, addressing Florence: "What more do you need to make you happy, with your people so rich, so wise, so much at peace? What were Athens and Sparta, for all their laws and civil life, compared to you? You make such finespun provisions in October that . . . they are worn out by the middle of November! You change your laws and customs as fast as you do your money and your men in office . . . You are like a sick woman tossing in bed to ease her pains."[27]

Florence had enjoyed ten years of quasi-democracy under Guelf leadership between 1250, the death of Frederick II, and 1260. It was this period that Dante has in mind when he speaks so movingly of Tegghiaio Aldobrandi, Jacopo Rusticucci, and the others "who set their minds on the common good."[28] The period ended with the disastrous defeat of the Guelfs at the battle of Montaperti, September 4, 1260. The Ghibellines returned to power and put a stop to con- stitutional progress. Dante has conveyed his feelings in regard to those later days of Ghibelline triumph in the canto devoted to the skeptical philosopher, Cavalcante Cavalcanti (father of Dante's friend, Guido), and the arrogant aristocrat, Farinata degli Uberti.

Farinata's voice issues mysteriously from one of the uncovered tombs in which Epicurus and his followers await the day of final judgment. "O Tuscan," he said, "may I beg you to pause for a moment. Your speech tells me you are a native of that noble father- land to which, I fear, I did much harm."[29] And meanwhile he raised himself to his full height so that his head and shoulders showed above the top of the tomb. On his face there was a look of scorn as though "he held even hell in great contempt."[30] Dante drew nearer to the tomb. Farinata, looking down at him, asked contemptuously: "And who were your ancestors?" Dante told him. "Fierce enemies," said

[27] *Purg.*, vi, 127–151.
[28] *Inf.*, vi, 81.
[29] *Inf.*, x, 22–27.
[30] *Ibid.*, 36.

Farinata, lifting his brows a little, "to me and to my family and to my party; so that twice I sent them into exile" — in 1248 and again in 1260 after Montaperti. "And both times," Dante quickly answered, "they returned"; as, indeed, the Guelfs did in 1251 and again in 1266. After a dramatic and emotional interruption by Cavalcante, during which Farinata remained coldly imperturbable, he continued: "It pains me more than hell to think that exiled Uberti should not return to so dear a place as Florence. But why," he asked, "are the Florentines so unforgiving?" Dante reminded him of the havoc and slaughter of Montaperti "that dyed the Arbia with blood." For that, said Farinata, I was not solely responsible; but when there was talk — as there was at the Ghibelline conference of Empoli — of wiping Florence off the face of the earth, "it was I and I alone who openly defended her."

And there in the Poem Dante leaves the story, content to have portrayed immortally the strange combination of pride and skepticism with civic loyalty and family love that wrought such harm to Florence. What actually happened after the battle of Montaperti, in 1260, was disastrous in the extreme. The palaces of the Guelfs were demolished and their properties outside the walls were robbed. Dozens of them, fearing death, went into exile. The Captain of the People who had given some appearance of democracy to Florence was cast into prison. The guilds on which all economic life depended were left intact, but the Ghibellines put back a *Podestà* in supreme authority, set up two Councils, manned with party men, and acknowledged an imperial vicar ruling in the name of Frederick's son, Manfred of Sicily.

Meanwhile, a new star rose above the political horizon of Florence. Charles of Anjou, brother of Louis IX of France, who had been invited in 1263 by Pope Urban IV to assume the crown of Naples, was urged by the new Pope, Clement IV, to come to Italy. In May, 1265, the month of Dante's birth, Charles reached Rome; in the January of the following year, with the consent of the Pope, he was crowned King of Sicily and Apulia. With a promise to send Manfred to hell or be dispatched himself to heaven, he set out to attack his rival. On February 26, 1266, at Benevento, Manfred was defeated and slain; his end is exquisitely told by Dante in the third canto of the *Purgatory*.

Charles of Anjou began his work in Florence as soon as he was safe on the throne of Sicily. He commissioned with supreme civic powers two Knights of Our Lady, "jovial friars," *frati godenti,* Catalano dei Talavolti and Loderingo degli Andalò. Dante puts them among the hypocrites in the sixth "pocket" of the eighth "circle" of hell. All he could say when he saw them was: "O Brothers, the ill you wrought. . . ."[31] The friars had managed, in the fair name of peace and reconciliation, to get rid of the imperial garrison; but, instead of peace, party rancor had raised its head higher than ever. In the scuffle for power the Ghibelline, Gianni de' Soldanieri, went over to the Guelfs, got himself named Captain of the People, and turned on Guido Novello who had done his best to keep some kind of order. This traitor, Gianni, is put by Dante deep down in hell, in the second zone of the ninth circle, along with the barking Bocca degli Abati who, at the battle of Montaperti, had treacherously gone over to the Ghibellines. Gianni and his new friends made some kind of pretense at establishing order, somewhat along the lines of the democratic constitution of 1250, and there was some attempt to settle family feuds by marrying Guelfs with Ghibellines. But the foreign influence both of Charles of Anjou and the French Pope, Clement IV, worked on the whole against popular government. The government was put in the hands of twelve Good Men (*buoni uomini*), and the powerful Guelf Party (*parte guelfa*) took over the real reins of power.

Better times appeared about to dawn when an Italian Pope, Gregory X, a Visconti, followed the two Frenchmen, Urban IV (1261–1264) and Clement IV (1265–1269). Peace of a sort was fixed up in 1273, but neither the Angevin king nor the factious nobles had much thought save for their own advantage; bloody brawl followed upon bloody brawl in the streets of Florence.

In 1277, an Orsini, Nicholas III, became pope, and three years later his nephew, Cardinal Latino Malabranca, was sent on a mission of peace to Florence. He remained in the city as peacemaker from October, 1279, to April, 1280. In November there was a great assembly in the *Piazza* of Santa Maria Novella, and the Cardinal was voted the most complete powers to execute his designs of peace. In January another meeting listened to the solemn reading of his decisions. In February, 1280, the leaders of the opposing families came to the *piazza* to give each other the kiss of peace.

[31] *Inf.,* xxiii, 109.

Dante was a youth of fifteen at the time. He must have watched
with enormous curiosity what went on that day. Two objects of his
hero worship — Brunetto Latini and Guido Cavalcanti — were there;
and also his guardian Manetto Donati. And there were many others
whom Dante would later condemn to hell: the Archbishop of Pisa,
Ruggieri degli Ubaldini, who was to leave Conte Ugulino and his
sons to starve to death in the "tower of hunger" in Pisa, and whose
head was to be eternally gnawed in hell by the murdered Count;
Bocca degli Abati, the traitor of Montaperti; Buoso Donati, who may
be the robber Buoso who spends his eternity in hell exchanging
shapes with a creeping serpent; and others.

Constitutionally, the peace of Cardinal Latino seemed of much
importance. Guelfs and Ghibellines lost their party power. A system
of checks and balances was introduced. The Podestà was to be aided
by two councils, picked from the six sections of the city. The guilds
were to help the Governor of the People in the task of keeping
order. Of the Ancients (*Anziani*) who formed the government (*Signoria*), eight were to be Guelfs and six Ghibellines. There was to be
a council to regulate the treasury. And so on. All this was in the
direction of democratic civic order. But, whatever the young Dante
may have hoped at the time, he later felt that this peace was no more
solid than previous attempts at pacification. The Pope of the peace,
Nicholas III, is damned in Dante's hell among the simonists, stuffed
into a hole in a livid rock, upside down and with flames burning
on the soles of his wriggling feet. One of the commissioners of the
peace, Andrea dei Mozzi, later Bishop of Florence in 1287, is ranked
by Dante with the unnatural sinners.

Another French Pope, Martin IV, followed Nicholas III in 1281.
He proved to be a servant of Angevin interests. Nevertheless, Florence began at last to feel strong enough to resist every outside
influence — whether of Pope or Emperor or the King of Naples.

In 1282, when Dante was seventeen, an important constitutional
measure was taken in Florence. The Priors of the guilds were em-
powered to aid the fourteen Ancients in the government of the
city, and before long the Priors took over the whole of the effective
government of Florence. The rule of each committee of six Priors
was to last two months. During that time they had to be at the
absolute service of the city. They were to live in the Torre della
Castagna, across the street from the Alighieri home, and have even

their food and drink regulated for them. Most of these Priors were merchants of great means, but at least, more than the nobles, they had the peace and prosperity of the city at heart. Among the earliest of the Priors was Folco Portinari, father of Dante's Beatrice.

IV

Citizen of Florence

In the year following the institution of the Priors, Dante may be said to have entered upon his mature citizenship of Florence. Being an orphan, he came of age at eighteen in 1283. This was the year of his first sonnet, *A ciascun alma presa e gentil core*. It was likewise the year in which his name first appears in a public document. It was a matter of no great moment — being merely a statement by a public notary, Spigliato Aldobrandini, that Dante son of Alaghiero, as heir of his dead father, made a settlement in regard to a small mortgage which Alaghiero had held against the property of Donato del Papa.

The 80's were for Florence mainly years of military activity, and Dante took his share both in the military parades that marked these years as also in actual battles. It is just possible, for example, that one of the sonnets in the *Vita Nuova, Cavalcando l' altr' ier per un cammino,*[32] may have been written on the occasion of the military aid that was sent by Florence in 1285 to help the Sienese raise the siege of Poggio a Santa Cecilia, attacked by the Ghibellines of Arezzo. What is more certain is that Dante had a part in the battle of Campaldino, fought June 11, 1289. Early in June, 1600 horse and 10,000 foot set out from Florence. The opposing Aretines had a smaller force of 800 horse and 8000 foot, commanded by the trained soldier, Buonconte da Montefeltro. The battle began with the assault of an Aretine company of horse, the attackers *(feditori).* This was met by a similar company of horse, commanded by Vieri dei Cerchi of Florence. In this company of Florentine *feditori* Dante Alighieri had a place. Later, he wrote in a letter that for a moment he was afraid, but that when the fight was over he was full of joy. He had good reason for fear. The Aretine attack was only driven back by the brilliant charge executed by Corso Donati with 200 horse of

[32] *Vita Nuova,* ix, 9.

Lucca and Pistoia. When it was over, some of the most famous of the Ghibellines lay dead on the field — among them Buonconte da Montefeltro.

Of Buonconte and the battle of Campaldino Dante has left us a memorable record in *Purgatory* v. On the second terrace of the antepurgatory Dante meets the souls of those who, in the moment of violent death, were given grace to repent of their sins. Fleeing on foot and bloodying the plain from a wound in his throat, Buonconte reached the point where the river Archiano joins the Arno. When he could no longer see nor speak, he fell — with the name of Mary on his lips. An angel of God snatched his soul, but a devil cried out: "O you of heaven, why do you rob me? Take if you must the immortal part of him — that one little tear has robbed from me; but over the rest of him sovereignty is mine." Satan, with thought linked to a will forever bent on ill, and with the power his nature gave him, moved the mist and wind and raised a storm. The swollen Archiano carried Buonconte's frozen body to the Arno. The waters tore apart the cross which he had made with his dying arms folded on his breast. The dead body swung from bank to bank on the bottom of the Arno, until the river rubble became his winding sheet.

The story, as far as we know, is wholly of Dante's fancy and is largely a counterpart to the story of Buonconte's father, Guido, who died with all the blessings of holy Church, but is damned by Dante for giving fraudulent counsel to Pope Boniface VIII.[33]

After Campaldino there were skirmishes made in the hope of capturing Arezzo; to these Dante may be alluding in the opening lines of canto XXII of the *Inferno*.

In August, 1289, Florence sent 400 horse and 2000 foot soldiers to help Lucca against Pisa;[34] and to the capture of Caprona, during this campaign, Dante makes allusion in some lines in *Inferno*.[35]

Along with war there was a great deal of economic and political agitation in Florence during the five years between 1288 and 1293. The year 1292 was particularly fateful. The five lesser guilds agitated against the concentration of power in the hands of the magnates who controlled the seven principal guilds. The agitations, led by Giano della Bella, ended in the Ordinances of Justice published January 15, 1293.

It was to defend the normal peace-loving citizens against the brawls

[33] *Inf.*, xxvii, 66–132.   [34] *Villani*, vii, 137.   [35] *Inf.*, xxi, 94–96.

of the *grandi* — nobles and *nouveaux-riches* — that Giano insisted, among other measures, on the formation of a citizen militia of a thousand men who could be called out by a sheriff (*Gonfaloniere della Giustizia*). The sheriff was to have a seat with the Priors in the Government and, like them, was to be elected for a period of two months.

Dante had no direct part in the formulation of the Ordinances, and there may seem to be something of contempt in his one allusion to Giano della Bella as a man who bears the "beautiful escutcheon" of the "great baron" (Hugh, the imperial Vicar in Tuscany who died in 1006), but who "today has ranged himself with the people."[36]

On the other hand, it was not long before Dante himself "ranged himself with the people." This he did by having his name inscribed in one of the lesser guilds, as soon as a reform of the Ordinances in July, 1295, made this possible. He was now thirty and eligible to serve on one or other of the five city councils. There were two councils of the Podestà — a Special Council of ninety members and a General Council of 300; and two of the Captain of the People — one of thirty-six members and the other of 150. Finally there was the Council of One Hundred, which gave advice on all major financial affairs. The minutes of many of the sessions of these Councils have long been lost, but the name of Dante appears as one of the thirty-six members of the Special Council of the Captain of the People in the session which began on November 1, 1295. That he was not particularly active seems evident from the fact that he is marked for six absences; for each he would have been obliged to pay a legal fine of ten *soldi*.

In December, 1295, his name appears in association with the Directors of the Twelve Guilds. At a meeting on December 14 of the outgoing Priors with fifty or so of the Directors and a commission of picked advisers (*Savi*), under the presidency of the Chief Justice, Dante was present in the capacity of an adviser. The meeting was concerned with the method to be adopted in the election of the new Priors; Dante is recorded as being in favor of the motion to put the election in the hands of the Directors and their advisers.

[36] *Par.*, xvi, 131.

V

BONIFACE VIII

Throughout the year 1296 Dante appears to have engaged more earnestly in political life. It was in many ways a critical year; not least, because it marked the entrance of the strong figure of Pope Boniface VIII on the stage of Florentine history. Appeal had been made to him by the *grandi* who feared that the government of Florence was about to rescind the decree of banishment and recall Giano della Bella. The appeal was successful. On January 23 the Pope issued a brief demanding that Florence continue to enforce the decree, and threatening excommunication and interdict if the demand were not respected.

At the time of the brief, Dante was still a member of the Special Council of the Captain. His term expired with the new election of May 1; but three weeks later, on May 23, he allowed himself to be elected to one of the vacancies in the Council of the Hundred. That he soon rose to a position of special authority in the Council seems clear from the minutes of a meeting of June 15. The debate turned on the outrages committed by certain of the *grandi* on plain citizens who, while in office, had been obliged to take action against the nobles. An active minority of the Council defended the *grandi*. At the end came Dante who was called upon to sum up the debate. His arguments clinched the case against the nobles.

Unfortunately there are no minutes preserved of any meetings of the Florentine councils for the early months of 1297. It is not possible, therefore, to know whether Dante was elected on November 1, 1296, to the Council of the Captain or on January 1, 1297, to the Council of the Podestà. He would not have been eligible for immediate re-election to the Council of the Hundred after the expiration of his office at the end of September. But, member of a council or not, he was stirred deeply by one event of 1297. In May of that year one of the Colonna family attempted to rob the papal treasure of 200,000 gold florins on its way from Anagni to Rome. Boniface VIII proclaimed a "crusade" against the Colonna family. Cardinal Matteo d'Acquasparta was sent to Florence to proclaim this "holy war." The sad memory of the fall of Acre in 1291 was but six years old. How little such a "crusade" was to Dante's liking appears in the bitter words he puts into the mouth of Guido da Montefeltro in the *bolgia* of "fraudulent counselors" in the *Inferno*: "The prince of the new pharisees [Boniface VIII], paying no regard to his supreme office nor to his holy orders, waged war, not with the Saracens or the Jews, but near the Lateran. All his enemies were Christians, not men who had helped to conquer Acre, nor traffickers in the Sultan's land."[37]

We have no documents dealing with Dante's political activity during the following year, 1298, but it is easy to believe that, whatever else he did, he watched with a good deal of horror the developments in the war between the Pope and the Colonna family. Boniface tricked the Colonna into surrendering their stronghold at Palestrina. He then had the palace leveled with the ground. The story got around that Count Guido da Montefeltro (who, in 1296, became a Franciscan) was asked by Boniface for counsel how best he could bring about the destruction of Palestrina. Guido answered: "Be long on promises and short on keeping them." Out of this story Dante's fancy created one of the most striking episodes of the *Inferno*.

In the eighth *bolgia* of the eighth circle, sinners flit about concealed in the form of flames, like fireflies in a dark valley, save that the flickering of these flames, like tongues, could utter words. From one such flame the spirit of Ulysses is made to tell his tale of sailing half around the world, out beyond the Pillars of Hercules to within sight of Dante's hill of purgatory.[38] When the tale was told, a second flame came up, giving forth muffled sounds of pain. The moanings became at last words with meaning: "O thou at whom I aim my voice . . . take it not ill to remain awhile and speak with me, even though I have come a little late. . . . Tell me if the people of Romagna are at peace or war." Dante answers: "O hidden soul down there, thy Romagna is not, nor ever was, without war in the hearts of its tyrants; but of open wars I left none there just now." When at last Dante asks the sinner in the flame his name, Guido da Montefeltro answers:

I was a man of arms and then became a follower of St. Francis, hoping by the wearing of his girdle to make amends; and my hope would have been fulfilled had it not been for the great priest (a curse upon him!) who set me back in my former sins. . . . There were no sly nor hidden ways I did not know and follow, as all the world now knows. But when I saw that I had reached a point in life when a man should lower sails and

[37] *Inf.*, xxvii, 85–92.   [38] *Inf.*, xxvi, 90–142.

coil the ropes, what had pleased me once now made me sad, and I repented, and was absolved, and took the friar's girdle. And Oh! what grief to think how well it might have been. . . . The prince of the new pharisees . . . reckless of his supreme office and his holy orders and of my religious girdle, called me like a doctor to cure the fever of his pride, much as Constantine once sought out Silvester on Mount Soracte to cure his leprosy. . . . He demanded counsel of me. I made no reply because his words seemed drunken. Then he insisted: "Let not your heart be troubled. I give you absolution now. Only, you must show me how Palestrina may be leveled with the ground. I can lock and unlock heaven, as you know. For that I have two keys — which my predecessor [Celestine V] esteemed too little." When his weighty arguments pushed me to a point where I felt silence to be wrong, I said: "Father, since you wash away the sin into which I now must fall, be long on promises and short on keeping them, and you will triumph in your lofty seat." Then I died, and St. Francis came to take me; but one of the black cherubim said to him: "Take him not; do me no wrong. He must come down among my minions, because he gave the fraudulent counsel. From that moment I have had him by the hair. You see, no repentance, no absolution; and to repent and will a thing at the same time is impossible — the plain contradiction not permitting it." Oh, woe is me! How I shook when he seized me, saying: "I guess you did not think I was so good at logic." He carried me to Minos; and Minos twined his tail eight times about his rigid back, and in his furious rage he bit his tail, saying: "This is a sinner for the enveloping flame." And so here I am, where you see me, lost; and in these clothes I wander broken-hearted.

And so his words were ended, and the flame passed on, writhing and tossing its pointed top in pain.[39]

In Florence a good deal happened during the winter 1298–1299 that made Dante unhappy. He found that he had, for the first time, to "put up with the stench of that yokel from Aguglione," who was a Prior in 1298. Baldo was a Ghibelline who turned Guelf to save his skin. Then, after taking a leading part in drawing up the *Ordinamenti della Giustizia,* when the wind turned, he helped to drive Gianno della Bella out of Florence. When Niccolò Acciaiuoli got into trouble for bribing the Podestà, Baldo conveniently tore out a page of the record that could have been used in evidence. Dante alludes to the unpleasant business in a line of the *Purgatorio.*[40]

This brings us to 1300. It is the year which is sometimes taken to mark the end of the Middle Ages and the beginning of the Modern World. It is the year which Dante later chose as the year of the "high fancy" which took him down to hell, up the hill of purgatory, and beyond the stars to paradise. It was the year when he was thirty-five, "halfway along the road of life," *nel mezzo del cammin di nostra*

[39] *Inf.,* xxvii, 67–132.   [40] *Purg.,* xxii, 105.

vita.[41] It was a year when no one in Florence could be indifferent to public affairs. Political passions ran high. The feud between Vieri dei Cerchi and Corso Donati was dividing the whole population within the walls; outside, the Ghibellines in the country were lining up with the Cerchi to oppose the alliance of the Donati party with the Pope. Deeper than all was the fear of the ordinary citizens lest the *Ordinamenti della Giustizia* should lose their vigor. It was not a Florence in which a poet and rigorous moralist like Dante could hope to play any immediately and decisively practical part. Yet nowhere could he better study the play of those passions that would one day fill the *Inferno*.

More threatening even than the factions within the walls seemed to Dante the secular ambitions of Pope Boniface VIII. There was talk of the Pope wanting the Emperor-elect, Albert of Habsburg, to cut off Tuscany from the Empire and make it a principality for one of the Pope's relations. And there were Florentine bankers in the Curia who were not opposed to the Pope's plans. An embassy was sent to Rome to congratulate the Pope, but with secret instructions to investigate the matter. When they returned they named names. Three bankers were accused of treason, and fined 2000 lire ($3,000) each. One of the important men on the embassy was a typical Florentine politician of those days. He had been in and out of many of the city offices, and finally on April 15 — three days before the punishment of the traitor-bankers — became one of the Priors. He belonged to the party of the Cerchi and, like many men in Florentine public life, was some kind of a poet. But he was not above taking an occasional bribe. It was this that Dante seems to have had in mind when he makes Cacciaguida complain that in the "good old days" a rogue like Lapo Salterelli would have been as much a wonder as an honest man like Cincinnatus would be a miracle in the Florence of Dante's day.[42]

It was during the priorate of Lapo Salterelli that Dante was chosen for no less important a mission than an embassy to San Gemignano. And it was his task to strengthen the Guelf League which at the moment was helping Boniface VIII in one of the least spiritual of his enterprises — the enrichment of his nephews at the expense of Ghibelline nobles.

Meanwhile, Pope Boniface seems to have been seriously preoccupied about the internal peace of Florence. He invited Vieri dei

[41] *Inf.*, i, 1.   [42] *Par.*, xv, 128, 129.

Cerchi to the Curia in the hope of reconciling him with Corso Donati. The Pope went further in sending Cardinal Matteo d'Acquasparta as a peacemaker (*paciaro*) to Florence, and the bull prepared for this occasion shows Boniface in a very different light from that cast by the bitter invectives of the *Commedia*. Yet Dante was, seemingly, in an excellent position to make up his mind on the sincerity of the Pope. It was, in fact, while Cardinal Matteo was at work in Florence that Dante reached the very height of Florentine political ambition. He was named as one of the Priors on June 14, 1300. According to the Christian custom of those days, the six newly elected Priors spent the night in vigil and prayer. Next day, June 15, they were installed in the *Palazzo della Signoria,* which was then being built.

Before the second week was up, a crisis of the first order occurred to tax the patience of the new Priors. The Feast of St. John the Baptist was then, as it still is, one of the most notable days in the Florentine calendar. On the eve, June 23, it was the custom for the consuls of the guilds and the guildsmen to form in procession and proceed to make an annual offering in honor of the city patron, St. John. As they moved down the street, they were startled by the clatter of armed horsemen. Followers of both Corso Donati and Vieri dei Cerchi united for the moment against their common enemy, the simple guildsmen. To the cry, "It is we who won the victory at Campaldino; and it is you who have deprived us of all office and honor in the city," the scuffle began. It was a scandal alike to the Cardinal and to the Priors. But the action of Dante and his associates was as prompt as it was impartial. Cardinal Matteo was called in to hear their decision. The ringleaders were seized and banished from Florence. Among the condemned was one of Dante's dearest friends, Guido Cavalcanti. He was sent to Sarzana in Lunigiana. There he caught fever in the rigorous summer heat. He was allowed to return to his native air, but died before the end of August, and was buried in Santa Reparata.

Meanwhile, word got to the Priors that the Cardinal was secretly in favor of the Donati party, and that he was stirring up the enmity of Lucca in order to embarrass Florence. Dante and his associates promptly countered by strengthening the guards and, in a letter drafted by Dino Compagni, they warned Lucca to beware. At no time did Dante and his associates fully trust the Cardinal. Immediately after the brawlers of the vigil of St. John had been condemned, the Cardinal had asked for plenipotentiary powers to proceed to a pacification of the city. The *Signoria* stood firm. It may have been Dante who formulated their position. The Priors were willing to back the Cardinal, if only he would try to effect at least a truce for the next two or three years between the factions, but they wished him to use his power with discretion. In other words, they were fully in favor of the papal purpose of civic peace, but they were against any extension of the Pope's political power within their city. Boniface thereupon attempted to strengthen the position of the legate by a letter, written in the increasingly vigorous style of his chancery, inveighing against the Priors and the people and the Podestà of Florence. The Priors maintained perfect politeness and even reverence in regard to the legate, but directed their policy by a cautious suspicion of all outside influences. The succeeding Priors were not so suave in manner. The Cardinal in disgust put the city under an interdict, shook the dust from his feet, and returned in a huff to the Curia.

In the early summer of 1301 Dante was once more active in Florentine politics. He is reported as one of the most effective speakers in a meeting of the Council of the Captain on April 14. Toward the end of the same month he was appointed a member of a commission for the repair of roads and bridges.

He was at the same time a member of the Council of the Hundred, for the session April 1 — September 30 of that year. The minutes show that he took an active part in the debates. At one meeting in particular, that of June 19, 1301, the question in debate was whether the Florentine troops in the service of Pope Boniface should have the term of their service prolonged. Dante, whether from animosity against the Pope or because he was fearful of the growing power of the nobles, wanted all Florentine troops for the defense of Florentine peace, and opposed the prolongation of the service. Later in the day, however, in spite of a second speech from Dante, the voting went 49–32 against him. In the Councils of the Captain and of the Podestà, the voting showed even a larger majority opposed to Dante's position. In the Council of the Podestà, of which a great many members belonged to the wealthy and noble class, the voting was overwhelming in favor of keeping the troops in the service of the Pope.

Events soon proved that Dante, though defeated in the councils, had rightly discerned the dangers ahead. Three weeks later, the French prince, Charles de Valois, arrived in Turin. Before long he was welcomed with open arms in Siena. In September he was closeted with Pope Boniface in Anagni. Every honest man in Florence at last realized that a crisis was imminent. On September 13, the Podestà called for an emergency meeting of the United Councils and the heads of all twenty-one of the guilds. This time Dante was listened to. A week later there was a question of strengthening the friendship with Bologna. Dante again spoke, this time with success, in a combined meeting of the Council of the Hundred and Heads of the Guilds. Still more important was a meeting of the Council of the Hundred on September 28. Dante there argued in favor of a number of emergency measures; and some of these were unanimously accepted.

The nature of the crisis became clear in October. Charles of Valois, who had been named by Pope Boniface as Captain General of the lands of the Church and Peacemaker in Florence, and who had written to various communes in the friendliest way, made his headquarters at Castel della Pieve, the very place to which the leaders of the Blacks had been banished by Dante and his associate Priors in 1300. In alarm, Florence sounded out a number of neighboring cities, only to find that — with the exception of Bologna — she was friendless. In the hope of achieving a leadership of experienced and moderate men it was decided to elect new Priors at once, anticipating the legal date. Among these was Dino Compagni. One of the first acts was to confirm a proposal of their predecessors to send an embassy directly to the Pope. Three men were chosen; of these Dante Alighieri was one.

It is perhaps in connection with this embassy that a story got about which has been preserved by Boccaccio. According to this story, when Dante was asked by the government to serve as ambassador, he remained for a long time silent and in deep thought. One of the councilors interrupted his reflections with some such expression as: "A penny for your thoughts!" Dante replied: "My thoughts? I was thinking, if I go, who is to remain; and if I remain, who is to go?" The story, if not true, was *ben trovato;* for likely enough many in the government felt just that way about the best and wisest man in their midst.

The main preoccupation of the ambassadors was to persuade the

Pope that at all times Florence had been faithful to Guelf traditions, but that the city was fearful of the return by force of the new friends of Charles de Valois. The Donati had proved too factious in the past. With a legal vacancy of the Empire, the city had no difficulty in admitting the claims of the Pope to overlordship in Tuscany, but faithful ministers of this overlordship could best be found among men who wanted the triumph of constitutional justice rather than of factious power.

As far as one can make out, Boniface was impressed by the arguments of the ambassadors. He answered that his own purpose was the peace of Florence; that two of the embassy should return to Florence to report; and that one should remain in the Curia. This last was Dante. In the meantime, however, Charles de Valois had acted. His lawyers had talked lawyers' language to the lawyers of Florence, and, with all sorts of promises on paper as their only guarantee, the Priors allowed Charles to enter the city. The date was November first. Three days later, the passions of faction were reawakened. Nobles began to ride about the city as though they owned it, and scuffles followed. The Priors felt impotent to act. It was still worse the next day. Corso Donati and twelve of his friends rode into the city. They began to behave like conquerors. With the "election" of new Priors favorable to the invaders on November 7, 1301, there was an appearance of peace; but in reality there was merely a change from injustice by violence to injustice by fraud. The new oligarchy was formed almost wholly of rich men and nobles. Keeping the letter of the Constitution as written in the time of Giano della Bella's revolution, they made it serve the ends of personal greed.

The Pope made some attempt to put a stop to the worst abuses. He sent Cardinal Matteo d'Acquasparta to attempt once more to put peace between the Cerchi and Donati. But the peace was but skin deep. Murders went on as usual; worse than the crimes of passion were the deliberate villanies according to "law." One by one, nearly all those who, like Dante, had tried to work for Florentine independence were proscribed. The Podestà was given power to act retroactively against all who had been in office during the past few years. Dante was bunched with four others under a general accusation of political corruption, *baratteria*. There was no question of any dated and documented evidence against him. All his enemies could say was that rumor had it that one or other of the group had "accepted something or other (*alcun che*) illicitly, unduly, or un-justly" from candidates for office; that "money had been spent against the Supreme Pontiff or for resistance to the coming of messer Carlo"; that things had been done against the peace of the city or the party of the Guelfs; that "one or other" had been against "those who are called Neri, devoted servants of the holy Roman Church"; that the guilty parties had failed to respond to a first summons and so for their contumacy to "the statutes of the com-mune and people of the city of Florence and to the *Ordinamenti di Giustizia*," were fined 5000 small florins apiece. In case of failure to pay within three days their property was to be expropriated. Even in case of payment, they must still suffer exile for two years outside of Tuscany. For all time, the culprits' names were to be registered as *barattieri*, and they were to be excluded from all public office in the future.

If Dante had been really guilty of any action even remotely re-sembling a crime, it is certain that the fact would have been seized upon by his accusers. He was condemned for having resolutely opposed factions within the city and attempts from without to use force or fraud to enter. As for contumacy in regard to the summons, that was the simplest common sense, considering the torture that would have been applied in order to secure confessions of guilt. Altogether there were fourteen other ex-Priors summoned as Dante was and, to a man, they preferred exile to the sort of justice they could expect in the Florence of 1302. As it was, they were all con-demned, in absence, to capital punishment. Should any of them fall into the hands of the Commune he was "to be burned with fire until he was dead," *igne comburatur sic quod moriatur*. The in-famous document is dated March 10, 1302.

Likely enough Dante heard of the whole affair only after the final sentence had already been passed. He had remained at the Curia when his two associates on the embassy returned. In the spring of 1302 he reached Siena. There he learned that Florence had behaved like a "cruel and perfidious stepmother"; that he must "abandon all that he loved most dearly"; that he must learn "how full of salt is the taste of other people's bread, how hard the steps on other people's stairs."[43] As far as we know he was never in Florence again.

[43] *Par.*, xvii, 46–60.

IV

Citizen of Christendom

"There is one task that only a world community can achieve — the never-ending and collective task of turning, first, into clear ideas *all* that human heads can think and, then, into concrete things *all* that human hands can make."[1]

I

RELICS, RUINS, WRITINGS

DANTE's banishment from Florence in 1302 forced him to be, in fact, what he had already become, in head and heart — a citizen of Christendom. This second citizenship began in 1300. That is the year in which Dante "dates" the vision described in the *Divine Comedy*. It was, apparently, a year of personal crisis. But the crisis was not moral, as many imagine. There is no evidence that Dante, who had been continuously engaged, since 1295, in the gravest responsibilities of domestic and political life, suddenly, in 1300, "came to himself" in a "dark wood" of personal pride and greed and lust. The crisis was mental. It was the same sort of crisis as that suffered, in the same year, by Dante's contemporary, Giovanni Villani, the chronicler of Florence. It was a crisis occasioned by a pilgrimage to Rome.

The year 1300 was the year of the "great indulgence." Pope Boniface VIII had conceived the grandiose idea of inviting every Christian who could ride or walk to visit the capital of Christendom. Inducements of a spiritual nature were offered to the faithful. The

---

[1] *Proprium opus humani generis totaliter accepti est actuare semper totam potentiam intellectus possibilis, per prius ad speculandum et secundario propter hoc ad operandum per suam extensionem. Monarchia,* I, iv, 1.

effect was astonishing. "It was the most wonderful thing that ever was seen," says Villani in his Chronicle, "for, not counting the pilgrims on the road, for a whole year together there were never less than 200,000 pilgrims in the city itself." And, lest we should doubt his word, he adds: "I was there, and saw them myself."[2] And being on "that blessed pilgrimage in the holy city" and seeing the relics and ruins and reading of the great deeds of the Romans and "the wonders of the whole world,"[3] Giovanni Villani was inspired with the idea of writing the history of Florence, "the daughter and creation of Rome."[4]

It is possible that Villani and Dante made the pilgrimage together. At any rate, the same relics and ruins and writings lit the same ardor in their hearts and minds and spirits. Like Villani, Dante knelt reverently, before Veronica's veil. To this day you can still feel his emotion in the exclamation he puts into the mouth of a pilgrim from the hills of Croatia: "And did you . . . really . . . look like . . . *that*, my Lord . . . my true God, Jesus Christ," *Signor mio Gesù Cristo, Dio verace, or fu sì fatta la sembianza vostra*.[5] Like Villani, Dante had no doubt that divine indulgence could be found on the banks of the Tiber. One can feel the pulsing of his faith in his vivid picture of an angel of God plying a sailless ship, "light and fast" and filled with souls, between the mouth of the Tiber and the hill of his poetical purgatory.[6] In the year of the Jubilee, pardon was abundant. The voyage was free for all who would enter the ship. And the ship, as swift as it came, returned for more. Its speed, as of wind, can be felt in the line: *ed el sen gì, come venne, veloce*.[7]

Like Villani, Dante learned to look on Florence as "a daughter of Rome."[8] There should not be, he felt, one kind of civilization in Florence and another in Rome.[9] More than Villani, Dante had an eye for the ruins of ancient Rome. "Assuredly," he wrote a few years after the pilgrimage, "I am firmly convinced that the very stones that are still in her walls are worthy of reverence and the soil on which she stands is more sacred than anything human that can be praised and approved."[10] It is typical of Dante to say, in describing the orderly march of the pilgrims back and forth across the bridge of

---

[2] *Cronaca*, VIII.
[3] . . . *strani dell' universo mondo*.
[4] . . . *figliuola e fattura di Roma*.
[5] *Par.*, xxxi, 107.
[6] *Purg.*, ii.
[7] *Purg.*, ii, 51.
[8] . . . *la bellissima e famosissima figlia di Roma. Conv.*, I, iii, 4.
[9] . . . *ut alia sit Florentina civilitas, alia sit Romana. Epist.*, vi, 8.
[10] *Conv.*, IV, v, 20.

Sant' Angelo, that those on the one side had their faces set on St. Peter's and those on the other were facing "the mount."[11] "The mount is the mount of Romulus,"[12] the Capitoline Hill, of which Dante was to say in the *Monarchia* that it was the "last refuge of the Roman name" when the Gauls had all but captured the city.[13] This mount was a symbol of Rome's civilization, as the relics in St. Peter's were the symbol of her religion, and as the ancient writings were a symbol of her culture.

Far more than Villani, Dante had read those ancient writings. He found in them, among other treasures of wisdom and law, the concept of the oneness of the world. Just as Villani alludes to "all mankind" and the "whole world," so Dante can say, after the pilgrimage: "As the ocean for the fishes, so for me the whole world is a fatherland."[14] Not that he loved Florence less, but that he loved Christendom more. He loved the city with all his heart. But he loved the world, as it were, with his head; and it is "on the head," he wrote, "more than on the heart that we must rest the shoulders of our judgment."[15] There was no place in all the world dearer to him than Florence — from the point of view of physical comfort and emotional satisfaction. Yet, the more he read of the poets and others who describe the world as a whole and in part,[16] the more he came to realize that "there are cities and regions more noble and delightful than Florence and Tuscany, and peoples and nations who speak lovelier and better-known tongues than Italian."[17]

Dante mentions in this passage the equator and the poles. In another place, he describes the position of Rome by saying that it was 2600 miles, "more or less," south of the North Pole and about 7500 north of the South Pole.[18] Thus from pole to pole the distance was about 10,200 miles. This gives a circumference of 20,400. Dante had a precise knowledge of the ninety days of polar night and polar day — and of how the sun seems to travel in circles about the polar horizons. He knew, too, of the great climatic zones, and of the Garamantes on the equator who found it too hot to wear clothes.[19]

[11] *Inf.*, xviii, 28–33.
[12] *Romuleus culmus.*
[13] . . . *quod solum restabat ad ultimum interitum Romani nominis.* II, iv, 7.
[14] *Nos autem cui mundus est patria velut piscibus aequor. De vulgari eloquentia,* I, vi, 3.
[15] *Rationi magis quam sensui spatulas nostri iudicii podiamus.*
[16] . . . *mundus universaliter et membratim.*
[17] *Ibid.*
[18] *Conv.*, III, v, 9.   [19] *Monarchia*, I, xiv, 6.

Of course, Dante's map of the world was defective. In the Poem, he puts an imaginary island at the antipodes of Jerusalem — and on it he pictures his symbolical purgatory. But, as far as he knew, all of the inhabitable land on the globe was in the northern hemisphere. His map of the world's land is shaped like a large half-moon,[20] bounded on the south by the equator, on the west by the shores of Africa, Spain, Britain, and Norway; on the east by India and China; and on the north by the arctic circle. Cadiz was the end of the inhabited world to the west, and the mouth of the Ganges was the end of the world to the east.[21] Dante thought, by an understandable miscalculation, that the Ganges and Cadiz were 180 degrees apart and that Jerusalem was just halfway between them. Thus, when he first looked down from the stars, during his poetical pilgrimage to paradise, he could see the sun setting in India and rising in Spain while it was midday in Jerusalem. From that height he could see the whole "threshing floor of fighting humanity."[22] Six hours later when he looked down again, the sun was setting in Jerusalem and was rising over his hill of purgatory; and he could see the whole course of the "vain voyage of Ulysses."[23]

The allusion here is to the symbolical voyage made, in Dante's imagination, by Ulysses and his bold companions from the Pillars of Hercules to the "world without people" beyond the setting sun. Feeling that men were not made to live like brutes, but to follow virtue and knowledge,[24] they turned the poop of their ship to the rising sun and, unlike Dante's angel, with nothing but their oars to help them, started. They rowed, and rowed into the southwest. The stars of the southern hemisphere came more and more into view. Those of the northern sky dipped lower and lower. For five long months they rowed. At last, in the dark distance they caught sight of a mountain. It was Dante's mount of purgatory. It was higher than anything the ancient world had ever seen.[25] Dante expresses the triumph and tragedy of that symbolic moment in the crescendo and staccato of one of his amazing lines, *Noi ci allegrammo, e tosto tornò in pianto.*[26] Triumph, because nothing so

---

[20] *Quaestio de Aqua et Terra,* 51.
[21] *Quaestio,* 54.
[22] *L'aiuola che ci fa tanto feroci. Par.,* xxii, 151.
[23] *Il varco folle d' Ulisse. Par.,* xxvii, 82.
[24] *. . . per seguir virtute e canoscenza. Inf.,* xxvi, 120.
[25] *Alta tanto quanto veduta non avea alcuna. Ibid.,* 135.
[26] *Ibid.,* 136.

daring had ever been done; tragedy, because all was in vain. A storm tore down from the mountain. Three times the boat was tossed about in the whirling waters — and the poop went up and the prow went down until, at last, all the waters of the ocean closed inexorably over them.[27]

And so the bravest effort of pagan antiquity came to naught — "as pleased Another," *come Altrui piacque,* says Ulysses, meaning God. No one without Redemption could reach the supernatural virtues of contrition, faith, hope, and charity. But besides this spiritual lesson we can learn from the story of Ulysses the size of Dante's world. It was a big world.

It was in no sense a uniform world. Take so human a thing as language. Dante had heard Germans, Saxons, English (and, as he thought, Croatians and Hungarians) say something like *iò* for Yes; while Provençaux said *oc;* and Frenchmen *oïl;* and Italians *sì;* and Greeks and people further east differed from all of these. Even in the "tiny corner of the world" called Italy, Dante counted no less than fourteen distinct dialects, and he felt there must be a thousand and more local variations of these.[28] And what was true of language was true of laws and customs.

Nevertheless, Dante felt, the world was one, one in its deepest roots and highest aspirations. What moved him when he visited Rome was the sense that Rome was meant to be the capital of the world, the center of a single society held together by a common purpose and by principles and values of universal validity. The relics, the ruins, and the writings of Rome were to Dante symbols of a universal religion, a universal civilization, and a universal culture; of a faith, a law, and wisdom, of a *Sacerdotium, Imperium,* and *Studium,* that were meant to be the organs of the whole world's peace and of all men's happiness.

II

JERUSALEM, ROME, ATHENS

Dante often enough speaks abstractly of faith, and law, and wisdom. In the Poem he speaks of them symbolically under the names of "Beatrice" and "Virgil." But he was fond of expressing his mean-

---

[27] . . . *infin che 'l mar fu sopra noi richiuso. Ibid.,* 142.
[28] *De vulgari eloquentia,* I, x, 9.

ing concretely, in terms of the historical traditions of three cities —
Jerusalem, Rome, and Athens. Jerusalem had given the world
revelation and redemption, faith in God's infinite power and wisdom and love, and the grace of a mysterious communion between
God and men. Rome had given the world a human revelation of the
wise and loving use of political power in the interests of justice,
temporal peace, and world unity. Athens had provided a human
revelation of a powerful and loving use of wisdom, in the light and
strength of which men could pursue, like the symbolic Ulysses, that
knowledge and virtue which alone promise peace to the mind and
conscience of men. Athens had ministered to men's minds, as Rome
to their wills, and Jerusalem to their immortal spirits. Athens had
not discovered the supernatural destiny of men in the beatific
vision of infinite truth and goodness and beauty — for that is possible only with divine revelation, with faith; nor had she succeeded
in working out the concrete, political means to the peace and
temporal prosperity of a world community — for that calls for the
Roman endowment of practical understanding, for the Roman
sense of public law and justice. But Athens had discovered man's
dignity, the rational perfection of his human life, the music that
comes into a man's soul when he lives according to the measure of
prudence, justice, fortitude, and temperance. She had discovered a
concept of personal, moral responsibility without which neither the
ministers of faith nor the administrators of law can long fulfill their
functions in a world society.

These three cities, so it seemed to Dante, had begun almost at the
same time to exercise providential roles in preparing for the coming
of Christ and the creation of the world-wide community of Christendom. And, in a metahistorical sense, all three cities would continue
in eternity, when time should be no more. Everlasting peace, Dante
thought, may equally be called the heavenly Jerusalem[29] or the
celestial Athens, or the "Rome of which Christ is a Roman."
Beatrice in the Poem will say to Dante: "For a short time only will
you wander in the wood of life; but afterward with me forever you
will be a citizen of that Rome of which Christ is a Roman."[30] In the
Convivio, speaking of the theological virtues of faith, hope, and
charity, Dante says it is by their means that we "soar to philosophize

[29] Epist., ii.
[30] . . . di quella Roma onde Cristo è Romano. Purg., xxxii, 102.

in that celestial Athens where Stoics and Peripatetics and Epicureans in the light of eternal truth will be at one in the utter peace of a single purpose."[31] Heaven can be called Jerusalem, Rome, or Athens because heaven is perfect and consummate peace; and peace on earth was the purpose of all these cities — peace for men's minds in truth, for their wills in justice, for their spirits in the grace of faith.

On earth, says Dante, Aeneas was called to found Rome just at the time when David was given the destiny of being the ancestor of the Virgin Mother of Christ. And on this it is well to listen to Dante at some length.

When the immeasurable goodness of divine nature [he says] willed to restore human nature to the image and likeness of God which had been lost by the sin of Adam, it was decreed in the high and united consistory of the Trinity that the Son of God should come to earth to bring about this concord. And because at His coming it was fitting that the . . . earth should be in most perfect disposition, and because the world is at its best when there is a world community (*monarchia*), that is, when all are subject to a single law . . . it was ordained by divine providence that the people and glorious city of Rome should be the means of bringing this to pass. And because it was proper that the inn where the heavenly king was to rest should be immaculate, a holy race was chosen in which, after the lapse of years, a woman above all other women should be born to serve as the resting-place for the Son of God. The race was the race of David, and from it sprang the boast and glory of the human race, that is, Maria. . . . And it was at one and the same time that David was born and that Rome began to be. For the coming of Aeneas from Troy to Italy was the birth of the city as the writings of Rome bear witness. And so the divine election of the Roman Empire is manifest by the fact that the birth of the holy city was contemporaneous with the planting of the root of the family of Maria. . . . And because there was universal peace, the like of which had never been nor ever will be again, the ship of world society was headed straight and on an even keel for the port toward which it should be sailing.[32]

It is in the light of thoughts like these that we shall best understand the *Divine Comedy* as a whole. The key can be found in the second canto of the *Inferno*. It is there said that Aeneas was granted by God a vision of the "immortal world," and that a "high effect" issued from the vision, namely, the providential rule of Rome and of her world empire.[33] A second vision was vouchsafed to St. Paul, the "vessel of election," for an even higher world purpose — that of

---

[31] . . . *in uno volere concordevolemente concorrono. Conv.*, I, xiv, 10.

[32] *Conv.*, IV, v, 3–9.

[33] [*Enea*] *fu de l' alma Roma e di suo impero*
ne l'empireo ciel per padre eletto. Inf., ii, 20, 21.

bringing vigor to the faith which is the beginning of the "way of salvation."[34] Finally, "Dante" himself is invited to a third vision. He
exclaims, of course, in some alarm: "But I, why should I come? Who
will grant the vision? I am not Aeneas. I am not Paul."[35] And yet
he goes. The *Divine Comedy* is the record of his going. In whose
name does he go? Not in the name of Rome or Jerusalem — but of
Athens; not in the name of Caesar or Christ — but of Aristotle; not
in the name of *Imperium* or *Sacerdotium* — but of *Studium;* not in
the name of law or grace — but of wisdom. He goes in the name of
human intelligence, conscience, and taste; of philosophy, ethics, and
art. He goes in the name of common sense — of intellectual honesty
and moral responsibility. He goes because, in spite of the manifest
destiny of Aeneas and St. Paul, of the Empire and the Church,
individual emperors and popes had failed to collaborate in pro-
ducing the peace of the world that all men longed for. World
ministers of law and grace had failed in wisdom, in moral responsibility to their world functions. There was need of a new vision —
a vision which would have the effect of fostering the collaboration
(without confusion or collusion) of temporal power and spiritual
authority. World unity was a moral imperative binding on the
consciences of emperors and popes.

III

The Crisis of 1300

This was the crisis (in the literal Greek meaning of the word), the
judgment of Dante Alighieri in the year of the jubilee, 1300. I like
to imagine that the crisis occurred late one afternoon as Dante was
returning from his prayers at the shrine which Constantine, the
successor of Caesar, had built to honor St. Paul the apostle of Christ.
"The day was departing and the brown air was taking the animals
that are on earth from their toils" and the pilgrim, of a sudden,
felt fearfully alone, with war in his head and woe in his heart.

[34] *Andovvi poi la Vas d'elezione,*
  per recarne conforto a quella fede
    ch' è principio a la via di salvazione. Ibid., 28–30.
[35] *Ma io perché venirvi? o chi 'l concede.*
  Io non Enea, io non Paolo sono. Ibid., 40, 41.

> *Lo giorno se n'andava, e l'aere bruno*
> *togliava gli animai che sono in terra*
> *da le fatiche loro; e io sol uno*
> *m' apparecchiava a sostener la guerra*
> *sì del cammino e sì de la pietate*
> *che ritrarrà la mente che non erra.*[36]

With the relics of St. Paul behind him and the ruins of Rome before him, and the visions of Aeneas and the "vessel of election" filling his soul, Dante trudged along in the dust and lengthening shadows on the Ostian Way. For a moment, in his dream, the whole world seemed one. In the basilica Dante, the "common man," the community man, the man of the world community, prayed to the apostle of the world Church in a shrine built by the ruler of a world Empire. That was as it should be. Now as he walked toward Rome, he recalled that Justinian was inspired to codify the laws of the Empire only when his feet were "in step" with the Church.[37] He remembered, too, that Charlemagne had deserved to be Emperor only after he had rescued the Church from the "fangs of the Lombards."[38] In all this there was a collaboration of politics and religion that common sense could understand. Dante looked up; and as the last ray of the setting sun caught both St. Peter's and the ruins on the Capitoline Hill, he knew that Rome was meant to be the capital of one world. This city and her empire, in very truth, were meant to guard the holy place where the successor of "great Peter" has his See.[39]

Then the sun set; and the dream of one world disappeared. Suddenly Dante found himself thinking of Boniface VIII in the Lateran Palace, and his neighbors the Colonna, and of the war that had ended in the ruins of Palestrina. *That* Pope seemed to the poet a "prince of the modern pharisees." He had warred not with Saracens, as Cacciaguida had done, but with Christians; and not in distant Acre but in the capital of the world.[40] Such a Pope — so Dante felt

---

[36] *Inf.*, ii, 1–6.
[37] ... *tosto che con la Chiesa mossi i piedi. Par.*, vi, 22.
[38] ... *quando il dente longobardo morse la Santa Chiesa. Par.*, vi, 94.
[39]   *Alma Roma e ... suo Impero ...*
  la quale e 'l quale, a voler dir lo vero,
  fu stabilita per lo loco santo
  u' siede il successor del maggior Piero. Inf., ii, 20–24.
[40] *Lo principe de' nuovi Farisei,*
  avendo guerra presso a Laterano,
  e non con Saracin nè con Giudei,
  chè ciascun suo nimico era Cristiano. Inf., xxvii, 85–88.

— had no sense of responsibility. He was not *true* to his "high office" nor to his "holy orders."[41] Even the sweet thought of the "great indulgence" soured a little as Dante remembered the money it brought to the "rich father." A dark shadow fell across his soul. There in St. Peter's Christ was being sold day after day — sold in His own temple.[42] In the basilica of St. Paul Dante may have thanked God for the conversion of Constantine and for the conversions of Justinian and Charlemagne. But now he began to feel that a convert's "dowry to the first rich father" had been the mother of much ill.[43] And why had Constantine left Rome for Byzantium? Why had he "made himself a Greek"? For the sake of the Pope! What bad fruit had come from that good intention![44] Was it not contrary to the plain duty of an emperor to carve up the Empire?[45]

And so the "war of the way and the woe" went on in the head and the heart of the "common man" of Christendom as he recalled these things to his "unerring memory." He had nothing but "reverence for the supreme keys";[46] and he knew "imperial majesty to be the highest human authority in the world community,"[47] but he also knew that the "virtue of truth is binding on every authority."[48] A song began to take shape in the poet's soul. He could still see the visions of Aeneas and St. Paul. But the new vision was a vision not only of law and grace, but of *truth*. It became suddenly clear to the poet that it takes not two but three authorities to run one world. Power without truth is a peril. The authority of wisdom must be joined to the power of the emperor.[49] What a mess is being made by our rulers today! And what misery for those who are ruled![50] Our rulers neither study nor take counsel. How many times a day do any of them reflect on the purpose of human life?[51] *This* is the truth that popes and emperors must learn. They must be told the truth,

[41] *Ibid.*, 91.
[42] . . . *là dove Cristo tutto dì si merca. Par.*, xvii, 51.
[43] *Ahi, Costantin, di quanto mal fu matre,*
    non la tua conversion, ma quella dote
    che da te prese il primo ricco patre. Inf., xix, 115.
[44] *Sotto buona intenzion che fè mal frutto,*
    per cedere al Pastor si fece Greco. Par., xx, 56, 57.
[45] *Contra officium deputatum Imperatori est scindere Imperium. Monarchia*, III, x, 8.
[46] *Inf.*, xix, 92.
[47] . . . *la imperiale maiestade e autoritade essere altissima ne l'umana compagnia.*
Conv., IV, iv, 7.
[48] . . . *la vertude de la veritate . . . ogni autoritade convince. Conv.*, IV, iii, 10.
[49] *Congiungasi la filosofica autoritade con la imperiale a bene e perfettamente reggere.*
Conv., IV, vi, 18.
[50] *Oh miseri che al presente reggete! e oh miserissimi che retti siete! Ibid.*, 19.
[51] *Ibid.*, 20.

the discovery of which made Aristotle the prince of philosophers and the "master of those who know," the truth that made him as much deserving of our "faith and following" as any ruler is.

Every man, whether pope or emperor — or, for that matter, parent or professor — is a human person, has free will, is responsible, deserves reward or merits punishment — is subject to eternal justice.[52] The song was taking the shape of a picture of souls after death. Its purpose would be to lead men to a better world out of the mess and misery into which bad leadership has brought them.[53] A hell, purgatory, and heaven full of emperors and popes burst upon the poet's imagination as he walked along the Ostian Way.

It would take courage to tell all that he saw, even "for the good of a wicked world."[54] But a voice within bade him not to be "a timid friend of truth."[55] "All falsehood set aside, reveal the vision whole, and let those scratch who feel the scab,"

> . . . rimossa ogni menzogna,
> tutta tua vision fa manifesta;
> e lascia pur grattar dov' è la rogna.[56]

As the dusk grew darker, so did Dante's vision. Throughout the whole world there seemed to him a blackout of virtue.[57] The "world was blind."[58] But in this blindness and darkness one thing was clear. The fault is not in men's stars but in themselves.[59] "Bad leadership is the trouble."[60] Bad leadership is a bad use of free will. Persons, not institutions, are to blame. In the past, Church and State have collaborated without confounding one with the other. In the good old days in Rome two suns shone clearly — one showing men the way of grace; the other showing them the path of law. But today one light has put the other out. The sword and staff have been twisted into a single and unnatural scepter.[61]

[52] *Homo prout merendo et demerendo per arbitrii libertatem est iustitie premiandi et puniendi obnoxius. Epist.*, xiii, 34.
[53] *Finis totius et partis est removere viventes in hac vita de statu miserie et perducere ad statum felicitatis. Ibid.*, 39.
[54] . . . *in pro del mondo che mal vive. Purg.*, xxxii, 103.
[55] *Par.*, xvii, 118.
[56] *Ibid.*, 127–129.
[57] *Lo mondo è . . . tutto diserto d'ogne virtute. Purg.*, xvi, 58.
[58] *Lo mondo è cieco. Ibid.*, 66.
[59] *Se 'l mondo presente disvia in voi è la cagione. Ibid.*, 82.
[60] . . . *la mala condotta è la cagione.*
[61] *Soleva Roma, che 'l buon mondo feo*
     due soli aver, che l' una e l' altra strada
     facean vedere, e del mondo e di Deo.
   L' un l'altro ha spento; ed è giunta la spada
     col pasturale, e l' un con l' altro insieme
     per viva forza mal convien che vada. Purg., xvi, 107–111.

To this bad leadership — and consequent world disorder — true, rational, ordered love, that is, moral responsibility, is the only answer. Institutions, whether of grace or law — or of love or learning — are of little avail unless popes in the Church, emperors in the State, parents in the home, and teachers in the school are obedient to their consciences, to the innate faculty that gives them counsel, to the power that stands on the threshold of assent, winnowing good and evil loves.[62]

Unless the rulers of the world discover their highest human dignity, not in their offices, but in themselves — in the depth of their own souls, in the freedom of their rational choices — there is no hope for morality in the world and, therefore, none for the ordered peace of a world community.[63]

These, at any rate, are the thoughts that Dante finally enthroned in the very heart of his Poem, in the central cantos of the *Purgatorio*. Some such thoughts occurred to him, I think, in the crisis in Rome in 1300. He saw then the outline and the purpose of the *Commedia*. With art and philosophy he would try to build a bridge between politics and religion. He would call in Athens to redress the balance between Rome and Jerusalem. Beauty and truth must help law and grace to build one world for the happiness of all mankind.

IV

MONARCHIA

From this point of view the best commentary on the *Divine Comedy* is Dante's Latin work, which he called in Greek, the language of Athens, *Monarchia*, that is to say, "World Rule" or "Leadership of the World Community."

By a "world community," Dante meant not merely a world that is one in space (geographically one), but a world that is one in time (historically one). For him unity was dynamic, not static. He felt

[62] *Amore sementa in voi d'ogni virtute*
  e d'ogne operazion che merta pene . . .
  che corre al ben con ordine corrotto. . . .
  innata v' è la virtù che consiglia
  e de l'assenso de' tener la soglia. Purg., xvii, 104, 105, 126; xviii, 62–63.
[63] *Color che ragionando andaro al fondo,*
  s'accorser d' esta innata libertate;
  però moralità lasciaro al mondo. Purg., xviii, 67–69.

that men were not likely to be good neighbors unless they realized their oneness with their ancestors and their descendants. He begins the *Monarchia* by saying that since it is truth and the love of truth that makes the whole world one, we who have been enriched by the truth discovered in the past must so work that the future may be enriched by us. His own share in this work, he says, will be not to rehash the conclusions of Aristotle, Euclid, and Cicero, but to dig in mines "unexplored by others."

It never occurred to Dante to say that the world is one because men can travel around it in sixty hours. However far or fast we travel, we are no nearer to our neighbors than our minds are near. The only real oneness of the world is the oneness of men's purposes, of their ideas and aspirations. Only a world purpose can make a world community. Dante argues that just as there is a purpose for a finger, a hand, an arm, a whole man, a home, a neighborhood, a city, a nation, so there is a purpose for mankind in its totality in time and space.[64] The nations of the world are as much a family of nations as a city is a family of homes, and a home is a family of persons, and a person is a family of human faculties. There is a work to be done by the family of nations as there is a work to be done by any other family.[65] This will be a human work, and if it is to hold the world together it must be man's highest work. It must be a work of men's minds. The work will not remain in the mind. The speculative intellect by extension becomes practical. Men's ideas will be realized in a concrete world of moral and political action ruled by prudence, and in the world of created beauty ordered by art. This progressive realization of a world civilization and culture is the purpose of historical humanity. It is a task that only a world community can achieve.[66]

A necessary condition, *propinquissimum medium*,[67] for the realization of such a purpose is world peace. World peace, in turn, calls for some kind of world authority. Dante insists on the democratic idea that world leadership will be a leadership based on consent, *consentientibus aliis*,[68] but authority, leadership, world law there must be if the household of the world is not to be divided against itself and so be laid waste.

[64] *Finis universalis civilitatis humani generis. Mon.*, I, ii, 8.
[65] *Aliqua propria operatio humanae universitatis. Mon.*, I, iii, 4.
[66] *Mon.*, I, iv, 1.
[67] *Ibid.*, 5.
[68] *Mon.*, I, v, 6.

Dante's rigorously syllogistic method of argument may have lost its appeal to the average modern reader. Dante's conclusions, however, are thoroughly up to date. Beginning from the abstract idea of order and of the relations of parts to the whole, he reaches the conclusion — as we have done, in a more roundabout way — that all nations are interdependent.[69] So, too, from the general principle that wherever there is room for a quarrel there ought to be a court,[70] he reaches the conclusion that a court with international jurisdiction is essential in a world community. One of his most metaphysical arguments reaches the practical conclusion that world rule is the best guarantee of personal liberty. "Liberty-loving peoples"[71] will best be served by a government that is the "servant of all," *minister omnium*. Liberty, of course, as Dante well understood, is not a gift of government, and least of all of world government. Liberty is the inherent, inalienable right of every person whose will is free, that is, of every person whose rational judgment is able to control his passions. This true liberty, the personal right (and duty) to be self-controlled, will best be respected by law which is fully international.

More important than this part of his work is Dante's handling of the difficult question of the relation of law and grace, of world politics and world religion. Religion in Dante's days was far ahead of political organization in the universality of its authority. Nevertheless, Dante argued, the function of the Church as such is not to achieve political order under law but to foster spiritual peace through divine grace.

Dante's root idea is that one God is the ultimate source of both law and grace — as He is also the ultimate source of all beauty and truth. Nevertheless, the Church and State, and even a world Church and a world State, are distinct because each has a purpose peculiar to itself. Men must pursue their temporal purposes under law. The same men should pursue their eternal destiny with the aid of grace. The highest authority in the State is reason, as the highest authority in the Church is revelation.

World peace seemed to Dante a temporal matter to be pursued by political means. Yet he realized that no political purpose can be fully achieved without philosophical and religious insights. The very last word of the *Monarchia* reminds the world ruler, not merely that he

[69] *Mon.*, I, vi, vii.
[70] *Ubicumque potest esse litigium ibi debet esse iudicium. Mon.*, I, x, 1.
[71] . . . *populi libertatis zelatores.* I, xii, 9.

is under the sovereignty of God, but that he will be well advised to eke out the light of reason by the light of faith.

V

THE ROMAN EAGLE

Echoes of these ideas can be found everywhere in the *Divine Comedy*, but the most continuous and concrete illustrations are those in the final cantos of the *Purgatory* and in the sixth canto of the *Paradiso*.

The sixth canto of the *Paradiso* takes the form of a song on the flight of the Roman eagle. It is put into the mouth of the Emperor Justinian, the codifier of the Roman law. The eagle, a symbol of power in the service of world peace, passes from Ilium to Latium, from Alba Longa to the seven hills, from Rome to the rest of Italy, from Italy to all the countries surrounding the Mediterranean. The story begins at the point where Virgil in the *Aeneid* left off, that is to say, with the death of Pallas, son of the Greek Evander. It continues, with gaps, to the time when Caesar established a world monarchy; and then, with more gaps, to the time when Charlemagne used a renovated Empire to ward off barbarian enemies from the Church; and, finally, with a longer leap, to Dante's day, when the cause of world peace was endangered by Guelf nationalism opposing the Empire and by the Ghibelline cupidity appropriating to a party what was meant for mankind.

Dante in the Poem meets the soul of Justinian in the planet Mercury. In the lower sphere of the moon, Piccarda Donati had expressed the fundamental idea in all of Dante's thinking: "In God's will is man's peace," *e 'n la sua volontade è nostra pace*. In the heavenly Jerusalem there is a perfect vision of peace, but the earthly Jerusalem, the Church Militant, can give men's spirits deep draughts of peace in the possession of the graces of faith and hope and charity. In the same way, this side of the "celestial Athens," there is an Athenian peace on earth, the peace of mind that comes from such an image of ultimate truth and goodness and beauty as is possible to human intelligence, conscience, and taste. So, too, this side of the "Rome of which Christ is a Roman" there is a Roman peace, the *pax Romana,* an image on earth of divine justice, a political peace that can bring men's discordant wills into temporal harmony and regional associations into a world society. It is a peace that is established by power; but by power made possible by divine providence and used in conformity with the divine will. Only such a power, Dante felt, had any real claim to authority, any real right to be heeded and obeyed. Any other kind of power, for Dante, was tyranny.

Justinian was chosen to sing of the Roman eagle because the Justinian code of Roman law seemed to Dante the most perfect human image of divine justice. Before Justinian reveals himself, he welcomes the pilgrim by congratulating him on the grace that has allowed him to "look upon the thrones of the eternal triumph" before the days of his earthly warfare are over. The same grace, as we saw, had been conceded to Aeneas, as the father of the Roman Empire, and to St. Paul, as the strengthener of faith.

Justinian describes himself in two ways, first, by his world office and, then, by his person. "Caesar I was and I am Justinian, who by the will of the primal love that now gives me joy" codified the laws. "I *was* Caesar," because the function of Emperor (like that of Pope or philosopher or poet) is a role that ends with death. "I *am* Justinian," because it is one and the same person who follows beauty or truth or justice or grace on earth and who rejoices eternally in the reward that follows these earthly responsibilities.

"As soon as I was in step with the Church," says Justinian, "God of His grace pleased to inspire me to undertake the high task." For all his scolding of individual emperors and of popes, Dante clearly wants the harmony of the two institutions in their respective roles of securing temporal and eternal peace.

Justinian in his song of the eagle has two purposes. The first is that Dante may understand what special gifts, *virtù,* have made Rome an authority with a right to men's obedience. The second is that Dante may understand with how little reason, *ragione,* with how little sense of moral responsibility, that authority has been both opposed and abused. Where history reveals a continuous use of practical understanding in the interest of world peace, as seemed to be the case with Rome, Dante concluded that divine providence had provided that gift for that purpose. He also argued that where divine providence had provided such a *gift* then its use was of right

(*Mon.*, II, vi, 11; *Conv.*, IV, iv, 8 ff.). Thus Justinian's enumeration of Roman victories from the triumph of the Horatii over the Curiatii to those of Charlemagne over the Lombard enemies of the Church is meant as a demonstration of the rightfulness of Rome's role as the guarantor of world peace. For Dante, the political *virtù* of the Roman heroes proved the validity of Roman law, much as the religious *virtù* (or miracles) of the apostles proved the divinity of the Christian faith (*Par.*, xxiv, 100–111).

And yet both emperors and popes could act against reason, against their conscience, against the responsibility which as persons they owed to their office. Still more could others act against reason in opposing the authority of the Empire or the Church. The Ghibellines were irresponsible in abusing imperial power for party purposes. The Guelfs were irresponsible in opposing the proper function of imperial authority.

After the triumphs of the Horatii, Justinian says, came those of the seven kings in the successful conquest of their neighbors.[72] Even more illustrious were the Roman leaders of the Republican period, Torquatus and Quinctius, the Decii and the Fabii, the conquerors of the Gauls and of Pyrrhus and of Hannibal.

Justinian is here implying what Dante had written in the *Convivio*: "The holy people in whom the high blood of Troy was mixed have proved by long experience that they are unequaled in that combination of strength, skill, and suavity which is needed for defense, for conquest, and for sovereignty. Therefore, God chose them for that office."[73] They conquered with "the very greatest virtue," and they have ruled with "most humane moderation." Their title is not force; not even human reason; but that divine reason which is called providence.

If divine providence can be read in the triumphs of the Republican heroes, still more, Justinian implies, can it be discerned in the all but miraculous achievements of Caesar and Augustus. The series of conquests that led up to the closing of the temple of Janus as a sign of world peace seemed to Justinian to have been made possible for three reasons: the capacity of the men themselves; the sanction of the will of the Roman people;[74] the fact that heaven had willed

[72] *Par.*, vi, 42.
[73] *Conv.*, IV, iv, 11.
[74] *Poi presso al tempo che tutto 'l ciel volle
    redur lo mondo a suo modo sereno,
    Cesare per voler di Roma il tolle. Par.*, vi, 55–57.

a single Empire made to the image of the divine monarchy that rules the cosmos. Only in such an Empire was it fitting for the Son of God to become man for the redemption of the world. The human race, says Dante in the *Monarchia*,[75] is best off when it is most like God; it is most like God when it is one; it is most one when it is under a single sovereign. And so it was that Caesar was but a tool of providence when his conquests extended from the Var to the Rhine, and from Spain to Egypt.

Even more of an instrument of God than Caesar or Augustus was Tiberius. And here Dante puts into the head of Justinian a most singular conception, namely, that the redeeming death of Christ required for its universal validity a condemnation by an authority with legitimate "universal jurisdiction."[76] If Christ had died at the hands of a judge without such jurisdiction, the death would not have been a legal punishment; Adam's sin, presumably, would not have been properly expiated! The argument is given in full in the *Monarchia*. Justinian summarizes by saying that the living justice of God conceded to Tiberius the authority and the glory of avenging the sin of Adam. The argument, Justinian hints, must be looked at with a "clear eye and a pure heart."[77] I am afraid, in this instance, Justinian (and therefore Dante) had a purer heart than a clear head. The argument becomes even more complicated when Justinian says that the destruction of Jerusalem under Titus was "vengeance for the vengeance of the ancient sin."[78]

With that Justinian leaps over the centuries to the restoration of the Empire under Charlemagne. It was still the same eagle, Dante thought, collaborating with God when Charles rescued the Church, bitten by the fangs of the Lombards. There is another leap over the next five centuries from Charlemagne to Dante's day. Justinian is vehement against both the Guelfs and Ghibellines. The "yellow lilies" of France are fighting the flag of the world. The Ghibellines are appropriating that flag to a party. It is hard to see which faction sins the more.[79] Let the Ghibellines ply their art under some other flag. It is an ill following of the world's ensign when one renounces

---

[75] *Mon.*, I, viii, 3.
[76] *Supra totum humanum genus jurisdictionem habens. Mon.*, II, xii.
[77] *Con occhio chiaro e con affetto puro. Par.*, vi, 87.
[78] *Vendetta . . . de la vendetta del peccato antico. Ibid.*, 93; cf. *Par.*, vii, 49-51.
[79] *L'uno al pubblico segno i gigli gialli,*
    oppone, e l'altro appropria quello a parte,
    si ch' è forte a veder chi più si falli. Par., vi, 100-102.

justice. And let Charles de Valois with his Guelfs remember that the eagle's talons have torn the skin from a prouder lion. The sins of both are "the cause of all your ills."[80]

To a modern ear that last phrase seems more cogent than all the rest. Dante's real starting point was not in abstract ideas but in the facts as he saw them, the facts of political disorder. His argument is the argument used at San Francisco in 1945. The necessity of world order here and now justifies power in the preservation of peace. "The ultimate foundation of world rule is, in truth, the necessities of human civilization. The argument for world organization is man's right to be happy; and happiness is impossible without collaboration."[81]

However, it seemed to Dante that both reason and faith could throw some light on this elementary political argument for law. He thought that both Athens and Jerusalem had something to say about Rome; or as we might say today that the scholars and the churchmen have something to contribute to politics.

VI

THE CHARIOT AND THE TREE

Another illustration of Dante's passion for peace through collaboration can be found at the end of the *Purgatorio*.

In canto XXVII Virgil speaks his last words to Dante, that is to say, ancient culture (of which Virgil is the symbol) says its last word to progressive humanity (of which Dante is the representative). Virgil says he has done the best that he could do with "genius and art," with speculative and practical reason, with ethics, conscience, and law. More light will come from the lovely eyes of "Beatrice," from faith. "Dante" has been freed from the tyranny of passion. He is out of the wood of ignorance. He is strong enough to pursue the journey of life by himself. His conscience is now ready for a crown and his intelligence for a doctor's cap. He has a constitutional soul under the

---

[80] *Falli che son cagion di tutti vostri mali. Ibid.*, 99.

[81] *Lo fondamento radicale de la imperiale majestade, secondo lo vero, è la necessità de la umana civilitade, che a uno fine è ordinata cioè a vita felice; a la quale nullo per se è sufficiente a venire sanza l' aiutorio d'alcuno. Conv.*, IV, iv, 1.

sovereignty of reason and the rule of will. He has achieved a sense of responsibility.[82]

Thereupon "Virgil" steps behind "Dante" and allows him to lead the way. All Virgil knows is that there is a sweeter fruit for Dante than he himself had ever tasted, a sweet fruit for which "the care of mortals seeks from branch to branch in order to put in peace their hungers."[83]

Dante, out of the "dark wood" was ready for a vision of a "supernatural forest,"[84] the garden where mankind, before the fall into ignorance, cupidity, and spiritual debility, had once been happy. Virgil had dreamed of a "golden age"; and so there was no reason why he should not remain with Dante a little longer. But Dante's guide is now the "mistress of the age of innocence," singing and plucking flowers as though she were here at home. She was luminous, not with the light of reason (as Virgil was), nor with the light of faith (as Beatrice will be), but with the light of love, with *raggi d'amore*.[85] Something about her reminded Dante of the *mother* of Proserpina and of the *mother* of Cupid. She was more like a parent than a teacher or a priest. The "lovely lady" tells Dante (and Virgil and Statius are listening) much that they had not known of the home of innocent happiness. Then "singing like a girl in love,"[86] she sang a song that neither Rome nor Athens had ever heard, a song that came out of Jerusalem, a song of King David, "Blessed are those whose sins are forgiven." Blessed, indeed; and forthwith Dante, separated as he was by a narrow brook, followed the "lovely lady" as a child toddles along with its mother, his "tiny steps in step with hers."[87]

Suddenly, there broke into his ken the "pageant of faith." The forest became luminous as with lightning that did not die, with a light that grew brighter and brighter; and a "sweet melody ran through the luminous air."[88] Dante thought with anguish of all the

---

[82] *Non aspettar mio dir più nè mio cenno;*
    libero, dritto e sano è tuo arbitrio
    e fallo fora non fare a suo senno;
    per ch' io te sovra te corono e mitrio. Purg., xxvii, 139–142.
[83] *Quel dolce pome che per tanti rami*
    cercando va la cura de' mortali
    oggi porrà in pace le tue fami. Purg., xxvii, 115 ff.
[84] *La divina foresta.* Purg., xxviii, 2.
[85] Purg., xxviii, 43.
[86] *. . . cantando come donna innamorata.*
[87] Purg., xxviii, 9.
[88] *E una melodia dolce correva per l'aere luminoso.* Purg., xxix, 22.

ineffable delights that had been lost when the first mother fell from grace. But the new light was but a foretaste of what was to come.

The whole air below the green branches seemed to turn into a great red flame, and the poet calls on all the muses of Helicon to help him and especially on Urania, the muse of heavenly things, so that he may "put into verse things too high for thought."[89] He saw what looked like seven trees of gold. He heard voices singing, in the language of Jerusalem, *Osanna*. In astonishment Dante turned to the good Virgil who stood behind him, but Virgil had no answer but only a look of silent wonder.[90] So Dante turned to the "high things" of the Vision. He had looked on Virgil for the last time. The age of antiquity was over. The Kingdom of God was at hand. The voice of John the Baptist would soon be calling for repentance. The dawn of Christendom was about to break.

But first came the age of the prophets. Outlined against the green of the foliage (symbol of Christian hope) and the luminous redness of the air (symbol of supernatural charity), Dante saw a procession of elders in white (symbol of revealed faith). And the waters of the stream, luminous with the new light, served as a mirror (symbol of conscience) when Dante looked into it. He stood on the very edge of this water and looked at the vision. From the seven lights at the head of the procession (symbol of the seven gifts of the Holy Spirit) streamers of light, like banners in a breeze, floated behind them farther than his eyes could reach. And under these banners of light came twenty-four elders crowned with lilies. They symbolize the twenty-four books of divine revelation contained in the Old Testament. When they reached the point where Matelda was they sang: "Blessed art thou among the daughters of Adam, and blessed may thy beauties be forever." They passed on. Next came four animals crowned with green leaves, symbol of the divine revelation contained in the Gospels; and in the space between the animals a triumphal two-wheeled chariot (symbol of the Church), drawn by a Gryphon, a lion with an eagle's head (symbol of the two natures, human and divine, in Jesus Christ). As the vertical wings of the Gryphon passed through the horizontal streamers of light, they formed a cross (symbol of the "age of grace"). The chariot was lovelier than Rome had ever known, lovelier even than the chariot

---

[89] *Forti cose a pensar mettere in versi. Ibid.*, 42.
[90] *Ibid.*, 57.

which the son of Apollo had once driven awry. By the side of one
wheel, singing and dancing, came faith, white as new-fallen snow,
and emerald hope and charity, red as a living flame; and sometimes
faith would lead the dance and sometimes charity, but always it was
the song of charity that gave the beat for the dance. By the side of
the left wheel of the chariot, prudence led the dance with justice,
fortitude and temperance keeping in step. Behind the chariot came
two elders, symbols of revelation in the Acts of the Apostles and the
Epistles of St. Paul. After four others (symbol of the minor Epistles),
came an old man (symbol of the Apocalypse of St. John).

The procession came to a halt. Dante had the chariot directly before his eyes. The twenty-four elders turned, so that all faces were
toward the chariot, as toward their peace, the object of their long
desires. The elder symbolizing Solomon's Canticle sings in Latin,
Come, Spouse of Lebanon. All the others take up the song. Forthwith a hundred angels, "ministers and messengers of eternal life,"
sing, again in the Latin of the Vulgate, "Blessed is He that cometh,"
and in the Latin of Virgil, *Manibus date lilia plenis.*[91]

The eighteen lines that follow are, in some sense, the most remarkable in the whole Poem. They constitute, in their literal sense,
a lyric song describing the apparition of Beatrice ten years after her
death, and the hunger of Dante's heart in the presence of his beloved. The same lines, under the lightest veil of allegory, describe
the first Christmas, the dawn of the new day of Christendom, the
return of grace to fallen humanity. The eastern sky is red — symbol
of grace; and the west is serene — symbol of peace under Roman law.
The divine Person in Christ — symbolized by the rising sun — is so
tempered with human nature that He can be seen by human eyes,
as a rising sun can be looked at through the morning mist. When
"Beatrice" (symbol of divine revelation) descends into the chariot,
"Dante" (symbol of longing humanity, of mankind that has been
without the graces of faith and hope and charity since the Fall)
feels, in virtue of a mysterious grace, the "full power of his ancient
love," *d'antico amor sentì la gran potenza.*[92]

Humanity felt once more the "high love that had filled its heart
in the childhood" of the world.[93] And Dante the poet, forever trying

[91] *Aeneid,* vi, 883.
[92] *Purg.,* xxx, 39.
[93] . . . *l'alta virtù che già m'avea trafitto
prima ch' io fuor di puerizia fosse. Ibid.,* 41, 42.

to harmonize Antiquity and Christendom, nature and grace, tried to think of a line in Virgil that would suit the occasion. Of course, he found it. He recalled the words of Dido, in love with Aeneas, *agnosco veteris vestigia flammae*.[94] In the Poem, "Dante" turns to say to "Virgil": "Every vein in my body is trembling; I feel the burning of the ancient flame," *conosco i segni dell' antica fiamma*.[95]

But Virgil was gone. Virgil, the "dear, dear father" to whom Dante had entrusted himself, had gone. Gone, of course, like stars when the sun has risen. Not that the world would no longer need reason and law, truth and beauty, philosophy and art; but because the new faith would be truer than reason, the new love higher than law. Humanism would be henceforth Christian humanism. That is why the convert poet, Statius, remained. But Virgil who had lived "before Christendom," *dinanzi al cristianesimo*,[96] who had "not adored God as God should be adored," had gone.

The name of Beatrice had not yet been mentioned. The face of the lady in the chariot was still concealed by the white veil (of faith) decked with a garland of olive leaves (symbol of the Roman peace). But she had spoken; and her voice was stern — like the voice of John the Baptist calling on mankind to prepare the ways of the Lord. Weep not for Virgil, she said, for a sword must pierce you more cutting than his going. And speaking "like a queen,"[97] she said (using, according to one reading, the "majestatic We"): "Look at us well, we are, we are indeed Beatrice."[98] Thereupon with symbols that may or may not have any personal applications to the historical Dante's moral failings, "Dante" makes an act of perfect contrition, a full confession of sins, and a sincere purpose of amendment.

The confession is too drawn out for lyrical poetry. If this were a meeting of the real Dante and the real Beatrice the scene would be slightly ridiculous. But the psychology of repentance is admirably analyzed; and the theology of the *contritio cordis*, the *confessio oris*, the *satisfactio operis* is equal to the psychology.

"Repent and be baptized," St. John had said in the desert. After repentance "Dante" is ready for baptism. It is administered symbolically by "Dante's" passage through the waters of the stream of Lethe.

---

[94] *Aeneid*, iv, 23.
[95] *Purg.*, xxx, 48.
[96] *Inf.*, iv, 37.
[97] . . . *regalmente ne l' atto ancor proterva*. Purg., xxx, 70.
[98] *Guardaci ben! ben sem, ben sem Beatrice*. Ibid., 73.

When he issues from the waters four nymphs at the side of the chariot — prudence, justice, fortitude, and temperance — show him a sign of their affection. They are handmaids of Beatrice, in the sense that nature is the handmaid of grace. They will lead Dante to look into her eyes; but, of course, the three nymphs on the other side — faith, hope, and charity — look more deeply into the beauty of divine revelation. "Dante" is led to the breast of the Gryphon, and is privileged to look, not long but deeply, into the lovely eyes of "Beatrice" that are, however, never taken for a moment from gazing on the Gryphon. "Dante" felt he was feeding — as in Holy Communion — on a food that, like all spiritual food, leaves not satiety but hunger in the soul. When both the "eyes" and the "mouth" of "Beatrice" are revealed to Dante, he can think of no better exclamation than in words modeled on the Christmas hymn that honors Jesus Christ, *Tu Lumen et Splendor Patris*.[99]

Meanwhile the procession wheels to the right and moves toward the morning sun. Matelda, Dante, and Statius find themselves on the right of the chariot with faith, hope, and charity for company.

The next point in Dante's symbolism is somewhat difficult. He speaks of a high tree with all its branches "bared of leaves."[100] It may be, in the literal sense, the tree from which Eve took the fruit when she committed the sin that, as the theologians say, left man *spoliatus supernaturalibus,* without grace and the power to merit. Symbolically, it would mean unaided human nature, that is, intelligence without faith, and conscience without the strength of the Holy Spirit; in other words, Athens and Rome in need of Jerusalem for their full flowering and fruit. When the Gryphon links the chariot to the tree by means of the cross-shaped pole of the chariot, the symbolic tree breaks into fresh foliage with the color of amethyst.[101] Amethyst, according to St. Bonaventure, is a symbol of supernatural *justitia* or grace. In other words, nature as known to antiquity is "regenerated." Wisdom and law burgeon with the new life of grace. Men without ceasing to be human become Christians, and the Roman Empire begins to be Christendom. To celebrate this harmony of wisdom, law, and grace, the whole procession breaks into a heavenly hymn. It lulled Dante into sleep, as Argo was lulled by the song of Mercury. Dante was overcome, like Peter, John, and

[99] *Purg.,* xxxi, 139.
[100] *Pianta dispogliata di foglie e d'altra fronda. Purg.,* xxxii, 38, 39.
[101] *Men che di rose e più che di viole. Ibid.,* 58.

James on the mountain of Transfiguration when they heard the words: "This is my beloved Son in whom I am well pleased."[102]

Meanwhile Beatrice had taken her place under the new foliage, sitting on the roots of the tree. The rest of the company, like Moses and Elias after the Transfiguration, had returned to heaven. Beatrice was left as the guardian of the chariot.[103]

"Beatrice" stands for the revealed faith and redemptive grace of Jerusalem as the tree stands for Athenian reason and Roman law. Around both Beatrice and the tree, like a wall, are the seven nymphs carrying in their hands the seven lights, that is, the seven gifts of the Holy Spirit.

That is Dante's vision of a perfect Christendom. Roman law, springing from the roots of the eternal law, is spread over the whole world. Protected by human justice, the ministry of grace is undisturbed. Statesmen, churchmen, and scholars are guarded, guided, and strengthened by prudence, justice, fortitude, and temperance, and by charity, faith, and hope; and all are illumined by the seven gifts of the Holy Spirit — wisdom, understanding, counsel, fortitude, knowledge, piety, and fear of the Lord.

"Beatrice" could now say to "Dante": "Here you will be but a short time in this wood of the world; and then with me forever you will be a citizen of that Rome of which Christ is a Roman." She adds: "And therefore for the good of the world that lives ill, keep your eyes fixed on the chariot, and what you see in your vision take heed that you write when you return to the world."[104]

What Dante saw in vision was a cavalcade of Church history. The bird of Jove (the pagan Roman Empire) tried to pluck the leaves and flowers from the new Christian civilization. The chariot of Christendom rocked like a ship in a storm under the blows of the Roman persecutions.[105] Next "Dante" saw the fox of heresy turned to flight by "Beatrice."[106] The donation of Constantine is symbolized by the eagle leaving some of its feathers in the chariot. Upon which a voice from heaven was heard to complain: "O my little bark, how ill thou art laden," *O navicella mia come mal se' carca.*[107] The dragon of Islam rends the bottom of the chariot. (And for this

---

[102] *Matt.* 17:5.
[103] *Sola sedeasi in su la terra vera*
    come guardia lasciata li del plaustro
    che legar vidi a la biforme fera. Purg., xxxii, 94–96.
[104] *Purg.,* xxxii, 100–105.   [106] *Ibid.,* 118–123.
[105] *Ibid.,* 112–117.   [107] *Ibid.,* 129.

Mohammed with a rent belly is eternally damned in Dante's hell.)

Christian penance, prayer, and good works suffer as the medieval Church is enriched; and seven heads as of a monster begin to replace the seven nymphs — that is, the seven capital sins, pride, envy, anger, sloth, greed, gluttony, and lust take the place of the seven virtues. In place of Beatrice there appears a harlot, *una puttana sciolta*[108] — symbol of the papacy in Avignon under the influence of French power. She looked appealingly to "Dante," but the giant, her lover, whipped her from head to foot. "Dante," says Lana, one of the earliest fourteenth-century commentators, here symbolizes the laity of Christendom, *il popolo cristiano,* to whom the papacy in the "Babylonian exile" appeals for help. Meanwhile, "Beatrice" (faith) sighs as she listens to the lament of the virtues. Then she says in Latin: "A little time and you will not see me; and then a little time and you will see me." She puts herself at the head of a procession formed by the seven virtues, followed by Dante, Matelda, and Statius. She takes ten steps — symbolizing, perhaps, the ten years between the beginning of the Babylonian captivity in 1305 and the year of imperial triumph which Dante hoped would occur in 1315. She bids Dante come closer to her so that he may hear her instructions. Nothing, she said, can stay the divine vengeance. Not for all time will the eagle be without an heir. She sees a helper sent by God that will kill the adulteress and the giant that sins with her. She calls the deliverer a "five hundred, ten and five," a *cinquecento diece e cinque.*[109] She may mean that five hundred and fifteen years after the coronation of Charlemagne in 800, that is, in 1315, there will be another restoration of the Empire, this time under Henry VII of Luxemburg. More clearly she gives Dante the mission to let the world know what his vision revealed, especially of the tree that was despoiled by Adam's sin and then again by the eagle and the giant.[110]

Dante's symbolism in the last canto of the *Purgatorio* is obscure and has puzzled the commentators from the fourteenth century to our own day. If we will remember that in the very last lines "Dante" is "remade like a young plant renewed with fresh foliage, pure and disposed to soar to the stars,"[111] we shall be inclined to see in the symbolic tree both individual human nature and the collectivity of mankind. "Dante" is the symbol of humanity in both these senses.

[108] *Ibid.,* 149.   [110] *Ibid.,* 52–57.
[109] *Purg.,* xxxiii, 43.   [111] *Ibid.,* 143, 144.

After the advent of "Beatrice" he is both Christendom and the Common Man of Christendom; just as before her advent he was "unregenerate humanity," singly and collectively, *civis Romanus* and *Imperium Romanum,* an "Athenian" and "Athens."

When "Beatrice" says: "Whoever robs or rends the tree offends God by blasphemy in deed,"[112] she is announcing what, as I have been trying to suggest, is the main theme of the whole Poem, namely, that an ordered world calls for integrated persons, that the synthesis of culture, civilization, and religion is only possible in a world society when in the souls both of leaders and common men there is an integration of intelligence, conscience, and supernatural life. Adam's sin brought about the first disintegration both in Adam as a person and in mankind as a society. Men and mankind remained disintegrated like "a plant with leafless branches" until the advent of grace in the Incarnation. Even then Christendom was subject to crises. The Roman eagle did its best to "rob" the tree; and in Dante's day the giant, Guelf political power, by attacking the Empire in the name of the Church, was "rending" the tree once more.

"Dante" is reproached by "Beatrice" for having followed a way and a truth as different from the divine way and truth as the earth is distant from heaven.[113] Athens, in a word, has as much need of the light as Rome has of the love of Jerusalem. Most of the scolding in the *Divine Comedy* is for princes who dispensed with supernatural grace and pontiffs who dispensed with secular law; but Dante knew that the philosophers, too, could "rob and rend" their souls and human society as easily and fatally as the others can. The complete citizen of Christendom understands that the world needs learning, law, and faith. He knows that if one world is to endure, beyond the truth of Athens and the justice of Rome men must have a vision of eternal truth and a hope of everlasting love. That is why "Beatrice" in the Poem leads "Dante" up to paradise.

[112] *Ibid.,* 58, 59.
[113] "Perchè conoschi," disse, "quella scola
    c' hai seguitata, e veggi sua dottrina
    come può seguitar la mia parola;
  e veggi vostra via da la divina
    distar cotanto, quanto si discorda
    da terra il ciel che più alto festina." *Purg.,* xxxiii, 85–90.

V

Glorious Mistress of My Mind

La gloriosa donna de la mia mente.[1]

I

BEATRICE PORTINARI

WHEN Dante was nearing the last of his fifty-six years and bringing to an end "the arduous matter"[2] of his Poem, worn out with the fatigues and failures of eighteen years of exile, he wrote this prelude to a famous canto: "If it should ever happen that the sacred song, in which both heaven and earth have had a hand and which has made me thin these many years, should overcome the cruelty that closed against me the blessed fold where, as a lamb, I slept . . . then with altered voice and whitened hair I shall return and, near the font where I was made a Christian, receive the poet's crown."[3]

It never occurred to Dante to think that he had written the Poem out of his head — or even his heart. He would have said, in absolute sincerity (and Scholastic language), that he, the poet, was the instrumental and secondary cause, but that God was the ultimate efficient cause, and that the men and women of the world in which he lived were the material and the final cause. His practical purpose — to write "for the good of the world that is living badly"[4] and "to lead men living in the world from misery to happiness"[5] — seemed to him as much a cause of the Poem as his inner determination never to be "a timid friend of truth."[6] So, too, the subject matter of the Poem, man, was a cause — man in the abstract, responsible to justice,[7] and

---

[1] *Vita Nuova*, ii, 1.
[2] *Par.*, xxx, 36.
[3] *Par.*, xxv, 1–9.
[4] *Purg.*, xxxvii, 103.
[5] *Epist.*, xiii, 39.
[6] *Par.*, xvii, 118.
[7] *Epist.*, xiii, 25.

man in the concrete, the actual men and women who are, here and now, in pain or bliss in hell or purgatory or heaven. Apart from the world in which the poet lived the Poem would not have been written. Heaven, too, had a hand, the Holy Spirit, the "high light,"[8] whose immediate inspiration made the poet's "tongue strong enough to leave to people yet unborn at least a tiny sparkle of the glory" that he saw — and God, as the author and end of all creation.

God, the world, the poet — these three produced the Poem. Pietro Alighieri, in calling his father a "glorious theologian, philosopher, and poet," implied that his father was at home in three worlds: the worlds of imagination, philosophy, and faith; the worlds of matter, mind, and supernatural mystery; the worlds of the real, the ideal, and the divine. Pietro also implies that, as a philosopher, Dante knew that the ideal was caused by the real; and, as a theologian, that the real was created by God. Dante, the artist, was a realist in philosophy, a creationist in theology. He believed that the world that lived in him was caused by the world in which he lived, and that both these worlds were caused by God.

It is with some such thoughts as these in mind that we turn to the problem of Dante's Beatrice. She was a part of the world in which he lived. She was likewise a part of the world that lived in him. She was, first, a dated and documented historical person — her beauty of face and purity of soul awakened a passionate love in Dante's heart. She was, second, an ideal in Dante's soul — an aesthetic conception, a vision of abstract beauty, a moral idealization, a model of perfect womanhood. She was, finally, a saint. She lived in grace on earth, in glory when she died. She was a cause (under God) not merely of the poet's romantic love and artistic perception, but also of his growth in grace, in supernatural contrition, faith, hope, and charity.

For the historical Beatrice our main document is Dante's *Vita Nuova*. She was eight years and four months old when Dante fell in love with her. Since her birth, he says, the stars had moved from west to east one twelfth of the distance they move in a hundred years. Dante at the time was not quite nine. Supposing that he was born on May 27, 1265, we can date the memorable meeting early in May, 1274. Beatrice died in the evening of June 8, 1290. She was then twenty-four. Her father died before her.[9] If, as Dante's son, Pietro, and Dante's earliest biographer, Boccaccio, tell us, her father

---

[8] *Par.*, xxxiii, 67.   [9] *Vita Nuova*, xxii.

was Folco Portinari (who died December 31, 1289) then Beatrice is the Bice mentioned in Folco's will. This Bice was married to a young banker, Simone de' Bardi. Likely enough the marriage feast mentioned in *Vita Nuova* XIV was that of Beatrice herself. Dante mentions no word that Beatrice ever uttered. The most he tells us is that on her lips the name of the Blessed Virgin Mary was ever in high esteem.[10] For the first nine years he loved her she never spoke to him. Only when he was nearly eighteen, in May, 1283, did Beatrice, now grown up into a "marvelous lady," *mirabile donna*, even bow to him. She did so with "indescribable graciousness," *ineffabile cortesia*. She was dressed in white. It was three in the afternoon.

The beginning of Dante's romantic affection is thus described in the *Vita Nuova*:

Nine times the heavens had revolved, bringing the sun almost to the point where it was when I was born, when, to my eyes there appeared for the first time, the glorious mistress of my mind. She was called Beatrice by many who could not think what else to call her. . . . She was near the beginning of her ninth year as I was near the end of mine. She appeared to me clothed in a most perfect color, a modest and becoming crimson. She was girt and adorned in a way that fitted her very tender age. I speak the truth when I say that at once the spirit of life, that dwells in the most secret chamber of the heart, began to tremble with such violence that it appeared fearfully in the least pulses, and trembling, said these words: *Ecce deus fortior me, qui veniens dominabitur mihi* [Behold a god stronger than I who is come to lord it over me]. At that instant the spirit of the soul, that dwells in the high chamber to which all the spirits of the senses carry their perceptions, began to marvel greatly, and speaking especially to the spirit of the eyes said these words: *Apparuit iam beatitudo vestra* [Now has your bliss appeared]. . . .

From that time on love was lord in my soul. . . . In virtue of the power my imagination gave him I felt obliged to do his bidding in all things. Often enough he bade me seek and see this young, young angel; so that while still a boy I often went in search of her, and I saw in her such perfect and laudable behavior that the word of Homer could certainly be said of her: "She seems not the daughter of mortal man but of God." And although her image which stayed constantly with me encouraged love to lord it over me, nevertheless, that image was of so perfect a virtue that not once did it permit love to rule me without the faithful counsel of reason in all these matters in which it was good to give heed to this counsel.[11]

When at last, in 1283, Beatrice bowed to Dante, he was so intoxicated with delight that all he could do was to retire to solitary medi-

---

[10] *Vita Nuova*, xxviii, 1.   [11] *Vita Nuova*, ii, 1–9.

tation. He was already half lover, half artist. In his solitude there came to the lover a marvelous vision which the artist put into song, his first sonnet, *A ciascun alma presa e gentil core.*[12] He had already "studied by himself the art of making rimes with words."[13] The point of the little poem was in the last line, "Then Love I saw go on his way aweeping." Something told Dante that Beatrice was not long for this life.

II

COURTLY LOVE

The young lover and poet was also a moralist. More than once he insists that Love commanded him "in accord with the counsel of reason."[14] Reason and romance, he felt, should go together. He saw in Beatrice a model of maidenhood. She was, he says, "the destroyer of vice and the queen of virtue."[15] He writes in one of his loveliest sonnets:

So lovely and so pure my lady seems when she but says "Good day" to passersby that men start trembling and their tongues turn mute; they dare not raise their eyes to look on her. She trips along and knows that she is praised, but she is veiled with such humility she seems a thing come down from heaven to earth — a very miracle for eyes to see. She shows such loveliness to those who look that, through their eyes, a sweetness fills their souls that none could guess who has not felt its force. And from her lips there seems to issue forth a voice so sweet, a spirit full of love, that whispers nothing to the soul but: Sigh.

> *Tanto gentile e tanto onesta pare*
> *la donna mia quand' ella altrui saluta*
> *ch' ogne lingua deven tremando muta*
> *e li occhi no l' ardiscon di guardare.*
> *Ella si va, sentendosi laudare,*
> *benignamente d' umiltà vestuta*
> *e par che sia una cosa venuta*
> *da cielo in terra a miracol mostrare.*
> *Mostrasi sì piacente a chi la mira*
> *che dà per li occhi una dolcezza al core*
> *che 'ntender non la può chi no la prova;*
> *e par che da la sua labbia si mova*
> *un spirito soave pien d' amore*
> *che va dicendo a l' anima: Sospira.*[16]

[12] *Vita Nuova,* iii, 10–12.   [14] *Vita Nuova,* iv, 2.   [16] *Vita Nuova,* xxvi, 5–7.
[13] *Ibid.,* 9.   [15] *Vita Nuova,* x, 2.

In another song he sings: "Of her Love asks: 'How can a mortal thing appear so lovely and yet be so pure?' Then gazing on her in his heart Love swears: 'God means to make a miracle of her. The color of her face is like a pearl that marvelously fits her maidenhood. Nature could make no second thing so fair — a perfect paragon of loveliness."

> *Dice di lei Amor: "Cosa mortale*
> *come esser pò sì adorna e sì pura?"*
> *Poi la reguarda, e fra se stesso giura*
> *che Dio ne 'ntenda di far cosa nova.*
> *Color di perle ha quasi, in forma quale*
> *convene a donna aver, non for misura:*
> *ella è quanto de ben pò far natura;*
> *per essemplo di lei bieltà si prova.*[17]

It is impossible to believe that Dante was not deeply in love with' Beatrice. It is difficult to believe that his love was sensual. It was "courtly" — not in the sense of some of the troubadours, but in the sense in which Dante himself speaks of "courtly" language. In *De vulgari eloquentia*, Dante the artist, in love with language, "hunts" among the "vulgar" modes of Italian speech, pursuing an ideal of beauty that "everywhere leaves a scent but nowhere has its' lair."[18] In the potentialities of "natural" speech the artist perceives the *ratio,* the essence, the "form," the spirit or soul of a language that is "illustrious, cardinal, aulic, and courtly."[19] Such language is "courtly" because it is artistic; it has about it the harmony and balance of artistic creation.[20]

Dante's love for Beatrice was a form of poetry. It began in passion; turned into vision; ended in song. The transition from passion to vision was a "transfiguration."[21] Passion that was fed on seeing passed through the "dark night," the "death," of the eyes to become a flame burning in the soul. Dante speaks in a song of the "dead sight of the eyes that desire their death."[22] And in prose he says that when he "imagines her miraculous beauty" a new desire is born in virtue of which "the previous passion to seek a *sight* of her no longer holds me back."[23] He can still see her, but not with his eyes — only

---

[17] *Vita Nuova,* xix, 11.
[18] *Illustrem Ytalie venemur loquelam . . . illud vulgare . . . quod in qualibet redolet civitate nec cubat in ulla. De vulgari eloquentia,* I, xi, 1, xvi, 4.
[19] *De vulgari eloquentia,* I, xvi, 6.
[20] *. . . quidquid bene libratum est curiale dicitur. De vulgari eloquentia,* I, xviii, 4.
[21] *. . . trasfigurazione, trasfiguramento. Vita Nuova,* xiv, 7, 10.
[22] *Vita Nuova,* xv, 6.   [23] *Ibid.,* 2.

with his soul. "The spirits of vision remain alive but not in the organs of sight."[24] All that "remained alive was a *thought* that spoke of my lady."[25]

Love had become art. The visible beauty of Beatrice was the inspiration, the occasion, the cause. Without a passionate love for *her*, there would not have been *this* artistic vision. At the same time, of course, it is Dante's "habit of art" that "makes" the vision into a song — just as it is a philosopher's "agent intellect" that makes a "phantasm" into an "idea," a concept, a *ratio*.

This is what Dante means in the sonnet beginning with a line that is usually translated, "Love and the gentle heart are one same thing," *Amore e 'l cor gentile sono una cosa.*[26] "Courtly love" and the artist's "heart" are one, as thought (*ragione, ratio*) and the philosopher's soul (*alma razional*) are one. True love is the ideal or "vision" in an artist's "heart" just as true thought is the idea or *ratio* in a philosopher's "head."

> True love is gentle heart and gentle heart
> True love, as sagely did the poet sing;
> Nor lives true love from gentle heart apart
> More than from mind the *ratio* of a thing.

> *Amore e 'l cor gentil sono una cosa*
> *sì come il saggio in suo dittare pone,*
> *e così esser l' un sanza l' altro osa*
> *com' alma razional sanza ragione.*[27]

Artistic vision and philosophic thought are reached by a similar process — by a passing from "potency" to "act." The first part of his sonnet, says Dante, deals with love "in so far as it is in potency," *in potenzia;* the second deals with love in so far as "from potency it is reduced to act," *in quanto di potenzia si riduce in atto.* In the second part of the sonnet he speaks of the relation of "love" and the "gentle heart" in terms of "form" and "matter."[28]

Thus in the *Vita Nuova* we have already a Dante who is lover, moralist, artist, and philosopher all in one. It is not that he loves Beatrice less, but that love means to him more than languorous looks and the touching of lips. Love means a "new life" in the soul. It means the true, courtly, artistic love, the ideal vision of beauty and

---

[24] *Vita Nuova*, xiv, 14. [26] *Vita Nuova*, xx, 3–5. [28] *Ibid.*, 6, 7.
[25] *Vita Nuova*, xvi, 3. [27] *Ibid.*, 3.

purity that goes to the making of song. Dante was faced — as what young artist has not been faced? — with the choice between passion and vision, sin and song. But he listened to the voice within him that said: "Good is the lordship of love because it draws the heart and mind of his servants from all vile things."[29] Long before "Virgil" met "Dante" in the "dark wood," the poet's conscience and art had led him safely through an "amorous errancy," *amorosa erranza,* in which lust made its bid — but in vain — to trap him. Dante's choice was a puzzle to some of the ladies of Florence. "What is the purpose of your love?" the ladies asked. Dante answered that his bliss was in song — "in the words that praise my lady."[30] It was in this mood that he wrote one of the greatest of all his *canzoni,* the song that begins "Ladies that have intelligence of love," *Donne ch' avete intelletto d'amore.*[31]

In this song we have the whole Beatrice, not only the girl the color of whose face was like a pearl, but the ideal of beauty and purity, the "perfect paragon of loveliness." She was even more than this. An angel calling to the intellect of God was heard to say that heaven itself was incomplete without her, *Madonna è disiata in sommo cielo.* God had given her, "as her greatest grace, that none could lose his soul who has talked with her."[32]

Beatrice was more than matter for a poet's song. She was a saint. That is why Dante passes from love, art, and philosophy to theology, from passion, vision, and poetry to prayer. Beatrice was an occasion for an increase of supernatural grace in Dante's soul. Her visible beauty, therefore, seemed a "sacrament," a symbol, of God's beauty, goodness, truth.

It does not matter whether we say that Beatrice is a symbol of grace in general; or of faith or hope or charity in particular; or a symbol of the source of these graces — the Redeemer, Jesus Christ; or of the channel of these graces — the Church founded by Jesus Christ; or of the divine wisdom of which Jesus Christ is the visible incarnation. It is simplest to say that she is a symbol of the supernatural order, of "Jerusalem," of the city of divine love, much as "Virgil" is a symbol of the natural order, of "Athens," the city of human light, and of "Rome," the city of human law.

From now on when Dante sings of Beatrice, the little girl will still

[29] *Vita Nuova,* xiii, 2.
[30] *Vita Nuova,* xviii, 6.
[31] *Vita Nuova,* xix, 4–14.

[32] *Ancor l' ha Dio per maggior grazia dato che non pò mal finir chi l' ha parlato.*

be in his lover's eyes and her ideal beauty will still be in his artist's
"gentle heart," but in his head he will have in mind not merely the;
symbol but what the symbol means. He will have in mind divine
wisdom or faith or Christ or the Church or the systematic knowledge
of these things — theology. Dante will always be aware of his real
meaning under the veil of allegory or the paint of rhetoric. "It
would be shameful indeed," he says, "for a poet to sing under the
cloak of allegory or rhetorical coloring and not to be able to take the
cloak from his words and to reveal his true meaning."[33]

Such a Beatrice was ripe for heaven; and, in fact, "the Lord of
justice called this most gentle creature to join the ranks of glory
under the banner of the blessed queen, the Virgin Mary, whose
name was held in the greatest reverence in the words of this blessed
Beatrice."[34] In his song, *Li occhi dolenti,* Dante sings that "Beatrice'
is gone to high heaven, to the realm where the angels are in;
peace. . . . The gentle soul full of grace was parted from the lovely
body and is in glory in a worthy place."[35] She was now, in the fullest
sense, the *glorious* mistress of his mind.

In another song, written for Beatrice's brother (but also, of course,
for himself) Dante sings: "Now that she is out of sight the radiance
of her beauty becomes a great spiritual loveliness, that spreads the
light of love through heaven to salute the angels, and their high
intelligences are made to marvel, so gentle is she there,"

> perchè 'l piacere de la sua bieltate,
> partendo sè da la nostra veduta,
> divenne spirital bellezza grande,
> che per lo cielo spande
> luce d'amor, che li angeli saluta,
> e lo intelletto loro alto, sottile
> face maravigliar, sì v' è gentile.[36]

Meanwhile, Dante's soul was not without human consolation. He
began to read, so he tells us in the *Convivio,* Boethius and Cicero
and, "looking for the silver of consolation, he found the gold" of
another kind of love, the love of human wisdom, the gentle and
merciful mistress whose name is philosophy — "the daughter of God,
the queen of all, most noble, most lovely philosophy."[37] He courted

---

[33] *Vita Nuova,* xxv, 10.
[34] *Vita Nuova,* xxviii, 1.
[35] *Vita Nuova,* xxxi, 8.
[36] *Vita Nuova,* xxxiii, 8.
[37] *Figlia di Dio, regina di tutto, nobilissima e bellissima filosofia. Conv.,* II, xii, 9.

his new lady very seriously. For three academic years he followed the
lectures in the schools of the religious and the disputations of the
philosophers.[38] At the end of that time he felt such sweetness in the
love of wisdom that he broke out into the song, *Voi che 'ntendendo
il terzo ciel movete.* He had fallen in love with "Athens," with the
life of learning, with truth which is the good of the intellect, with
the life which, as Aristotle said, is the second and ultimate perfection
of a human being as such.[39]

What seems to have moved Dante most in this study of philosophy
was the Commentary of St. Thomas Aquinas on the *Ethics* of Aristotle. Moral philosophy seemed to Dante the *primum mobile* of
mental life. It orders us in regard to all other learning. Without it,
he says, there would be no pursuit of mental life, no intellectual
creation, no real human happiness. Athens would become a city of
the dead.[40] Of course, the *primum mobile* is not so high as the
empyrean, moral philosophy is not so high as the "divine science
that is full of peace."[41] Yet Lady Philosophy was "full of sweetness,
adorned with virtue, wonderful in wisdom, glorious in liberty."[42]
When she flashes her eyes upon her lovers, she "delivers them from
the death of ignorance and vice."

What Dante says of philosophy in the "temperate and virile" style
of the *Convivio,* he had said in the *Vita Nuova* in a style he describes
as "fervent and passionate." In the *Vita Nuova,* philosophy is symbolized by "gentle lady young and very beautiful," who looked
from a window, showed great compassion, and reminded him of
Beatrice. He began to have scruples. At one moment it seemed that
it was "the will of Love himself that a lady so gentle, lovely, young,
and wise should set his soul in peace." At another moment he would
feel that reason was yielding to appetite. In the end, he says, the
victory went to Beatrice. He was now in the mood to write the last,
marvelous page of the *Vita Nuova,* the sonnet, *Oltre la spera,* and
the prose epilogue. In the sonnet his sighing heart seeks Beatrice
beyond the stars. His pilgrim spirit finds her as a light in heaven
too brilliant for human eyes to look on; yet it speaks so subtly to his
sorrowing heart that he recognizes, in the heavenly Beatrice, the
Beatrice of his romantic devotion and his artistic dreams.

[38] *Conv.,* II, xii, 7.   [41] *Ibid.,* 19.
[39] *Conv.,* II, xiii, 6.   [42] *Ibid.,* xv, 3.
[40] *Conv.,* II, xiv, 18.

Beyond our space and all the spheres in motion
    Passes the sighing of my sorrowing heart;
Over the waters of which skiey ocean
    Love, and love only, plies the pilot's art.

Then when it reaches where desires surrender,
    Seeing the lady of this starry goal,
Her radiance of light, her heavenly splendor,
    Captures the senses of my pilgrim soul.

Not but the mind were baffled to recover
    Sights past the power of memory to hold
Did not my dumbness, in desire, discover
    A tongue to utter what the vision told.

This (for so much the mind remembers) this
Lady of the dream was Beatrice.[43]

After Dante had sung that song, he saw in a vision such things as made him wish to sing no more of his blessed Beatrice until he should be more fitted to sing her praises.

And to come to that I study all I can, as she right truly knows; so that, should it be His will for whom all things live to give me a few more years on earth, I hope to sing a song such as never was sung of any woman. After which, may it please Him who is the Lord of *cortesia* to let my soul go forth to see the glory of this lady, my blessed Beatrice, who now, in beatific vision, looks into the face of Him who is blessed for ages without end.[44]

III

DIVINE LOVE

The song that was sung is the *Divine Comedy*. The "Beatrice" who makes it so lovely is still the red-robed child of eight, the white-dressed girl of seventeen, the emerald-eyed miracle of beauty and virtue who died at twenty-four. She is also the "blessed soul" who serves under the banner of the Queen of Glory. She is, finally, a symbol of our Saviour, a symbol of His truth and grace communicated to the Church, a symbol of eternal wisdom. The "Dante" who meets her on the summit of his poetical purgatory is the wide-eyed lad of eight, the lover of seventeen, the artist and moralist of the *Vita Nuova*. He is also the grown-up citizen of Florence and of

[43] *Vita Nuova*, xlii.   [44] *Ibid.*

Christendom. Finally he, too, is a symbol. He stands for humanity in history, groping for personal, political, and spiritual peace, longing for a better peace than even truth and justice here on earth can give, for the peace that only infinite love can confer.

This groping humanity at the beginning of the Poem is lost in a "dark wood," lost in the sense of fallen from grace and wounded in mind and will. "Dante" is in need of light for the mind's ignorance — in need of Athens, *Studium,* culture; law for the will's concupiscence — in need of Rome, *Imperium,* civilization; grace to lift him to the height from which he fell — he needs Jerusalem, *Sacerdotium,* religion. Life for fallen humanity had become like a dark and pathless wood in a deep valley. Humanity, of course, could still look up to the high hill above which a new dawn seemed imminent, but unaided efforts to reach that height would be met by the light, fleet-footed, spotted leopard of envy (or lust); the high-headed, hungry fearsome lion of pride; the thin, peaceless, wolf of covetousness. Humanity would find itself constantly driven back into the dark valley "where the sun was silent," where there was no light of faith, and too little of reason and law.

It was this "Dante" that "Virgil" came to rescue, this humanity that Athens and Rome would try to restore to human normalcy. The voice of "Virgil" was weak from want of exercise.[45] "Dante" asked him whether he were a "ghost or a living man," symbol or an historical person. He was both, like all the other symbols. He tells "Dante" that he must take another path. Concupiscence is wedded to all the passions; she will haunt the wood of human life until the Greyhound, the *Veltro,* comes to kill her. This redeemer will not hunger for property or pelf, but only for wisdom, love, and moral power, and he will belong not to this or that nation but to all the world. He will be an image of God, who is infinite wisdom, love, and power.

> *Questi non ciberà terra ne peltro*
> *ma sapienza, amore e virtute,*
> *e sua nazion sarà tra Feltro e Feltro.*[46]

He will push the beast of concupiscence back into hell from which the devil's envy first let her loose.

Therefore, for your good, I think and decide that you should follow me; and I shall be your guide and shall lead you from here through an

[45] *Inf.,* i, 63.   [46] *Inf.,* i, 100–102.

eternal place, where you will hear the hopeless lamentations, and see the ancient spirits in their pain that makes them plead for a second death. And, thereafter, you shall see souls content to be in pain, because they hope to reach, however long it takes, the saints in peace. And to these saints, if you should wish to soar, a soul more able than I to help you will come, and with her I shall leave you when I must depart. For you must know that the Emperor who reigns up there has willed that none should reach His city with me as guide, since I was not submissive to His law.[47]

The soul more able to help was "Beatrice." She had come down from paradise to limbo, urging Virgil to begin the rescue.

Her eyes shone brighter than the stars and her voice was soft and low like an angel's voice, and she began, "O gracious spirit from Mantua, whose fame will live as long as lasts the world, my friend (but not the friend of fortune) is hindered in the desert place and too afraid to climb. Please move . . . and help him so that I may be consoled. I am Beatrice, who bids thee go. I come from a place to which I long to return. Love has moved me and makes me speak."[48]

Throughout the dialogue between Beatrice and Virgil, he is a man of lovely words, *parola ornata,* but she is a lady of power, *donna di virtù,* the power by which, as Virgil says, "human nature can rise higher than the circle of the moon." She is also called "true praise of god,"[49] another name for acts of faith. And yet she makes willing use of Virgil's words of human wisdom.[50]

Under the veil of symbol we can see the lovely eyes of Beatrice, and especially when she turns to hide a tear from Virgil, *li occhi lucenti lacrimando volse.*[51] And, of course, that only made Virgil come the quicker. It made Dante, too, all the more willing to follow where Virgil led. "Lead on," he says, "we two have but one will; you are my leader, my lord, my master."[52]

And so they turned to the portals of the city of loss and pain. Dante finds written on it the words: Power, Wisdom, Love. Added together they make up divine justice. The power was divine and, therefore, irresistible; the wisdom, supreme and, therefore, unanswerable; the love was the source and measure of all other love and, therefore, inexhaustible. From this Justice there was no escape. Therefore, "leave all hope ye who enter here," *lasciate ogni speranza voi ch' entrate.*[53]

In hell, the home of the "dolorous folk who have lost the good

[47] *Inf.,* i, 112–125.
[48] *Inf.,* ii, 55–72.
[49] *Ibid.,* 103.
[50] *Ibid.,* 113.
[51] *Ibid.,* 116.
[52] *Ibid.,* 139, 140.
[53] *Inf.,* iii, 9.

of the intellect," the place of "sighs and plaints and cries of woe,"[54] the name of Beatrice is never mentioned. Only once is there even an allusion to her. That is when Virgil says to Dante: "When you are in the presence of the sweet light of her whose lovely eyes see all, from her you will learn the path your life must take."[55] Even in purgatory, before the apparition in the "garden of innocence," the name, Beatrice, is mentioned only five times.[56] In canto VI, Virgil tells Dante that for the solution of his difficulties he must wait for "one who will be a light between his intellect and truth," for Beatrice whom he will find at the top of the mount, smiling and happy. Whereupon Dante says: "Let us go with greater speed, for already I am less tired than before." There are two allusions to Beatrice in those central cantos that constitute the heart of the whole Poem and which are dedicated to the themes of law, liberty, and love. These cantos represent "Virgil" at the summit of his rational insight. However, he finds himself face to face with problems that only Beatrice can fully answer in the light of faith.

In canto XV, in the presence of a supernatural angel of mercy, Dante's eyes are dazzled. "You must not marvel," says Virgil, "if the ministers of heaven dazzle you. . . . You will soon be used to looking at realities like this and you will take delight in them the more your nature is disposed."[57] As Virgil and Dante climb from the terrace of envy to that of anger, Dante wonders how best he can profit from Virgil's words. There is still echoing in his mind a question posed by Guido del Duca: "O human race, why do you set your heart on things that cannot be both owned and shared?"[58] In answer, Virgil proceeds to explain the difference between the possession of material and of spiritual goods. When we set our hearts on material things, he says, the more persons there are to share the less can each one get; so it is that envy puts the bellows to the fire of greed. But there is no place for envy when love lifts our desires toward heavenly possessions. In the "supreme sphere" the more there are to share in God's love the more of charity fills that cloister. Dante was still puzzled. How could more possessors make each one richer? With the metaphor of a light reflected in a multitude of mirrors, Virgil says that "the infinite and ineffable goodness" pours itself out on souls in

---

[54] *Ibid.*, 22.
[55] *Inf.*, x, 130–132.
[56] *Purg.*, vi, 46; xv, 77; xviii, 48; xxvii, 36, 53.

[57] *Purg.*, xv, 28.
[58] *Purg.*, xiv, 86–87.

proportion to their ardor of desire. The more each one wants of love the more there is of love for each and all.

It was a good answer. It can be found, in fact, in St. Augustine's *City of God,* just as Dante's difficulty can be found in Boethius' *Consolation of Philosophy.* But in the Poem Dante makes Virgil say: "If my reason does not satisfy the hunger of your mind, you will see Beatrice, and she will fully satisfy this and every other longing." Dante was about to thank his guide, but he fell into an ecstatic vision. When he recovered, he finds Virgil speaking of opening "the heart to the waters of peace that flow from the eternal well."[59]

In Canto XVII "Virgil" pronounces a long discourse on love, natural and rational, and on free choice. It is reminiscent of St. Thomas Aquinas' treatment of the will and love in God and the angels.[60] It is a discourse that is important for the understanding of Dante's love of Beatrice. Dante's earliest love was "natural." The love in his *cor gentile* was "rational" or, as Virgil says, *amore d'animo.*[61] The discussion is also important for an understanding of what Dante felt to be the main achievement of Aristotle and, there- fore, of Athens — namely the idea of moral responsibility rooted in the human person's freedom of choice. When Virgil has finished the demonstration that love is the root of all virtues, but likewise of the seven capital sins, the "high doctor," "the true father," looks to see if Dante is satisfied. Dante replies: "O master, my seeing is so sharp- ened in your light, that I discern clearly all that your reason implies or proves."[62] Yet he feels that more can be said on the nature of love itself. Virgil explains (very much as Dante does in the *Vita Nuova*) that love "in potency" is "actuated" by beauty, *Da piacere in atto è desto.*[63] The cognoscitive faculties draw from an external reality a mental representation, *Da esser verace tragge intenzione,* and un- fold this within us. Then begins a spiritual movement in the soul. This inclination is love. There is a difficult phrase that seems to mean: "Love is a new life that is born of beauty," *quell' è natur che per piacer di novo in voi si lega.*[64] This love grows into desire and in the end it produces the fruit of joy. At this point responsibility enters. The first inclination of love is a natural and inevitable con- sequence of knowledge. When does the inevitability cease? *Must*

[59] *Purg.,* XV, 131.
[60] *Summa Theologica* I, XX, 1; I, II, XXVII, 4.
[61] *Purg.,* XVII, 93.
[62] *Purg.,* XVIII, 10.
[63] *Ibid.,* 20.
[64] *Ibid.,* 26, 27.

desire turn into fruit? Or can the spiritual movement be stopped? To this question Virgil answers: "As far as reason sees in this matter, I can tell you, but the matter involves a knowledge of faith, and so you must wait for Beatrice."[65]

This much Virgil could say. We have "within us a power that counsels and can guard the threshold of assent."[66] This power winnows out the chaff of evil loves and gathers in the good. Those whose philosophy went to the bottom of things recognized this innate liberty and, therefore, saved morality for the world. Love arises of necessity; but we have the power to restrain its movement. "By the noble virtue," says Virgil, "Beatrice understands free choice. Be sure you keep this in mind if she should speak of it."[67]

Obviously the "Virgil" of this philosophical discourse has very little to do with the poet of the *Aeneid*. He is the symbol of Athens; not merely of the Athens of Aristotle, but of an Athens on tiptoe waiting for the coming of St. Paul. A little later Virgil tears open the siren's dress to reveal the ugliness of sensual desire, and says to Dante: "Spurn the earth with thy heels; turn thine eyes to the lure which the eternal king spins around with the great spheres."[68] The Virgil of the fourth *Eclogue*, has become a symbol of the *anima naturaliter Christiana*.

From now on Virgil has little more to say. But he makes two allusions to Beatrice. When all the sinners on the slopes of purgatory have been seen, there is for "Dante" a symbolical purification to be gone through. It is a wall of fire. Dante hesitates. "Now look, son," says Virgil, "between Beatrice and you is this wall."[69] Dante flung himself into the flame when he heard "the name that like a flower springs up ever in my mind."[70] Virgil is now ready for his last words to Dante. "This day," he says, almost in the words of Boethius,[71] "the sweet fruit that the care of mortals searches on so many branches will put in peace your hungers."[72] And shortly after, in the speech that declares Dante a doctor of philosophy, a ruler and teacher of himself, he alludes to the "lovely eyes that, weeping, made me come to help you."[73]

We have already seen the reapparition of Beatrice and her lovely

[65] ... *Quanto ragion qui vede*
dirti poss' io; da indi in là t' aspetta
pur a Beatrice, ch' è opra di fede. Ibid., 47–48.
[66] *innata v' è la virtù che consiglia*
e de l' assenso de' tener la soglia. Ibid., 62, 63.
[67] *Purg.,* xviii, 73–75.

[68] *Purg.,* xix, 61–63.
[69] *Purg.,* xxvii, 36.
[70] *Ibid.,* 42.
[71] *Cons. of Phil.,* iii, pr. 2.
[72] *Purg.,* xxvii, 115–117.
[73] *Ibid.,* 136–137.

eyes. The eyes, however, are the eyes of faith. The *Paradiso* in which Beatrice guides Dante as Virgil had guided him in the *Inferno* is, in reality, the story of man's growth in grace, just as the earlier part, was the story of man's growth in rational responsibility. It is still, of course, a part of the love story Dante promised to write at the end of the *Vita Nuova*. The only trouble is that, as Beatrice says herself, "not in my eyes alone is paradise," *non pur ne' miei occhi è paradiso*.[74] Even though the beauty of her laughter grows as she rises with Dante to each new step on the stairway of the eternal palace,[75] she cannot quite compete with the celestial beauties all around her. When at last she comes to the triumph of Christ, Dante cries out "O Beatrice, sweet guide and dear!"[76] but his heart was carried away by a "power against which he has no defense." Here was the reality of which Beatrice was the symbol. "Here is the wisdom and the power that opened the road from earth to heaven, the love that was so long yearned for." "Open your eyes and see what I am,"[77] says Beatrice. And yet, symbol though she is, Dante's old tenderness breaks through. When the full beauty of the beloved disciple is too great for Dante's eyes and he is blinded by excess of light, he cries out: "Ah! what it meant to me when I turned to look for Beatrice and found that I could not see her, close as I was to her and in the world of bliss."

> *Ahi quanto ne la mente mi commossi*
> *quando mi volsi per vedere Beatrice*
> *per non poter veder, ben che io fossi*
> *presso di lei, e nel mondo felice.*[78]

Dante is singing of both the real Beatrice and the symbol when he says: "My enamored mind, always in love with my lady, burned more than ever to bring back my eyes to her; but all the lures of nature or of art that capture eyes and so possess the mind, whether in the beauty of the human face or in pictures — if all were put together they would seem as nothing compared to the heavenly beauty that glowed upon me when I turned me to her laughing face,"

> *La mente innamorata, che donnea*
> *con la mia donna sempre, di ridure*
> *ad essa li occhi più che mai ardea:*

[74] *Par.*, xviii, 21.   [76] *Par.*, xxiii, 34.   [78] *Par.*, xxv, 136–139.
[75] *Par.*, xxi, 7–9.   [77] *Ibid.*, 46.

> e se natura o arte fè pasture
> da pigliare occhi, per aver la mente,
> in carne umana o ne le sue pitture,
> tutte adunate, parrebber niente
> ver lo piacer divin che mi refulse
> quando mi volsi al suo viso ridente.[79]

Even when he speaks of Beatrice as "the one who doth emparadise my mind,"[80] he still thought of "the beauteous eyes from which love made the noose to capture me."[81]

In the canto where the symbol of revealed faith is to give place to the symbol of mystical experience, Beatrice to St. Bernard, Dante's poetry continues to fuse into a single beauty both his love for his lady and his yearning for supernatural beauty and truth.

Seeing naught and love constrained me to turn my eyes to Beatrice. If all that had been said so far of her could be included in a single act of praise, it would be too little for what I want to say. The beauty that I saw in her was so transcendent, so far beyond our powers, that I think that only her Creator could enjoy it fully. At this point I must admit defeat — worse than the thrust of any theme that ever overcame a comic or a tragic poet. For the remembrance of her sweet smile blots out my mind as the sun blots the vision of a trembling eye. From the first day when in this life I saw her face until this vision my song has followed her without a break. But now the poetry that followed in the wake of beauty can go no farther. For every artist there is an ultimate he cannot pass. Such as she is I leave her to a greater music than that of my little reed that is now with difficulty reaching its highest notes.

She had led Dante beyond the world of time and matter to the heaven "of pure light, an intellectual light full of love, a love of true good full of joy, a joy that transcends every other sweetness.

> . . . tornar con li occhi a Beatrice
> nulla vedere ed amor mi costrinse.
> Se quanto infino a qui de lei si dice
> fosse conchiuso tutto in una loda,
> poco sarebbe a fornir questa vice.
> La bellezza ch' io vidi si trasmoda
> non pur di là da noi, ma certo io credo
> che solo il suo fattor tutta la goda.
> Da questo passo vinto mi concedo
> più che già mai da punto di suo tema
> soprato fosse comico o tragedo;
> chè, come sole in viso che più trema,
> così lo rimembrar del dolce riso
> la mente mia da me medesmo scema.

[79] Par., xxvii, 88–96.   [80] Par., xxviii, 3.   [81] Ibid., 12.

Dal primo giorno ch' i' vidi il suo viso
in questa vita, infino a questa vista,
non m' è il seguire al mio cantar preciso;
ma or convien che mio seguir desista
più dietro a sua bellezza, poetando,
come a l' ultimo suo ciascuno artista.
Cotal qual io la lascio a maggior bando
che quel de la mia tuba, che deduce
l' ardua sua matera terminando,
con atto e voce di spedito duce
ricominciò: "Noi siamo usciti fore
del maggior corpo al ciel ch' è pura luce:
luce intellettual, pien d' amore;
amor di vero ben, pien di letizia;
letizia che trascende ogni dolzore.[82]

What was beyond this required not merely the light of grace but the "light of glory," the *lumen gloriae.* All Beatrice could do was to point to the seats of the blessed that seemed like golden petals in a sempiternal rose. She pointed in particular to a seat, empty as yet, but marked with an imperial crown. There she said would be the soul of the high Henry, who had come to give peace to Italy before Italy was ready for it. Then she reveals the moral purpose of her allegorical role. As she had proclaimed so faithfully the mission of the Church, she has the right to scold the pastors who had been unfaithful to their trust. Her last fearful and unforgettable words condemn to hell a pope who failed to co-operate with the emperor for the common good of Christendom. She had in mind Clement V. He will be cast down, she says, where Simon Magus suffers for his sin, and he will push him of Anagni still further down, *e farà quel d'Alagna intrar più giuso.*[83]

With that she takes up her seat in paradise next to Rachel. Dante saw her face reflecting the eternal rays; his last words to her were these: "O lady in whom my hope grows strong, and who for my salvation deigned to walk in hell, it is to your power and goodness I owe the grace and strength to see the things that I have seen. You led me from captivity to freedom by all those ways, by all those means, which you had power to use. Guard these gifts which you have lavished on me, so that my soul which you have healed may issue from my body pure enough to please you." Beatrice from her far seat smiled and looked at Dante; then turned to the "eternal fountain."

[82] *Par.,* xxx, 14–42.   [83] *Ibid.,* 148.

> *O donna in cui la mia speranza vige,*
>   *e che soffristi per la mia salute*
>   *in inferno lasciar le tue vestige,*
>
> *di tante cose quant' i' ho vedute,*
>   *dal tuo podere e da la tua bontate*
>   *riconosco la grazia e la virtute.*
>
> *Tu m' hai di servo tratto a libertate*
>   *per tutte quelle vie, per tutt' i modi*
>   *che di ciò fare avei la potestate.*
>
> *La tua magnificenza in me costodi,*
>   *si che l' anima mia, che fatt' hai sana,*
>   *piacente a te dal corpo si disnodi."*
>
> *Così orai; e quella, si lontana*
>   *come parea, sorrise e riguardommi;*
>   *poi si tornò a l' etterna fontana.*[84]

Whoever she was, and whatever she was, she led Dante to love that good beyond which there is nothing for the heart to yearn for,

> *. . . ad amar lo bene*
>   *di là dal qual non è a che s'aspira.*[85]

[84] *Par.*, xxxi, 79–93.
[85] *Ibid.*, 23.

VI

Grandchild of God

"Man's art is, as it were, God's grandchild."[1]

I

ART AND LANGUAGE

BEATRICE, then, is another name for inspiration — romantic, aesthetic, moral, and religious. She inspires passion, vision, virtue, and, in the supernatural order, love of God. How she did it was Dante's secret — and hers. Of the fact and its effects nearly all the poet's works bear witness.

Beatrice is closely related to Dante's art. She is, I think, the key to its proper understanding. Dante's art is multidimensional. He reached for beauty with his eyes, his mind, his will, his spirit. He saw beauty in four worlds — in matter, in his mind, in morals, and in supernatural "mysteries." When he says of Beatrice that "she is the limit of nature's handiwork," he is inspired by her eyes and lips. When he sings: "She is the model by which to measure beauty,"[2] the vision is in his soul. When she "became a great spiritual loveliness that lit up heaven and made the angels fall in love with her,"[3] he is in a world of moral idealism. When, at last, he begs that "his soul which she has saved" may finish life unscarred,[4] the artist passes from poetry to prayer.

Beatrice is not the whole of Dante's art. Poetry is more than inspiration. Along with passionate vision in the heart there must go an intellectual habit in the head and a practical craftsmanship of hand. When "love whispers to the heart," the poet's head must

[1] *Inf.*, xi, 105.
[2] *Vita Nuova*, xix, 11.
[3] *Vita Nuova*, xxxiii, 8.
[4] *Par.*, xxxi, 89, 90.

119

"heed" and the poet's hand "retell the lessons to the rest of men."[5]
Eyes, heart, head, and hand make poetry. Without the whisper of
inspiration poetry could never soar. With a "hand that trembles,"
even the "habit of art"[6] would be nothing but a speechless awe.

The relationship between intellectual habit, practical craftsmanship, and poetic inspiration is discussed by Dante in a Latin work
on "The Art of Writing Italian," *De vulgari eloquentia*. It is a work
that has been much debated and misunderstood. Until quite re-
cently few of the critics showed any penetration of its medieval and
Scholastic spirit. The Renaissance saw nothing in the book but an
unsuccessful philological attempt to turn the Tuscan dialect into
a national tongue. In the nineteenth century, it was taken for a
rhetorical discussion of poetic diction pure and simple.

Dante, in fact, starts from philosophy. His major premise in Book
I is that language belongs to God, to nature, and to art. Speech is
as natural as any other need that God has put in human nature — as
natural as love, knowledge, and sociability. But to the natural, un-
self-conscious expression of ideas that we learn in the nursery, art
adds a second kind of language. Language is made precise, polished,
permanent by grammarians, rhetoricians, and artists. So it was,
Dante felt, with classical Latin and Greek. This suggested to him
that art could do for Italian what it had done for Latin. Not that
he thought of excogitating a new and "artificial" language that
could be created by a single crank. True "artistic" language can
only come "by the common consent of a whole society."[7] What art
does for language is to reveal a hidden and inherent beauty. Just
as the "act," the "form," the beauty, of true, "fine," "courtly,"
artistic love is "educed" from the "potency," the "matter," of
natural passion, so is true, fine, courtly, artistic language educed
from the potency of natural speech, from the matter, body, in-
dividuality of this or that particular way of talking. Dante counted
in Italy no less than fourteen local modes or dialects — not to mention innumerable minor variations. The Roman mode seemed to
him as corrupt as Roman morals. The good folk of Istria butchered
the language, *crudeliter accentuando eructuant*.[8] Even the Italian

---

[5] *Purg.*, xxiv, 52–54.
[6] *Par.*, xiii, 78.
[7] . . . *de communi consensu multarum gentium regulata, nulli singulari arbitrio
obnoxia. De vulgari eloquentia*, I, ix, 11.
[8] *De vulgari eloquentia*, I, xi, 5.

ot the average Tuscan was disgraceful. Dante's word for it is *turpiloquium*.[9] As for the Genoese, if they forgot how to pronounce z they would be speechless. On the whole, the Bolognese talked the best "municipal" Italian in the peninsula. But even this was not to be compared to the artistic creation of the poets of Sicily and Tuscany.

The splendor of true Italian shone brightest in the poems of Dante and his friends, Guido Cavalcanti, Lapo Gianni, Cino of Pistoia. This ideal, artistic diction is called by Dante "illustrious, cardinal, aulic, and courtly," *Illustre, cardinale, aulicum et curiale*.[10] Poets, he says, like kings and scholars, are men of light and leading (*Illuminati . . . illuminant*). Their artistic language, like ordered law and brilliant learning, is both an inner vision and a beacon for the rest of men. Out of a mass of "regional vocabulary, intricate construction, faulty phrasing, and boorish pronunciation" the poets have elicited a language that is noble, simple, polished, and courtly. And what a power their poems have over human wills and hearts! What glory and renown reward poets' effort! That is why both they and their language are "illustrious."

Their diction is "cardinal" in the literal sense that it is the hinge (*cardo*) on which the whole door of local language swings or comes to rest. It is "aulic" in the sense that it is fit for the palace of an emperor. It is "courtly" because it has about it the poise and rhythm of finished art, *Librata regula eorum quae peragenda sunt*.[11]

Of the sweet odor of artistic Italian there was a whiff, as it were, in every local form, but the full, rich odor of the living language could be found only where there was taste to distinguish the fair from the foul and "intelligence and learning" enough to organize beautiful parts into a living whole.[12]

This opens the question of inspiration, native taste, cultivated habit, and rhetorical adornment as elements of poetic style. Here Dante lays down as a first principle that technique and inspiration, rhetoric and poetry, learning and intelligence, care and taste, *cautio* and *discretio*, must be wedded to each other like body and soul, matter and form. No kind of caparison will make an ox beautiful; no sort of belt will improve the looks of a pig, *nec bovem epiphyatum nec balteatum suem dicemus esse ornatum*.[13] Ornament in art

---

[9] *Ibid.*, xiii, 3.
[10] *Ibid.*, xvi, 8.
[11] *De vulgari eloquentia*, I, xviii, 4.
[12] *De vulgari eloquentia*, II, i, 8.
[13] *Ibid.*, 9.

is never merely tagged on. It is an "appropriate improvement." *Est enim exornatio alicuius convenientis additio.*[14] The right kind of rhetoric can add something to the beauty of poetry. The fact is that rules of rhetoric are laws of reason discoverable in the works of supreme artists. They can be learned by "long study and great love" of the masters of style. It was thus that Dante himself did not disdain to learn from Virgil, his "master and authoritative model."[15]

Dante's discussion of style is characteristically philosophical. He begins, in the concrete, with Bertram de Born, Arnald Daniel, and Giraut de Borneil as the best of the Provençal poets. Then he generalizes. Their main themes have been three: arms, love, and righteousness. These themes correspond to the classical *utile, delectabile, honestum*. These distinctions, in turn, are correlative to the three levels of life in man — vegetative, animal, rational. On the lowest level man seeks what is useful (*utile*); on the animal level what is pleasant (*delectabile*); on the rational level what is right (*honestum*). Security, the best of all useful things, is defended by valor in arms; ardor in love is the most precious of all delights; order in virtue is the highest of rational achievements. Hence valor, love, and virtue are the proper themes of great poetry. In Italy, says Dante, Cino da Pistoia was the best of the poets of love; Cino's friend — Dante himself — the outstanding poet of rectitude.[16]

For these high themes — valor, Venus, virtue — the best medium is the *canzone*. It is at this point that Dante introduces a definition of poetry as "vision fashioned into song by means of rhetoric and music," *fictio rethorica musicaque poita.*[17] The *poita* in this definition is a word coined from the Greek *poiein*, "to make," from which our own word *poetry* is derived. Poetry, not as inner passion and vision but as outer expression, as song, is something that is "made," *poita*. Art is that habit, quality, or power of intelligence by which it is made. Art, in the language of Dante's philosophy, is an "operative intellectual virtue," *virtus intellectualis operativa*. The first part of the poet's "work" is to decide what style fits his theme, whether "tragic," "comic," or "elegiac" — sublime, temperate, or emotional. If the theme calls for the high, "tragic," style, it is part of the poet's work to achieve the right co-ordination of "significant meaning,

[14] *Ibid.*, 10.
[15] *Inf.*, i, 85.
[16] *De vulgari eloquentia*, II, iii, 6–10.
[17] *Ibid.*, iv, 2.

superbness of music, rhetorical construction, and choice of words."[18]
It is not enough for the poet to have drunk at the Pierian spring.
He must tune his strings before he begins to play. Poetry calls for
care and judgment. And "this means work." Poetry calls for a
vigorous mind, assiduous exercise, a life of learning.[19] Lazy geese
should keep to the ground and let the eagles soar.[20]

A simple illustration of Dante's own assiduity is his care in the
selection of words. A poet, he says, must "sift" his words — the
"virile" from the "feminine" and "childish"; the "urban" from the
"rustic." Words can be soft as wool, rough as serge, tough as hemp,
hispid as a hairshirt. Dante learned to mix his words — the "well
combed" with the "shaggy," but he preferred sounds like *amore,
donna, disio, vertute, donare, letitia, salute, securitate, defesa* — with
no aspirates, no sharpness, no doubled z. Occasionally, he says, a
very long word will do, especially a hendecasyllable like *sovramag-
nificentissimamente* that exactly fills a line. However, *honorifica-
bilitudinitate* is one syllable too long. The best rule in all such
matters is, however, good taste, *ingenua discretio*.[21]

Another illustration is Dante's effort to make his songs singable.
Each stanza in a *canzone* is made a perfect line-by-line, syllabic echo
of the first. Sometimes a single melody was meant to run through
the whole of each stanza. A common arrangement, as in *Donne ch'
avete intelletto d' amore*,[22] was to have the melody of the first four
lines repeated in the next four; with a new melody for the following
three lines, and this repeated in the last three lines. Such a stanza
was said to have two "feet" and two "turns" (*volte*). Sometimes, as
in *Li occhi dolenti per pietà del core*,[23] two "feet" of three lines
each were followed by a long tail (*cauda*) of eight lines. In this
matter of melodic division the best poets, Dante tells us, followed
no single rule. There was still more liberty in the matter of the
arrangement of the rimes. Dante himself liked the first line of the
"tail" to rime with the last line of the second "foot." This he called
"concatenation." In the same way he liked two riming lines at the
end of his stanzas, much as Shakespeare did in his sonnets.

[18] *Cum gravitate sententiae tam superbia carminum quam constructionis elatio et
excellentia vocabulorum. De vulgari eloquentia*, II, iv, 7.
[19] . . . *numquam sine strenuitate ingenii et artis assiduitate scientiarumque habitu
fieri potest. Ibid.*, 9.
[20] . . . *nolint astripetam aquilam imitari. Ibid.*, 10.
[21] *De vulgari eloquentia*, II, vii, 7.
[22] *Vita Nuova*, xix.
[23] *Vita Nuova*, xxi.

Dante never finished his work on vernacular eloquence. This may be a proof that he was not fully convinced of the value of elaborating rules of rhetorical and poetical composition. However, it may be merely evidence that the writing of the *Divine Comedy* began to absorb his whole attention. The fact remains that the great Poem itself is full of rhetoric, and even of rules and arrangements more complicated than those of rhetoric. The very name *Commedia* is taken from the workshop of the rhetoricians. Apart from the meaning that the Poem was to end pleasantly, the name *Commedia* was meant to imply that the style was pitched between the "high" style of tragedy and the "homely" style of elegy. In accord with a prescription of Horace's *Ars poetica* Dante could allow himself to raise the tone on certain occasions without attempting to sustain it.[24] He recognized that the *Paradiso* had to be "higher" in style than the rest of the Poem. In fact, he speaks of it as "sublime."[25] It is worth adding that, in this context, he also makes a firm declaration of poetic independence: "Those who live on the level of intelligence and reason are endowed with a kind of divine liberty and are bound down by no rules. The reason is not far to seek. How can they be led by laws since the laws are based on them."[26]

II

BEAUTY, JUSTICE, TRUTH, AND GRACE

There was for Dante no more contradiction in wanting both rhetorical laws and poetic liberty, than there was in wanting both political laws and personal rights, logical laws and intellectual liberty, ecclesiastical laws and "the freedom of the sons of God." Whether in art, politics, philosophy, or religion there was, for Dante, no fundamental difference between liberty and law, since there was no fundamental difference between reason and rule. A rule is not valid unless it is an insight of reason, just as reason is not reason unless it, in turn, is a reflection of the light of God. Art, like politics, philosophy, and religion, only gets its meaning from

[24] *Epist.*, xiii, 30.
[25] *Ibid.*, 11.
[26] *Nam intellectu ac ratione degentes, divina quadam libertate dotati, nullis consuetudinibus astringuntur; nec mirum, cum non ipsi legibus, sed ipsis leges potius dirigantur. Epist.*, xiii, 7.

the fact that beauty (like law, truth, and grace) is primarily in God, only secondarily in art. Ultimately, the most real art is the art of God, the supreme artist. When God created nature, divine beauty became open to the contemplation of human artists. Since nature is the child of God and since the creative visions of human artists follow the ways of nature, "man's art is, as it were, God's grandchild."[27]

It may help us to understand Dante's philosophy of art if we notice how he relates art to politics, philosophy, and religion. In all these fields Dante starts from the mind and will of God, the Creator. Dante looked upon man-made art very much as he looked upon man-made law. Both are reflections of something in God. Human law is an "image of the divine will."[28] Whatever is repugnant to the divine will is by that fact no law at all.[29] So with art. It is an image of divine beauty. Human art, like nature, which is divine art, is found on three levels: first, in the mind of the artist; second, in the tools he uses as means; third, in the matter that is ordered or informed by art. So, too, nature can be contemplated on three levels: first, as nature is in the mind of the Prime Mover, God; second, in the heavens as in the organs by means of which the likeness of the eternal goodness is unfolded; finally in malleable matter informed by nature.[30]

What is true of beauty and justice is true of truth and grace. This or that conception of truth may err as this or that matter may fail to take the form an artist wishes to impose upon it; but the "idea" of truth can never be wrong, since an idea is a reflection of divine truth as truly as an artist's vision is a reflection of divine beauty. In the same way this or that conception of the Church may be influenced by pride or cupidity, but the "idea" of the Church is an image of God. "The form of the Church," says Dante in the *Monarchia*, "is nothing but the life of Christ, of what He said and of what He did. For His life was the idea and exemplar of the Church on earth, especially of her pastors and above all of the supreme pastor to whom it belongs to feed the sheep and the lambs."[31] Saints have before them the infallible model of the incarnate Word of

[27] *Inf.*, xi, 105.
[28] . . . *jus in rebus nihil est aliud quam similitudo divinae voluntatis.*
[29] *Mon.*, II, ii, 4–6.
[30] *Ibid.*, 2.
[31] *Mon.*, III, xv, 2–4.

God; but artists have to rely on their taste, as philosophers rely on their intelligence and kings on their conscience. But in all these cases, what is seen, however dimly, is the truth or the goodness or the beauty of God. This is why, for Dante, art, politics, philosophy, and religion are autonomous, each in its own sphere of beauty, justice, truth, or grace. It is also the reason why the rules of art, if they are rational and traditional rules, can be as respectable as personal inspiration. Rules, in fact, result from the history of high inspiration, just as laws result from the history of good conscience, and logic from the history of right reasoning.

In Dante's mind the artist and the saint were closely related. Grace, in the full theological sense, makes a saint "deiform," "godlike," a "sharer of the divine nature." On an infinitely lower level, and yet on a level immeasurably above any other level in created things, artistic inspiration (like ethical and metaphysical insight) makes human persons as like the Creator as is possible to human nature as such. We can reject artistic inspiration as we can reject the prompting of conscience and the perception of abstract truth. Today, we call the rejection of metaphysics positivism, and the rejection of conscience naturalism. Dante had another word. He called such rejections "bestiality." And of all forms of bestiality the worst was to reject the divine gift of immortality. "Of all the forms of bestiality the most foolish, the lowest, and the most harmful is to deny that after this life there is no other life; because if we consider all the writings of philosophers and other wise men, all will be found to agree in this that there is a part of us that is immortal." Such a denial is bestial because, Dante adds, even philosophical insight (at least in Aristotle and Cicero) could discern immortality; because poetic inspiration as in the case of the pagan Virgil had intimations of it; because all law implied it, whether of the Jews, the Saracens, the Tartars, or any others "who lived according to reason." Finally, the denial of immortality is irrational because we are made certain of it by "the most veracious doctrine of Christ, who is the way and the truth and light." As for himself, says Dante, "I so believe, I so affirm, and I am certain, that I am to pass to a better life when this is over, to a life where that glorious lady lives of whom my soul was enamored."[32]

This paragraph of the *Convivio* in which Dante brings together

[32] *Conv.,* II, viii, 8, 9, 14, 16.

the witness of poetry, philosophy, law, and religion may serve as an introduction to the question of the so-called "four senses" — literal, allegorical, moral, and anagogic. When Dante speaks of poetry as "vision expressed with the help of rhetoric and music," we have to recall that he meant vision in the fullest sense, vision with all eyes open and all lights turned on. As he saw Beatrice in her immortal life with the help of faith, philosophy, morality, and artistic inspiration, so he saw her in temporal life; so he saw all beauty. She is, first, a fact or, at least, a myth for his imagination. The expression of this fact or myth is the "literal" sense of the *Divine Comedy*. She is, at the same time, seen as a "meaning" for his mind, an allegory. This meaning is expressed in the "allegorical" sense of the Poem. Somehow, he felt her with his conscience as immediately as he saw her with his eyes, his imagination, and his mind. In so far as she was a model, an ideal, she was a reproach to any deliberate rejection of that ideal.

This is a point on which modern taste is troubled. We are shy of any kind of propaganda, of any form of preachment, of any degree of moral purpose. But it is well for us to remember that we shall miss what Dante himself felt was the main point of his art if we try to forget *his* purpose. To forget the moral purpose of his art is like taking out one of the lenses from a telescope. In the case of Beatrice herself we store up for ourselves a bad dose of bathos — her last words in the Poem — unless we accept, with complete artistic surrender, both Dante's allegorical meaning and his moral purpose. We might expect at the end of the Poem some kind of celestial kiss wafted from Beatrice to Dante. What Dante actually saw and heard was quite different. *His* Beatrice, the Beatrice of the Poem, spends her last moment with Dante in canonizing a Holy Roman Emperor, and in condemning to hell two Roman pontiffs. Her very last words, strengthened with contemptuous staccato, have the force of a kick.

e farà quel d'Alagna intrar più giuso.[33]

The effect is sublime if we are in love with Dante's whole Beatrice — literal, allegorical, moral, and anagogic; the effect is ridiculous and disconcerting if we can find poetry only in the myth that touches our imagination. More than the allegorical and moral senses, it is the anagogic sense that reveals the climactic character of that line.

[33] *Par.*, xxx, 148.

By *anagoge* Dante means the lifting of the mind from the world of matter to the world of supernatural mystery. If we can feel, as an effect of Dante's art, that Beatrice is divine wisdom incarnate, that the apparition at the end of the *Purgatory* is the advent of Jesus Christ, that "Beatrice" is the "life of Christ," the "idea," the "form" of the Church, the model particularly of supreme pontiffs, then her last line has about it the sound of the trumpet on the day of doom. We can hear in that line something of what we see at the center of Michelangelo's "Last Judgment," in that fearful lifting of Christ's hand, as though it were about to strike.

It is with Beatrice as it is with immortality. Dante caught a vision of immortality wherever and however he could, in the intimations of poetry, in the insights of philosophy, in the implications of morality and law, and, clearest of all, in the revelation of divine truth. We see immortality, he says, perfectly by faith; by reason we see it with some shadow of obscurity because of the mixture in us of the mortal and the immortal.[34] So is it with beauty.

III

Sight, Insight, Inspiration, Ecstasy

There is a somewhat subtle intimation of this aspect of Dante's art in the *Purgatory*. As soon as Dante reaches the gate of St. Peter, he stops to remind the reader that he is about to lift his matter higher. "Reader you see clearly how I am lifting my subject, and therefore do not wonder if I bring to it the force of greater art."[35] When he reached the first terrace, Dante saw most marvelous carvings on the sides of the hill. First, he saw the Annunciation so vividly that he could have sworn that he was not merely looking with his eyes at a silent image but that he could hear the words, "Hail, full of Grace," spoken "to her who turned the key that opened the high love" when she said, "Behold the handmaid of the Lord." "Do not keep your mind on one place only," said Virgil. Dante turned and saw a second *intaglio* representing David and the ark of the covenant. Dante's eyes said: No, I cannot hear, I can only see; but his

[34] *Conv.*, II, viii, 5.
[35] *Purg.*, ix, 70, 72.

ears said: Yes, I hear the song. So, too, with the incense. His nostrils seemed to sense as much as his eyes could see. With a third *intaglio* it was even more remarkable. Dante could hear the whole dialogue between the Emperor Trajan and the poor widow pleading for her son, and he could see the imperial banner floating in the breeze. Then Dante comments: "He that never looked on anything new" — meaning, of course, God — "produced this visible speech," *esto visibile parlare.* And Dante took delight in looking at these images, beyond the power of human art and precious because they were the work of God.

There is here and in what follows an implicit distinction between sight, vision, and inspiration. All that Dante's eyes could see were carvings; by some deeper insight the artist's vision could see movement and hear sounds and understand deep meanings. It was even more so when Dante looked at the carvings below his feet. They seemed to be of better craftsmanship and revealed a closer following of nature.[36] "What a master of brush or scalpel he would be who could represent the shadows and the lines which there would make the subtlest artist marvel. The dead seemed dead and the living seemed alive. No one who saw the reality could have seen it clearer than I did."[37]

Still more remarkable was the art revealed to Dante on the second *cornice.* This time there was nothing for his eyes to see. Beauty came like voices in his mind, "flying spirits, sensed but unseen, that uttered courteous invitations to the banquet of love,"

> *e verso noi volar furon sentiti,*
> *non pero visti, spiriti, parlando*
> *a la mensa d' amor cortesi inviti.*[38]

The beauty was all in the *mind.* It was a case of vision and inspiration, of beauty in the mind, without any counterpart in the world of visible things. This was a preparation for a still higher artistic experience. "I seemed to be smitten by a reflected light in front of me; from which my eyes were quick to turn away. 'What is that light? sweet father,' I said, 'from which I am trying in vain to screen my sight, and which seems to be moving closer toward us?' 'Marvel not if the realities of heaven still dazzle you,' Virgil replied. 'It is an angel that is coming to invite us to go higher. Soon it will not be

[36] *Purg.,* xii, 22.   [37] *Ibid.,* 68.   [38] *Purg.,* xiii, 25–27.

so hard for you to behold such things, but rather a delight for you in proportion as nature has disposed you to enjoy it.' "[39] A little later Virgil hints that there are higher things to be seen if only we could close our eyes to the things of earth. "Because you fix your mind merely on the things of earth," he said, "you draw darkness from true light."[40] He went on to say that we see the things of heaven as a bright surface reflects the light of the sun. The better the mirror is polished the more light is reflected. So is it with the light of the ineffable good. It enters us and is reflected in proportion to the ardor of our longing to receive it.[41]

Dante was now ready for the highest level of artistic experience. Higher than sight and insight, higher than "visible speech" for his eyes and ears, higher than the inspiration of "invisible voices," was the experience of "ecstatic vision." "I seemed of a sudden to be caught up into an ecstatic vision, and to see in a temple persons and a woman about to enter with the tender ways of a mother and to say: 'My son, why hast thou treated us so.' " Here, apparently, was an intimation of beauty beyond seeing, vision, and ordinary inspiration. When the ecstasy was over, Dante realized that he had touched a different kind of world — the world of supernatural mystery. He found it to be as true, as real, as the worlds of sense and thought. "O sweet father," he said to Virgil, "if you will listen I shall tell you what I saw when I seemed to you intoxicated." But somehow Virgil understood. "What you saw," he said, "was but to urge you to open your heart to the waters of peace which flow from the eternal fountain."[42]

It is to these "waters of peace from the eternal fountain" that Dante's art is ever inviting us. "O you, who in your tiny skiff — longing to listen but with an eye on your visible shore — have followed behind my ship that, singing, sails the sea, venture no farther in the deep — lest, losing me, you may be lost. This ocean is uncharted. Apollo is the pilot, nine muses watch the stars, Minerva is in the breeze. But you other few — you who strain your necks, reaching for the bread of angels that feeds the saints without satiety — you may trust your boat to the deep, following my wake in the unruffled sea."[43] The bread of angels is the immaterial world, including what Dante calls in the *Convivio*,[44] "the supernal realities of eternal glory."

[39] *Purg.*, xv, 22 ff.
[40] *Ibid.*, 64–66.
[41] *Ibid.*, 67–72.
[42] *Ibid.*, 130–132.
[43] *Par.*, ii, 1–15.
[44] *Conv.*, II, i, 6.

An illustration of the way he leads us on from the shallows to the deep, from "matter" to "form" and, finally, to faith is the progressive immateriality of the apparitions in the *Paradiso*. Piccarda, whom he meets in the moon, appeared to him like an image in a mirror or in a shallow pool.[45] Justinian, who appears in Mercury, was more like a silhouette than a photograph — a shadow full of joy enclosed in light.[46] In Venus, Carlo Martello was merely color and movement and song without shadow or shape.[47] By the time the poet meets St. Thomas in the sun, he can hardly find a word to convey the immateriality of what he saw. Here was light without even color, beauty beyond the reach of genius, experience, fancy or art, a beauty only for the eyes of faith.[48]

IV

THE CANTO OF PAOLO AND FRANCESCA

Even in the *Inferno* this light higher than our fancy is seldom absent. A good illustration is the canto of Paolo and Francesca. Dante sets himself the problem of picturing a tragedy of love on the three levels of sense, thought, and faith. On the lowest level there is a mere tragedy of blood — the visible and violent death of two lovers caught in illicit embrace by an outraged husband. Higher than this was the tragedy in the lovers' heads and hearts: Why had Paolo and Francesca to *steal* their moment of romantic ecstasy? Highest of all was the "mystical" tragedy. More than anything in the worlds of matter and mind, love is meant to lead us to that love "beyond which there is nothing for the heart to long for." That had been so with Dante and Beatrice. With Paolo and Francesca love was to end — in loss and everlasting hate. Dante's art keeps the three tragedies quite distinct, but they are never separated. The four "senses" — myth, meaning, moral, and mystery — are struck, all together, like the notes of a single chord.

Dante and Virgil come to a place "where no light speaks." They can hear nothing but a "moan as of a sea in a storm when the waters are tossed with warring winds." Dante feels vaguely that there are spirits near, blown about by hellish blasts. A little nearer, and he

[45] *Par.*, iii, 10–16.   [47] *Par.*, viii, 25–30.
[46] *Par.*, v, 107–108.   [48] *Par.*, x, 43–45.

can hear the cries, complaints, and lamentations blaspheming the power of God. Finally, he is aware that these are the souls of carnal sinners, damned because they permitted passion to trample on their reason. Next he sees individual spirits, tossed like starlings in the winter wind, "now here, now there, now up, now down, with no hope of any kind to comfort them, no hope of rest, no hope even of lesser pain." In three marvelous lines the poet shows what he can do with onomatopeia:

> di qua, di là, di giù, di su li mena;
> nulla speranza li conforta mai,
> non che di posa, ma di minor pena.[49]

By a skillful transition he passes from the ancient Semiramis — by whose fate our sympathy is utterly untouched — first to Dido and Cleopatra, who move us somewhat, and then to Helen and Isolde. The increasing contrast between the sinners' fate and our feelings reaches a climax when the poet sees a pair of lovers "light upon the wind" with whom he longs to speak. "Beg them in the name of love," says Virgil, "and they will come." For a moment our feelings of affection make us forget their fate. But Dante calls us to attention. Into his single appeal he puts both the full force of human sympathy and the inexorable power of eternal justice. "O wearied souls," he pleads, "come and speak with us, unless Another [he means God] denies you this." Again, for a brief moment we forget all tragedy. We are in love with the two lovers. "As doves, called by desire and carried by their love, sweep on poised wings through the air to their sweet nest, so did the lovers issue from the troop where Dido is and move through the malignant air — for such was the force of my affectionate appeal."

> Quali colombe dal disio chiamate,
> con l' ali alzate e ferme al dolce nido
> vegnon per l' aere dal voler portate,
> cotali uscir de la schiera ov' è Dido,
> a noi venendo per l' aere maligno,
> sì forte fu l' affettuoso grido.

Then bringing together the whole pathos of the triple tragedy, Dante makes Francesca say: "O living creature gracious and benign, who come through this black air to visit us who stained the world with blood, if only the king of the universe were our friend, we

[49] *Inf.*, v, 43–45.

would pray to Him for your peace — because you have such feeling for our tragic fate."

Francesca tells her story. Thinking, furtively, of that ocean of infinite peace into which the rivers of all human lives are meant to flow, she says that she was born near the point where the Po and its tributaries come to rest in the sea at the end of all their flowing. She was born . . . but of the rest of her life she had nothing to relate but love. "Love that takes quick root in the gentle heart caught him with the lovely body that was robbed from me — robbed in a way that still afflicts me. Love that compels us to return love for love caught me so strongly with his beauty that, as you see, even here love will not leave me. Love led us to a single death — but a deeper pit in hell awaits our murderer!" *Caina attende chi a vita ci spense.*

When Dante hears the cacophony of those last words he knows that hell is the abode of hate. This thought weighs down his head until Virgil speaks to him: "What are you thinking of?" He was thinking of the dreadful contrast between the lovers' thoughts and sweet desires in life and the dire results in hell. "Francesca," he says "your torments make me weep for grief and pity. But tell me: In the time of the sweet sighing, how did love grant you to know the dubious desires?" To which Francesca answers: "There is no greater pain than to recall, when one is sad, a time of happiness,"

> . . . *nessun maggior dolore*
> *che ricordarsi del tempo felice*
> *ne la miseria.*

She tells how she and Paolo read together the story of Lancelot and Guinevere — up to the point where the Arthurian lovers kissed. What follows in Dante's song seems to me six of the most extraordinary lines in all literature. It is as though Dante wanted to condense a five-act play into six lines. The first act is contained in two lines that sing, with the fresh melody of daybreak, the pastoral scene of the lovers reading of the "longed-for laugh" of Guinevere kissed by such a lover as Lancelot was,

> *Quando leggemmo il disiato riso*
> *esser bacciato da cotante amante. . . .*

Then the curtain falls. It rises on a scene in hell. An altogether different music is in the air. The repetition of the sharp vowels *e* and *i* suggest a violin playing in a minor key, *questi che mai da me non fia diviso . . .*

"He that shall never, never be parted from me." The key word is *never*. They cannot escape each other's company — ever; because they are alike and forever damned to a life of hate and blasphemy in a place where, as Dante has already been told by Virgil, one can hear the "wailings of despair and see the ancient spirits in their pain, crying for a second death" of sheer annihilation.

> *ov' udirai le disperate strida,*
> *vedrai li antichi spirit dolenti,*
> *che la seconda morte ciascun grida.*[50]

On that scene of the helpless, hopeless lovers in hell the curtain goes down. When it rises for the third scene, we are back on earth, back to the lovers in their ecstasy of romantic but illicit love. In the line that says simply "he kissed me on the lips all trembling," Dante the artist manages to convey by sound, especially by the alliterative *b* and *t*, first the soft and feminine passivity of Francesca and then the hard, masculine, aggressive passion of Paolo,

> *la bocca mi baciò tutto tremante.*

Again the curtain goes down. It rises on the day of judgment. In an explosion harsher even than the explosion in the line, *Caina attende chi a vita ci spense,* Francesca curses the book that led her into sin, curses the author who turned her weakness into wickedness,

> *Galeotto fu il libro e chi lo scrisse.*

The line violates every rule of poetical diction laid down in *De vulgari eloquentia*. There is not a single trisyllable in the whole line. There is the harsh four-syllable name, *Galeotto,* that like Dante's example, *greggia,* has about it something of the "wildness of the woods."[51] There is *libro,* which like *corpo* has the roughness of lining. There is not a single one of the "well-groomed" words like *amore, disio, salute* which Dante liked, and which, as he says, "leave a kind of sweetness in the mouth."[52] There are four of those hispid monosyllables which are only justified in poetry by necessity, *fu, il, chi, lo.* And finally there is the terrible *scrisse* at the end of the line, with its combination of consonants that make a sound like the hiss of a snake.

With that line we know — with whatever anguish — that Fran-

[50] *Inf.,* i, 115–117.   [51] *De vulgari eloquentia,* II, vii, 4.   [52] *Ibid.*

cesca is as definitely damned as Semiramis. And so the curtain goes down. It rises on the actual murder scene on earth. As Dante seems to have conceived the story of Paolo and Francesca, there was no more outward sin than the stolen kiss. He implies, of course, that both sinners consented to a more consummated infidelity; but he heightens the romantic aspect of the triple tragedy by denying the lovers the full solace of their sin. In Dante's myth the lovers are caught and killed in the act of kissing. But that is conveyed to us only by the sound of the line. It is conveyed unmistakably. If you read the line aloud, with a slight emphasis on the explosive sounds and on the decreasing intensity of the continuant breathings, you will feel that Dante is suggesting the sudden stab of the sword, the first loud gasp of the victims and the *rallentando* of their dying breaths.

Quel giorno piu non vi leggemmo avante.

V

ULYSSES AND UGOLINO

Allusion has been made to the story of Ulysses in Canto xxvi of the *Inferno*. It may be taken as a second illustration of what I have called Dante's "multidimensional" art. In the "literal" sense it is a yarn of men who go down to the sea in ships. The same words, under a light veil of allegory, tell a tale of the brave old world of "Rome" and "Athens" — of humanity's daring in the worlds of will and mind, of virtue and knowledge, *virtute e conoscenza.* The allegory has a moral purpose — to teach us that even noble daring that begins in "folly" must end in failure. Divine grace is as far beyond the reach of Roman "virtue" as divine revelation is above Athenian "knowledge." And here the "moral" passes into the "mystery" of divine predestination and the unfathomable depths of the will of God.

Even in the speech that Ulysses addresses to his companions,[53] there is a passion in the pleading that tells us that Dante was thinking far less of reaching the tangible "world without people beyond the setting sun" than of grasping the invisible values in the soul.

[53] *Inf.*, xxvi,112–120.

"O brothers," Ulysses begins, "who through a hundred thousand perils have reached the west, to this short, short vigil of our senses that remains do not deny the experience of the world without people beyond the setting sun." There the voice of the mythical seafarer ends. What follows is the voice of Aristotle. "Think of your dignity as men. You were not made to live like brutes. The goals of life are the good and the true" — virtue and knowledge. The "little prayer" made his men so eager for the venture that Ulysses could hardly, if he tried, have held them back. So they began. "We turned our poop into the morning sun; we made of our oars wings for the foolish flight; we kept steering always to the left." That makes good sense in the yarn — in the "literal" sense. But, of course, what Dante has in mind is something else. Ulysses had turned his back on the light of God. So, too, when Ulysses mentions "oars for wings," Dante has in mind the angel who had "no oars nor even sails but only his wings" and who "disdained all human aids" and whose ship reached Ulysses' destination with a "speed that no human flight could equal."[54] When Ulysses says "left," Dante is thinking (and all his readers remember) that "left" and "right" mean in the language of allegory, "nature" and "grace," "human" and "divine." What is said of the stars and the poles and the night and the sea brings our emotion and imagination back to the myth, but the "five" slow months and the "light beneath the moon" and, above all, the mysterious music of the alliterative line, *lo lume era di sotto da la luna,* prepare us for the intimations of the "anagogic" sense. The "mountain, brown in the distance" and higher than anything man had ever seen is Dante's purgatory, the beginnings of the "way of salvation," of the world that can only be entered by the portal of faith. "We were filled with joy," Ulysses cries, "and all at once it turned to woe." From the "new" land, the supernatural land, the world of divine will, a "storm" came down. "Three times it turned the boat about with all the waters." It makes a good story in the myth, and in the onomatopoeia of the line, *tre volte il fè girar con tutte l' acque,* the ear can hear the churning of the inexorable water. But the operative word is "three." "Three, that is Father and Son and Holy Spirit," as Dante puts it in the *Vita Nuova.*[55] The ship went down — "as pleased Another." The "Other" was God. The wind and the waves were His will — the will that, like the bottom of the

[54] *Purg.*, ii, 18.   [55] *Vita Nuova*, xxix, 3.

ocean, is too deep for "eyes that can reach but a span." The last line of the story has the slowest beat of any line that Dante ever wrote. Every foot but the last is a spondee. It is like the slow, staccato, muffled tolling of a *de profundis* for the dead, *infin che 'l mar fu sopra noi richiuso*. Ulysses and his companions are not merely dead but "damned" — in the technical theological sense of "lost."

One can read the story as one would read a song of the sea by Masefield. Or one can hear the music and see the meaning that Tennyson put into his tale of Ulysses. Or one can read it as a moral counterpoint to Dante's tale of the angel that carries souls to the symbolical mountain of purgatory. Or one can read it, as Dante wanted his Poem to be read, as a myth with a meaning and a moral, set to a music that is inspired by a passionate vision of the mysteries of faith.

There is a pathos here which only those can feel who have experience of faith. It is the pathos that occurs so often in connection with Virgil: "The Emperor that reigns up there wills not that I should come into His city — because I was a rebel to His law — Oh, blest is he who is predestined. . . ."[56] They did no sin — nor did their merits matter, because they lacked the baptism which is the portal of the faith which you believe. They lived before Christ came. They adored God ill — and of these I, too, am one. For lacking grace, not for doing wrong, have we been lost and, painless as our punishment is, we live in hopeless longing. . . ."[57] Vain is the man who thinks that human reason can walk the infinitely distant way where a trinity of persons treads in unity of substance. Enough, O man to know the *what* without the *why* or *how*. Could man as man know more, there had been no need for Mary to bear her Child; nor would the ones you saw in hopeless longing — I speak of Aristotle and Plato and many more — have had their thirst unslaked. But, alas! their hopelessness is everlasting. Here Virgil hung his head and, deeply moved, he said no more."[58]

It is the same pathos that appears when the symbolic eagle sings to Dante in the heaven of the righteous rulers: " 'You say a man is born in India, and there is none to speak to him nor read to him nor write to him of Christ. All his thoughts and deeds are good and, as far as reason sees, his life and words are sinless. He dies unbaptized and lacking faith. Where is the justice that condemns him? Where

[56] *Inf.*, i, 124–129.　　　[57] *Inf.*, iv, 34–42.　　　[58] *Purg.*, iii, 33–45.

is his fault if he has not faith?' . . . O animals of earth, O minds too gross, the primal will is of its nature good — supremely good — and from itself cannot depart. What else is justice if not conformity to it?"[59]

Of course, not all of Dante's poetry is allegorical. For example, in the tale of Count Ugolino, the "anagogic" element is negligible. Dante brought to the tale a vehement medieval hatred of all kinds of treachery and, in a very general way, he has a moral purpose; but his feeling is only remotely related to religious emotion. He took the bones of a drab tale of brutal murder, in which a father and his sons were left in a tower to starve to death. Into those bones the poet breathes the very soul of tragedy. There is a virtuosity in the telling of the tale that has made this the best known episode in all the Poem. The problem Dante set himself to solve was this: What does the tenderest of all fathers do when, having watched, with irrepressible emotion, his children die about him, he is faced with irresistible pangs of hunger? No clear answer is given beyond the exasperating line: "More than the power of grief was the pang of hunger." It may mean that Conte Ugolino died, not of a broken heart, but of hunger. It may also hint that, in spite of his affection, hunger made a cannibal out of Ugolino. It is the play of the two motifs of hunger and affection that makes the tale inexpressibly tragic.

Quite apart from Dante's religious faith and human feeling, which can be relished even in translation, there is a technical perfection in his verse which can be appreciated only in the original. Take so simple a matter as speed of movement. When Dante wants to say: "We moved along with paces slow and far between," he writes the heavy-footed line, *Noi andavam con passi lenti e scarsi.*[60] When he wants to say: "Let us quicken our pace in accord with the kind invitation," he writes the anapestic line, *Ora accordiamo a tanto invito il piede.*[61] For a combination of passionate feeling with sheer virtuosity take these lines:

> *L'oltracotata schiatta che s'indraca*
> *dietro a chi fugge, e a chi mostra 'l dente*
> *o ver la borsa, com' agnel si placa,*
> *già venia su, ma di picciola gente.*[62]

[59] *Par.*, xix, 58–88.
[60] *Purg.*, xx, 16.
[61] *Purg.*, xvii, 61.
[62] *Par.*, xvi, 115–118.

"The outrageous gang pursues you like a dragon — if you run away; but if you show your teeth — or else your purse — they lie down like a lamb. Well, they were already riding high — the guttersnipes!" The opening polysyllabic words and the run-on line convey a perfect picture of the dragonlike pursuit. Then the abrupt monosyllable and the staccato: *e–a–chi–mostra 'l–dente,* makes you fairly see the teeth sticking out from the page. After that comes the insinuating *o ver la borsa;* and then the silken-soft *com' agnel si placa.* There is a rising inflection in *già venia su* which makes you see the social climbing of the family. This is followed by the contemptuous *picciola gente* — which puts them back in the gutter.

By way of contrast read the lines:

> *Quale allodetta che 'n aere si spazia*
> *prima cantanto, e poi tace contenta*
> *de l' ultima dolcezza che la sazia.*[63]

"Like the skylark climbing and spreading its wings in the air, singing at first, then suddenly ceasing — content with the last sweetness that fills its throat." The succession of *l*'s in *quale allodetta* lifts the bird out of sight as its sings. There is a struggle between song and silence in the *tace contenta;* the *ultima dolcezza* fills the very reader's throat; and the triumphant finale, *che la sazia,* leaves you with the conviction that the whole poetry of skylarks has been compressed, once and for all, into those marvelous lines.

Thus it is that Dante's art reaches from technique and rhetoric through feeling, fancy, passion, purpose, insight, and vision to religious inspiration, prayer, and ecstasy. The "power of the high vision failed" only when song was silenced in sanctity, when Dante's soul (like the skylark's throat) was filled with an "ultimate sweetness" — that of union with the "Love that moves the sun and all the stars."[64]

[63] *Par.,* xx, 73–75.
[64] *Par.,* xxxiii, 145.

VII

Love of Wisdom

"Philosophy is living speculation with truth for its body and love for its soul."[1]

I

PHILOSOPHY OF ART

WHATEVER elements went to the making of Dante's poetry — passion, imagination, music, vision, inspiration, faith, and prayer — he thought of art, primarily, as a work of reason. Even as a boy, trembling under the impact of a love that lifted his heart to "the limits of blessedness," he set about the craft of song-making in the spirit of a philosopher. "I *decided* to *make* a sonnet," he says, "since I had *studied* the art of putting words in rime."[2] Art, for Dante, was intelligence pursuing a human purpose by means of rules established by reason. St. Thomas Aquinas had written something very like that in his commentary on the *Posterior Analytics* of Aristotle: "Art is an order achieved by reason in which human action reaches a definite end by determined means."

Dante nowhere speaks expressly of his philosophy of art. Yet, as we saw in relation to his sonnet, *Love and the gentle heart are one same thing*, he thought of art as a kind of Scholasticism of the heart. He thought of the poet's taste — the *cor gentile* — being awakened to delight in ideal beauty, much as he thought of a philosopher's intelligence being awakened to rational knowledge by truth. In both cases the mind passes from "potency" to "act." In both cases an intellectual habit is involved. In both cases what is perceived is not

[1] *Conv.*, III, xiv, 1.
[2] *Vita Nuova*, iii, 9.

merely a concrete thing, but the form, the soul, the life, the spirit of a thing. Before art becomes a making of beauty, it is a perception of beauty. In this perception an artist becomes one with the beauty he perceives, just as a philosopher becomes one with the truth he perceives. M. Maritain, speaking of the medieval view of art, says that "through the presence in the artists of the virtue of art, they *are*, in a way, their work before they create it; to be able to form it, they have to conform to it."[3] St. Thomas says much the same thing of the philosophers and truth. Dante says in one of his songs that no one can paint a face until he has become that face, *poi chi pinge figura, se non può esse lei, non la può porre.*[4]

Art, for Dante as for St. Thomas, was the work or craft of impressing ideas on matter; this activity supposed, in the artist, an intellectual habit, a permanent quality of the operative intellect. As inevitably as a philosopher tends to perceive truth, a statesman justice, and a saint holiness, so the artist perceives beauty. In a way the artist is between the philosopher and the saint. Like the philosopher his habit is intellectual; like the saint, what he sees is rather the good than the true. Again, like the saint (and unlike the philosopher), he perceives for the sake of doing something — not merely for the sake of contemplation. An artist is more like a moral philosopher than like a metaphysician, because art is more like prudence than like speculation. As prudence inclines us to *do* what is right, so art inclines us to *make* what is beautiful.

When Dante speaks of the artist who has "the habit of art and a hand that trembles," *C' ha l'abito dell' arte e man che trema,*[5] he makes it clear that art is less in the hand than in the head, less in execution than in intuition. On the other hand, when he says that art is the "grandchild of God" he relates the intuition in the mind to reality in nature. "Philosophy to any one who has ears to hear declares, and not on one page only, that nature takes her course from the divine intellect and from God's art; and if you study your *Physics* [of Aristotle] carefully, you will find near the beginning that human art follows the divine art as a pupil follows the master; so that your art is, as it were, God's grandchild."[6]

This does not mean that a work of art is a photograph of a scene in nature. It means that the artist tries to see the ideas, the forms, that

[3] *Art and Scholasticism*, p. 12.
[4] *Conv.*, IV, *Le dolce rime*, 53, 54.
[5] *Par.*, xiii, 78.
[6] *Inf.*, xi, 97.

are realized in the works of nature. It also means that, as nature realizes God's ideas, so does art realize the artist's ideas. The student does not paint the master; or *what* the master paints; he paints *as* the master paints.

This leaves room for artistic creation — but not for willfullness. An artist, like God, creates what he sees. But whereas God sees beauty in Himself, the artist can see beauty only in or through what God has created. The artist, of course, can select and can synthesize. But it is as true of the artist as of the philosopher that, ultimately, there is nothing in the intellect that was not first in the senses.

II

PHILOSOPHY OF HAPPINESS

The real danger, in relating Dante's art to his philosophy, is to imagine that he was as great a philosopher as he was an artist. Nothing could be further from the truth. It is enough to compare the artistic perfection of the poems in the *Vita Nuova* with the philosophical comments in the accompanying prose to realize that Dante's philosophy was, in the beginning at least, somewhat superficial. He picked up the philosophical tags of his day much as literary persons today pick up tags of science. He speaks of matter and form, of act and potency, much as many of us speak of relativity or of splitting the atom. For example, when Dante quotes the tag, *nomina sunt consequentia rerum,* "names follow the named things,"[7] or when he speaks of "local motion according to the Philosopher,"[8] or of "the second book of the *Metaphysics*,"[9] we need suppose no more information than could be acquired in occasional reading or in casual conversation with friends who had studied in Paris or Bologna. The references to the "heaven of the moon" and the "heaven of the stars,"[10] imply no special knowledge of the works either of Aristotle or Albertus Magnus. Such phrases as the "faithful counsel of reason" and the "limit of beatitude,"[11] could have been picked up from any of the preachers of Florence. So, too, the distinctions between substance and accident in chapter xxv of the

[7] *Vita Nuova,* xiii.
[8] *Vita Nuova,* xxv.
[9] *Vita Nuova,* xii.
[10] *Vita Nuova,* ii, 1.
[11] *Ibid.,* 9; viii, 1.

Vita Nuova and between appetite and reason in chapter xxxviii imply no special familiarity with the writings of St. Thomas.

It was different when Dante came to write the *Convivio* more then twenty years later. In that work he tells us of his first serious philosophical study of Cicero and Boethius. He found it hard, he says, to make out the meaning at first, but by dint of native talent and a little Latin he made some progress. As he says, he widened his vocabulary; he began to realize the importance of philosophy; he was moved to make a more systematic study. The result was that at the end of three years he found himself head over heels in love with wisdom. He found that "philosophy has for its soul an all but divine love of understanding."[12] This new kind of love inspired the canzone, *Voi che 'ntendendo il terzo ciel movete.* His heart became a battleground. On the one side were memory, imagination, and emotion feeding on the beauty of his dead Beatrice now in heavenly glory. On the other was his intelligence captivated by a new-found truth that seemed jealous of any rival. His memories were in danger of being dispersed by a new mistress of his mind. "The glorious Beatrice," he says, "still held the rock of my mind."[13] Nevertheless, a new queen appeared "before the eyes of his intellectual affection."[14] In her eyes was paradise, but a paradise that must be purchased at the price of "anguish and sighs."

In the *Vita Nuova* the new queen had been described as a compassionate lady looking at Dante from a window. All that, he says, in the *Convivio,* was allegory. The lady in reality was "the daughter of God, the queen of all, the most noble and beautiful love of wisdom."[15] Just as love of beauty had been for Dante a new life, a *vita nuova,* so, too, was love of truth. It was more than a new life, a second perfection. It was his ultimate natural perfection as a rational creature. Truth was the good, the end, the perfection, the final "act" of the intellect. Truth, he found, was more than any lovely lady. Truth is full of sweetness, adorned with virtue, wonderful in wisdom, glorious in liberty.[16] The demonstrations of philosophy shine brighter than any lady's eyes; wisdom's power to draw the will to what is good is more persuasive than any lovely lips.

Dante was more in love with the "lips" than with the "eyes" of

[12] *Conv.,* III, xi, 13.
[13] *Conv.,* II, ii, 4.
[14] *Ibid.,* vii, 11.
[15] *Conv.,* II, xii, 9.
[16] *Ibid.,* xv, 3.

this new lady — more drawn, that is, by the persuasions than by the demonstrations of philosophy. He was more interested in ethical direction than in metaphysical insight. He thought of philosophy as a deliverer from the death of vice even more than from the death of ignorance.[17] That is why, in arranging his hierarchy of knowledge, he puts moral philosophy above metaphysics. Metaphysics he compares to the heaven of the stars and especially to the Milky Way, to the unseen pole and to the all but imperceptible movement of the stars from west to east. These suggested to Dante the idea of realities known rather by their effects than by their appearances — as metaphysical realities are known. But beyond the stars is the crystalline heaven, the *primum mobile*. To this highest heaven (this side of the empyrean) Dante compares ethics or moral philosophy. As the order of the heavens depends on the movement of the *primum mobile*, so does the order of the sciences depend on ethics. Without the movement of the *primum mobile* there would be neither night nor day, nor weeks, nor months nor years, but only a universal disorder — movement without meaning. So, too, without moral philosophy there would be a night of knowledge, there would be no life of happiness, there would be no value in the wisdom and writings of the past.

Another reason for the superiority of ethics to metaphysics appealed to Dante as an artist. The beauty of philosophy, it seemed to him, was in morality. Beauty in a physical body results from the harmony or order of the parts. So it is with wisdom which is the "body" of philosophy. The beauty of wisdom lies in the order of the moral virtues. It is in the beauty of moral truth that the striving for what is right is born. Thus vices and even natural instincts are overcome. The result is happiness which, as Aristotle defines it, is activity in accordance with virtue in perfect life.

With this conception of the happiness of human life we reach the center of gravity of all Dante's philosophical thinking. He knew that for most men, in the concrete conditions of ordinary life, human happiness must be found rather in moral action than in mental contemplation, in virtue rather than in knowledge, in loving more than in learning. It seemed to him more immediately important to reduce men's passions to peace than to dissipate doubts by the light of abstract truth. He knew, of course, that it took a

[17] *Ibid.*, 4.

great deal of speculation to reach the truth, that Aristotelian happiness (rather than Epicurean pleasure or Stoic calm) was the end or purpose of human living. But it was the product of Aristotle's speculation rather than the process that seemed to Dante of special value.

This is merely to say that what interested Dante was not so much thought as life, not so much mental maneuvering as man — man as individual person and man in society, man as a rational and social animal.

It is here that Dante comes closest to the central interest of our day. Nothing on earth seems so important to our generation as the safeguarding of the dignity of human persons by the right ordering of world society. Freedom in a world at peace; personal liberty under international law; an international Bill of Human Rights — whatever slogan we use, all seem agreed that world order under law is the only guarantee of individual happiness. This was Dante's central preoccupation. The supreme temporal value for any man is to be happy and, after that, to have happiness guaranteed by freedom from outside interference. To be happy was, for Dante, mainly a matter of ethics; to have that happiness guaranteed was a matter of world politics.

III

"VIRGIL"

Dante's interest in both personal virtue and public law is symbolized in the *Divine Comedy* by Virgil. Virgil is a synthesis of Athens and Rome, of Aristotle and Augustus, of moral perfection and political peace, of conscience and law. Virgil's main role is to lead humanity to the peace of ethical insight and moral purification, but he would not have been chosen as guide had he not established his right to speak for the need of world rule as a condition of peace and happiness.

Dante strikes the keynote both of his Poem and of his philosophy when he pictures himself in the dark wood of ignorance and vice assailed by human passions — the leopard, the lion, and the she-wolf. He is rescued by Virgil — by human reason. Virgil stands for reason in all its forms — as speculative and practical intelligence, and as

practical intelligence in its forms of prudence and art. Virgil represents human intelligence as thinking, doing, acting, making. He
represents the insights of metaphysics, ethics, politics, and art. He
is the guide to such peace as can be reached by truth, righteousness,
justice, and beauty.

What troubled Dante most was "the beast without peace."[18] His
rescuer represented himself as one who had lived at Rome under
the good Augustus, and as the poet who had sung of Aeneas, the
righteous son of Anchises. He is a representative, that is, of law,
art, and prudence. Dante, in the Poem, seizes upon Virgil's character
as a poet, as one who had been a "deep well to a wide river of song,
the honor and light of other poets." But Dante calls the poet a
"famous philosopher,"[19] and invokes his help against the beast of
passion. Virgil, poet and philosopher, in his reply makes clear that
he is no less interested in politics, in the rule of justice in society
at large, in the kind of peace that only law based on wisdom, helped
by love and backed by power, can guarantee. He speaks of the
greyhound, the *Veltro*, the deliverer who is to come, who will spurn
the low appeal of property and pelf and will be nourished by
"wisdom, love, and power" and whose realm will be the whole
world.[20] The immediate task for Dante was to see why he should
avoid evil and do good. For this reason he must be led through hell.
He must hear the hopeless wailing of the damned. He must climb
the hill of purgatory. He must see the penitents who are glad to
bear the pains of purification. After that, says Virgil, there will
come a soul worthier than he is to lead Dante to still loftier heights
of blessedness.

It is not difficult to see in this symbolism Dante's conception of
the role of philosophy in human life. That role is primarily practical. Philosophy is a means to inner peace, to the happiness that is
possible to a man whose mind has been illumined by truth and
whose will — freed from the tyranny of passion — has been made
straight and strong by the proper kind of love. When Virgil's task
is over, after his prudence and art, speculative and practical reason,
his *ingegno* and *arte* have led Dante through both "the eternal
and the temporal fire" to a point beyond which reason can "see no
further," Dante's power of moral choice is declared to be "free,
straight, and strong." From that point on Dante's heart might serve

[18] *Inf.*, i, 58.   [19] *Ibid.*, 88.   [20] *Ibid.*, 103–105.

for guide. The heart is not only in complete conformity with the head, with the "faithful counsel of reason," but even with the external norms of moral tradition and political rule. Dante is now ready to be both king and counselor to himself, to wear both a crown and a professor's cap — symbols of imperial and philosophical authority.

Virgil acts at the bidding of Beatrice, as Beatrice acts at the bidding of the "gentle lady of compassion," the mother of Jesus. Dante had no illusion that philosophical beatitude could ever be a substitute for eternal peace. On the other hand, he was equally clear that eternal peace begins only when men are dead. While life lasts we have human purposes to achieve — to learn truth, love justice, do right, make beauty. While waiting for God's grace to make them saints, men must try to be philosophers, moralists, statesmen, artists.

That Virgil could have no positive part in making Dante a saint is clear from the picture of limbo in canto IV of the *Inferno*. Limbo is Virgil's home; the home, too, of Homer and the great poets of antiquity, of Aristotle and the great philosophers; of Hector, Aeneas, Caesar, and other heroes. When all the labor of human thinking, artistic creation, moral and political effort is over, this is the highest happiness that man, as man, can hope for. This is as much as he can deserve, although it is not all he can desire — life without suffering but not without sighing.[21] These noble thinkers, artists, heroes "did nothing wrong," but their merits won them neither grace on earth nor glory in the world to come. So it is that "without hope they live in desire." A great pain went through Dante's heart when he realized how relatively little is the happiness that science, art, philosophy and law can give us. There is, indeed, in Dante's limbo a "noble castle" set in a green field and surrounded by a lovely river. Here in a place "open, luminous, and lofty" the very great spirits dwell. Above all the rest, is Aristotle, "the master of those who know."[22] But that place is not paradise.

It seems to have been part of "Virgil's" reward that he came to know more than the philosophy of Aristotle could ever have taught him. Perhaps we have to remember that, until the Resurrection, limbo was the home of Adam and Eve, of Abel and Noe, of Moses the lawgiver, of Abraham the patriarch, of David the king, of Israel

[21] *Inf.*, iv, 26.   [22] *Ibid.*, 131.

and Rachel, and of all the others who were destined to be saved.[23]
Virgil speaks familiarly of theological truths, of the last day, the
angel's trumpet, the resurrection of the body.[24] Like a good Scholastic philosopher, he even makes the same logical deductions that
St. Thomas does in the *Summa Theologica*[25] concerning the effects
of the resurrection of the body.

Virgil is half philosopher, half theologian, in his insistence on
the idea of divine providence. When Minos tries to bar Dante's
entry into hell, the monster is bidden by Virgil not to impede the
providential journey. It is willed, says Virgil, "in a place where what
is willed can be fulfilled."[26] So, too, to Pluto, Virgil says that the
journey is backed by reason, that it is willed on high where Michael
wrought revenge on "the proud adulterer."[27] In the same way,
fortune, like fate, is turned into an aspect of omniscient and
transcendent providence.[28] Virgil seemed to Dante a very "ocean
of all wisdom."[29] Yet Dante is reminded often enough by Virgil
himself that his wisdom and his will are in need, for certain
purposes, of a light and force beyond the powers of nature. In the
critical point where he must pass from the upper hell to the city
of Dis, Virgil's brave words, "it is up to us to win this battle," taper
off into an "If not . . . well, help has been offered us. . . . Oh! how
slow it seems to me in coming."[30] Sure enough, like a gust of
irresistible wind, an angel of God came to the rescue, and by a word
he tamed the violence of the furies. Up to that point, Dante had
been careful to contrast the "power" of Beatrice[31] with the mere
"words," however wise or lovely, of Virgil.[32] But once the angel has
come to the rescue of Virgil, Dante addresses his guide: "O high
power."[33] Virgil, however, knew his own limitations. He knew that
Dante could learn much more only when he should be before the
"sweet ray of her whose lovely eye sees all things."[34]

Virgil reveals himself fully in his role of moral philosopher when
he outlines for Dante the ethical topography of hell. The division
of sin which he indicates is, of course, Dante's own invention. It is
as good an indication as any that, although Dante most commonly
relied on St. Thomas Aquinas for systematic philosophy, he was

[23] *Inf.*, iv, 55–61.
[24] *Inf.*, vi, 95–99.
[25] *Summa Theologica*, I, II, q. iv, a. 6.
[26] *Inf.*, v, 22–25.
[27] *Inf.*, vii, 10–12.
[28] *Ibid.*, 73.

[29] *Inf.*, viii, 7.
[30] *Inf.*, ix, 7–9.
[31] *Inf.*, ii, 76.
[32] *Ibid.*, 67, 112, 126, 138.
[33] *Inf.*, x, 4.
[34] *Ibid.*, 130.

not opposed to a good deal of eclecticism. Dante was inclined to think that the value of ideas, like the value of institutions, could be tested by their historical persistence and geographical universality. The division of sins in canto XI of the *Inferno* makes uses of ideas taken from Aristotle and Cicero, from the Christian theologians and the canon lawyers, and from the code of medieval chivalry.

The three main divisions of hell were suggested by Aristotle's distinctions between incontinence (*akrasia*), bestiality (*theriotes*), and malice (*kakia*). The lustful like Paolo and Francesca, gluttons like Ciacco, misers and the spendthrifts, irascible spirits like Filippo Argenti, and the deliberately slothful are reckoned as incontinent. Between these and the souls guilty of malice, Dante places the heresiarchs. If we take literally what he says in the *Convivio* of the "bestiality," the utter irrationality, of those who reject divine revelation, and of the "foolish and vile beasts . . . that presume to speak against our faith,"[35] we may perhaps reckon the heretics like Frederick II and the Cardinal Aldobrandini as guilty of "bestiality." The lower part of hell is filled with the malicious.

Dante goes to Cicero[36] for a further distinction. The end of malice is injury to others; this injury is done either by violence or fraud; because fraud is more specifically human than violence it is a more grievous evil. Virgil, in the Poem, gives a Christian twist to the thought by saying that it "is more displeasing to God."

Of the violent there is a threefold division taken from the medieval theologians: the violent against one's neighbor; against oneself; against God. Each of these forms of violence is subdivided by the dichotomy found in all manuals of law, namely, "persons" and "property." Thus tyranny does violence to people's property, but murder to their persons; suicide is a violence against one's person, squandering is a violence against one's property; blasphemy is a violence against the person of God, sins against nature and art are sins against God's property.

Of the fraudulent there is a twofold division. There is fraud that is forbidden by law; there is likewise fraud that is forbidden by that higher allegiance we call loyalty[37] — the sin of treason in all its forms. There is a final distinction which Dante does not name between fraud that affects a few and fraud that affects the

---

[35] *Conv.*, IV, v, 9.   [36] *De officiis*, I, xiii.   [37] *Inf.*, xi, 53.

whole world. This last treason was that of the murderers of Caesar and of the apostle who betrayed Christ. In these cases the intended injury affected the universal institutions, in one instance, of State and, in the other, of the Church. Disloyalty to these supreme guarantors to man's happiness here and hereafter seemed to Dante the very depth of moral turpitude.

Virgil deals at some length with the sin of usury. The root idea is from Aristotle:[38] art follows nature as far as it can. To this is added the notion that nature itself is a product of the divine mind and, therefore, may be regarded as God's art. Nature is a revelation of God's delight in order and purpose. Hence the deduction that human art, delighting in the order it makes out of the purposes it conceives, is a grandchild of God. The point of this bold simile is that art not merely does, but ought to, follow nature — as a pupil ought to follow his teacher. But Dante's Virgil must have known that there is nothing in the physical premises to warrant the ethical conclusion. Revelation is called in to eke out the inconclusiveness of reason. Genesis 2:15 commanded that man should "work" in the garden of Eden: agriculture became a moral duty. In the same way Genesis 2:19 commanded that man should eat bread in the "sweat of his brow." Man was commanded to collaborate, to work with nature, that is to join his art to God's art, nature. The sin of the usurer is to despise both art and nature. He wants an increase of wealth without human labor — that is, in contempt of art. He wants a "barren breed of metal" to bear a progeny of profit — in contempt of nature. Perhaps, what Dante had in mind was that man is meant to live by agriculture and industry, the former depending mainly on nature and the latter on art. He delighted in complicated reasonings of this sort. That he was willing to put the argument into the mouth of Virgil is further evidence that Virgil as a symbol of philosophy is, at many points, without any relation to the historical poet.

Another case in point is the philosophy of history that is expounded by Virgil in his account of the Old Man of Crete who holds his shoulders turned toward Damietta and looks to Rome as to a mirror. The picture of a statue with head of gold, chest of silver, stomach of bronze, legs of iron, and right foot of terra cotta is modeled in part on the Book of Daniel. The conception of fissures

[38] *Physics*, I, 2.

shedding tears and blood that form the rivers of Dante's hell —
Acheron, Styx, and Phlegethon — and finally the frozen lake Cocytus
was added by Dante. The point is that when time is over, Satan will
be frozen under the ice made of the tears and blood which his
malice caused to flow. He will have nothing left but his hatred. He
will be a prisoner in a darkness and coldness of his own creation.
He will thus be an eternal caricature of the light and love and life
of God, an inversion of God's power and wisdom and love, a
monster of ignorance, impotence, and hate.

Four things are here implied. First, that the course of history,
for all its signs of progress, is a record of repeated degenerations;
second, that the cause of this is human sinfulness; third, that sin is
traceable ultimately to the malice and envy of the devil; fourth,
that behind all history is divine providence and the ultimate
triumph of divine justice. This is not the whole of Dante's philosophy of history; since over against the "fall" he insisted on man's
power of progress, and over against divine providence he placed
man's freedom.

Notice, in all of this, Dante's reiteration, in Virgil's words, of
the final insufficiency of philosophy as a complete guide to human
life. Virgil needed the angel's aid to get past the furies into the
city of Dis; he needed the back of Geryon to carry him from the
last circle of the violent to the "pockets" of the malicious; the
giant Antaeus helped him reach the "depth that devours Lucifer
and Judas."[39]

The limitations of Virgil become more apparent in the *Purgatory*.
When Cato at the foot of the hill asked Virgil and Dante what
light had served them to issue from the deep night that keeps the
infernal valley dark, Virgil answered: "I came not of myself, a lady
came down out of heaven and through her prayers I helped this
man with my companionship."[40] He added: "From on high descends
a power that helps me to lead him to see you and to listen to you."
When the newcomers to purgatory asked: "If you know the way,
show us how to travel about the mount," Virgil answers: "You
think, I suppose, that we are familiar with this place; we are
pilgrims just like you."[41] Not even with philosophy can we always
discern the clear dictate of conscience. Still less can we find the
force to obey the dictate when we know it.

[39] *Inf.*, xxxi, 142.   [40] *Purg.*, i, 43–54.   [41] *Purg.*, ii, 60–63.

Philosophy is impotent in matters of divine revelation. "It is vain," says Virgil himself, "to hope that our reason can reach to the end of the road that brings us to three persons in one substance. Be content, O human beings, with the knowledge of the fact. If you could have known more there had been no need for Mary to bear her child. You have seen the vain longings of the great philosophers. Their curiosity is given them as an eternal sorrow. It is never to be assuaged. I mean Aristotle and Plato and many others." And when Virgil said this he bowed his head, and said no more, and remained disturbed.[42] Dante senses Virgil's hesitations when the first sufferers at the foot of the hill of purgatory appear. "Look, there is one that might give us advice, if you yourself should be in need of it."[43] And, in fact, Virgil asks them the way.[44] As Virgil gets higher up the hill he still stands for philosophy, but he reminds one rather of St. Thomas than Aristotle. Like a medieval Christian philosopher he is aware not only of natural love but of supernatural charity.

Because your desires are focused on things that suffer by being shared envy moves the bellows to your sighs. But if only the love of the empyrean could turn your love upward that fear would vanish from your heart; for the more there are in heaven who say "ours," so much more of good does each one possess and the more does the flame of love burn in that cloister. . . . Because you fix your mind on things of earth you pluck darkness from the very light. The infinite and ineffable good that is on high goes out toward proffered love as a sunbeam meets a mirror. God gives himself in proportion to the love he finds, so that however far our charity extends eternal power exceeds it. And the more people there are up there who love each other the more there is for all to love and the more there is of mutual love, each like a mirror reflecting the other. And if my reason does not take away your hunger you will see Beatrice and she will take away completely this and every other longing.[45]

Within his normal limits, however, Virgil stands for illumination of mind and force of will in the light and warmth of reason. "Why is your spirit so worried that you slacken your pace," said the master. "What does it matter to you what people say of you. Follow me and let the people talk. Stand up like a strong tower whose steeple no wind can topple down. Remember that the man who lets his thoughts sprout one upon another gets further from the mark because each intention is weaker than the last."[46]

[42] *Purg.*, ii, 34–45.   [44] *Ibid.*, 75.   [46] *Purg.*, v, 13–18.
[43] *Ibid.*, 61–63.   [45] *Purg.*, xv, 49–78.

More and more, as the problems facing Dante's mind become too difficult for unaided reason to answer, Virgil has to be content rather with exhortation than with explanation. When, for example, Dante raises the difficulty of reconciling the unchanging decrees of providence and the efficacy of human prayer, Virgil bids him not to let his mind dwell on such deep doubts until he can get the answers from her who is a "light between his mind and the truth. I am not sure that you understand. I speak of Beatrice; you will see her above, happy and smiling, on the summit of the mount." And Dante lifted up by this hope said: "My Lord, let us move at a greater pace; already I feel less fatigue than before."[47]

Virgil is shown to be increasingly conscious of how much nature stands in need of grace, reason of faith.

I am Virgil; and for no other fault but to have lacked the faith did I lose heaven. . . . By all the circles of the dolorous realm have I come here; the power of heaven moved me and with its aid I come. Not for doing wrong but for not doing have I lost the right to see the high sun that you long to see and which I came to know too late. There is a place below made sad not by any pain but by darkness merely, where there is grief but no murmur of complaint beyond a sigh. . . . There is my home with those who were not clothed in the three holy virtues, but who knew every one of the other virtues and practised them and avoided sin.[48]

There is no hint in all this that Dante doubted that philosophy was an autonomous intellectual discipline or that it could provide real motives for the will. What it does imply is that, in the concrete conduct of life, it is folly to separate philosophy from faith, nature from the aid that grace alone can give. A philosopher is not less a philosopher because he knows that reason has its limitations; a moralist is not less a moralist because he experiences the need of grace. So it is that in the Poem Lucia comes by night and takes Dante in her arms and carries him up a difficult part of the mount and shows to Virgil the gate of purgatory.[49] The gateway was, in fact, one that philosophy by itself could never enter. Its three steps were the steps of confession, contrition, and satisfaction. The porter was an angel with a sword unsheathed and with the two keys of sacerdotal wisdom and power. With "good will"[50] Virgil led Dante up these steps, because nothing could be more rational than to make use of supernatural means when these are made available.

[47] *Purg.*, vi, 43–50.   [49] *Purg.*, ix, 55 ff.
[48] *Purg.*, vii, 7–36.   [50] *Ibid.*, 106.

As with truth so with beauty. Art can no more "redeem" men than philosophy can. Nevertheless, art plays its part in the drama of "Dante's" purification. "Here it is needful to use a little art," says Virgil.[51] He meant by "art," merely human skill and ingenuity. But Virgil also draws attention to the need of art in a more technical sense: "Cast your eyes down," he says to Dante, "it will do you good and make the way more easy if you see the bed on which your feet are resting."[52] What Dante saw was inlaid work of rare artistic perfection — the lines and shadows "would have made the subtlest artist marvel."[53] The carved figures seemed as alive as living men. On a higher level Dante would be helped not by sculpture but by song, by the "spirits who were heard but not seen, singing courteous invitations to the table of love."[54] All this is but to say that beauty (like justice, truth, and grace) has its role to play in human life.

IV

HUMAN DIGNITY

Virgil reveals himself most fully in his role of philosophic guidance in the central cantos of the whole Poem, cantos XVI to XVIII of the *Purgatory*. Dante has reached the terrace of the sinners who "go untying the knot of anger."[55] He found himself in a fog of smoke-like thickness so that, like a blind man, he had to keep close on the heels of Virgil, his "wise and trusty guide." They meet Marco Lombardo, a man of whom little is known but who serves here as a symbol of chivalrous loyalty and public law. He describes himself as a man who knew the world and loved the kind of valor that he felt was disappearing. He asks for prayers. Dante, in accordance with the code of chivalry, replies: "By my faith I bind myself in loyalty to do what you demand of me."[56] Dante agrees that the world is "empty of virtue" and full of wickedness, but he asks Marco to point out the reason, so that he may show it to the rest of men. He wants to know if responsibility is in men's wills or in the stars. Not in our stars, says Marco. Men are not determined. If that were so, free choice would be destroyed and there would be no justice in rewarding good

---

[51] *Purg.*, x, 12.
[52] *Purg.*, xii, 13.
[53] *Ibid.*, 66.
[54] *Purg.*, xiii, 26–27.
[55] *Purg.*, xvi, 24.
[56] *Purg.*, xvi, 52–53.

with bliss and sin with woe. The first movement of our wills is determined, but there is in every man an inner light to distinguish
good from evil. The will, in a word, is free; if the will but battle
with its first impulses freedom will be nourished. We are bound, of
course, to God, to a greater and better force than nature. Yet, even
in this subjection, we are free. Our dependence on God gives us a
mind no stars can control. And, therefore, if the world goes wrong,
the responsibility is man's.[57]

When the simple soul, he says, comes from the hand of its joyous
Maker, it naturally turns to whatever promises joy. It tastes the savor
of the first slight good it meets and, without a thought, pursues it.
It is here that deception may begin, unless love is guided and controlled. Man needs law as a bridle; man needs a guide whose business it is to discern at least the high towers of the true city.

> *Onde convenne legge per fren porre,*
> *convenne rege aver, che discernesse*
> *de la vera città almen la torre.*[58]

The trouble, continues Marco, is not the lack of law, but the
overflow of spiritual authority in the temporal sphere. The Church
has taken over the functions of the State. As a result its pastors give
a bad example: their main pursuit is self interest. Bad leadership,
la mala condotta, is the real trouble. In the old days Rome had two
suns, one to show the way on earth, the other to show the way to
God.

> *Soleva Roma, che 'l buon mondo feo*
> *due soli aver, che l'una e l' altra strada*
> *facean vedere, e del mondo e di Deo.*[59]

The sword has been joined to the crozier. Mutual respect has been
lost. The results are obvious. The secular virtues of valor and
chivalry are gone. The Church, under the double load of political
power and ecclesiastical authority has sunk in the mire.

With these thoughts in mind, Dante passes to the terrace of the
slothful. It is here that Virgil pronounces his longest philosophical
discourse. He takes up where Marco left off, but instead of dealing
with personal liberty and public law, Virgil faces the profounder
problem of reconciling liberty and love. Neither the Creator nor
any creature was ever without love. In the creature this love is twofold, instinctive and rational. Instinctive love turns infallibly to

---

[57] *Ibid.,* 58–81.　　　[58] *Ibid.,* 94–96.　　　[59] *Ibid.,* 106–108.

what is good. Rational or reflective love can wander: it can choose a wrong objective; it can err by excess or by deficiency, by loving too little or too much. Love is the root of all morality. We cannot do wrong when our love turns toward God the creator, nor when we truly love our own good. But love can be perverted, when we love the evil that our neighbor suffers. We can love to see our neighbor lowered — in order that we may seem to excel. This is the sin of pride. We can love to see our neighbor lose power, favors, honor, fame; so we sin by envy. We can love to see him suffer pain; this is the root of anger and revenge. So it is that the lower slopes of purgatory are filled with the proud, the envious, the angry. Sloth is the sin of loving too little. Finally, there are the sins of excessive love — greed, gluttony, and lust.

When Virgil had finished his account of the moral topography of purgatory, Dante said that his sight was made so clear by this light that he could see all that Virgil's reason described or implied. But Dante wanted Virgil to pursue the matter of love "to which all good action and the contrary can be reduced."[60] The soul, says Virgil, is created for love and so turns instinctively to all that pleases it, as soon as by beauty it is awakened into act. Our apprehensive power draws a mental representation (*intenzione*) from some being that is true. To this image the soul turns. This inclination is called love. It is "a new life awakened in you by the presence of beauty."[61] As naturally as smoke goes up so does love turn to desire. A spiritual movement is started that tends to the joy of union with the loved object.

At this point responsibility enters. It is not easy to see how, since love is awakened inevitably, and turns into desire with equal inevitability. Virgil acknowledges the difficulty. As far as reason can see he will speak, leaving to Beatrice to examine the matter more deeply.

The soul, being a substantial form united with matter, has a specific power which can be easily discovered by the way it works, by its effects. The soul produces thoughts and desires. Just what provokes the first thoughts and the first desires we do not know. They are as instinctive as the instinct of the bee to make honey. And, of course, they deserve no praise or blame. Other desires are related to definite objects. In relation to these we have an innate "power of

[60] *Purg.*, xviii, 15.   [61] *Purg.*, xvii, 26.

counsel" that stands on the "threshold of assent." Our morality depends on the way we gather in good desires and keep the bad ones out. The philosophers who went deep enough to discover this innate power found the root of our liberty and so left morality in the world. We are moved to love by necessity but we have the power to control desire. This free choice is, for Beatrice, the noble virtue — because, of course, it is this that makes us persons, that gives us our human dignity.

This is the climax of Virgil's leadership. He has discovered in man's intelligence the root of his moral freedom and, therefore, the root of his personal dignity. He has put his hand on the value of human personality as the supreme value in the world of created things.

There are other lessons given to Dante in the *Purgatory*, but they are given by Statius. Virgil, in fact, asks Statius to be the "doctor to Dante's wounds."[62] Statius gives a long lecture on the "physics" of the soul as Virgil has given one on its metaphysics. The lesson is taken directly from St. Thomas. After this lesson of Statius, Dante is ready for Virgil's last words, making Dante a king and counselor over himself. Conscience has become his law. Philosophy has done for man the best that philosophy can do.

[62] *Purg.*, XXV, 29–30.

VIII

Divine Knowledge Full of Peace

... la divina scienza che piena è di tutta pace.[1]

I

REASON AND FAITH

AS A symbol of philosophy in the conduct of human life, Dante's "Virgil" confessed his merely partial competence. He was not entitled to reach the "empyrean." He could not reach the garden on the top of the hill of purgatory without a great deal of divine aid. He was struck by the contrast between the supernatural flight of the angel from the Tiber to purgatory and the purely human, slow, and "foolish" flight of Ulysses. Again and again Virgil leaves a discussion unfinished. He knows that only Beatrice can give the final solution. He knows that it is vain to hope that reason could ever discover the mystery of the Trinity.

On the general question of the relation of "Virgil" to "Beatrice," reason to faith, philosophy to religion, nature to grace, Dante took three definite stands. First, by distinguishing so clearly the personality and guidance of Virgil and Beatrice, he declared that philosophy and theology are distinct, autonomous disciplines, starting each from its own principles and reaching its own conclusions. Second, by the frequent confessions of Virgil's need of supernatural aid, Dante declared that philosophy, for its function of ethical guidance, needs the illumination of faith. Third, by making both Virgil and Beatrice serve as guides in a single continuous journey, Dante repudiated the idea that there could be any contradiction between the conclusions of reason and the revelations of divine wisdom.

[1] *Conv.*, II, xiv, 19.

So, too, in the practical question of the separation of State and Church, Dante argued for the autonomy of civil government, but added that this autonomy was not to exclude all dependence of secular power on spiritual authority. The fact remains that human happiness (which is the final purpose of the State) is related to immortal beatitude. Consequently Caesar will be well advised "to show that reverence for Peter which a son owes a father." Justice will shine clearer if it is illumined by the light of grace. There need be no conflict in this co-operation since all authority in both State and Church depends on God, the Author and end of "all things temporal and eternal."[2]

Dante felt, in regard to the practical relation of nature and grace, that the more nature disposes itself toward its own perfection the more bountiful will God be in the bestowal of further blessings. In the *Convivio,* he writes: "When . . . God sees a creature disposed to receive His gift, He bestows on it as much as it is disposed to receive."[3] "O wonderful and benign Sower," he exclaims, "who waits but for human nature to prepare the soil for Thy sowing, and happy those who cultivate the seeds which have been sown."

Human life is ultimately one, though it runs in three channels, animal, intellectual, and divine. Happiness, too, must be sought on three levels: first, in human activity, in the operations of the moral virtues; second, in contemplation, by means of the intellectual virtues; third, in "the supreme beatitude, which cannot be enjoyed on earth."[4] Life must "grow in all its potentialities, vegetative, sensitive, and rational; it must branch out into the powers of them all, seeking the perfections of them all, and persevering up to the point when, with that part of our soul which can never die, life returns to the highest and most glorious sower of all life who is in heaven."[5]

In the pursuit of threefold perfection and happiness life must be lived in four phases — in boyhood, manhood, maturity, and old age. In adolescence, perfection and happiness must be sought in obedience, urbanity and modesty, eagerness to learn, self-control, sorrow for sin. In the second period of human life, in the vigorous manhood that reaches its perfection at thirty-five, the virtues called for are temperance and fortitude along with the chivalrous qualities of the lover, the gentleman, and the soldier. In this period, obedience must

---

[2] *Mon.,* III, xvi, 18.
[3] *Conv.,* IV, xxi, 11.
[4] *Ibid.,* xxii, 18.
[5] *Ibid.,* xxiii, 3.

be paid not so much to parents and teachers as to reason, revealed in conscience, custom, and law. Reason must ride our appetite with the "spurs and bridle" of temperance, fortitude, and magnanimity.[6]

In the third period of life, man needs for his happiness prudence, justice, and generosity in relations with his fellow men. So it was, Dante notes, that Cato was born not for himself but for his country and for all the world.[7] In these years it is proper for a man to "open like a rose that can no longer remain in the bud and that spreads its good odor about it."[8]

In the fourth phase, in old age, happiness must be sought in the soul's return to God — to the "port from which it departed to enter on the sea of this life"[9] — and in blessing God for all His gifts. An old man should prepare to have his soul leave his body and drop into the arms of God as ripe fruit drops, lightly and without violence, from a tree. And as a pilgrim returning to his city is welcomed by his fellow citizens near the gate, so the noble soul should be met by the citizens of eternal life.[10] In these years man prepares to leave the inn in which he has been dwelling to return to his own home. In a sense, all old men enter a monastery. They need not, of course, take the habit of Benedict or Augustine, Francis or Dominic, but they become religious with all that God wants — with their hearts.[11]

Just as Dante in the *Inferno* seems to symbolize vigorous manhood, and in the *Purgatorio* the third and first periods of life, so in the *Paradiso* he seems to symbolize the soul's return to God. The citizens of eternal life come to meet him, and he blesses God for the blessings of faith, hope, and charity in this life and for the vision of God in the life to come.

II

Divine Law and Human Liberty

As the main interests of the *Inferno* and *Purgatorio* are political, philosophical, and artistic, so the main interest of the *Paradiso* is theological. Its main theme is expressed in the opening and closing lines; "the glory of Him who moves all things . . . the Love that

---

[6] *Conv.*, IV, xxvi, 6.   [8] *Ibid.*, 4.   [10] *Ibid.*, 5.
[7] *Ibid.*, xxvii, 3.   [9] *Ibid.*, 2.   [11] *Conv.*, IV, xxviii, 9.

moves the sun and all the stars." The theme of the *Paradiso* is religious, too, in the sense that in his high vision Dante has experiences which he has neither the wit nor the words to express,

> *vidi cose che ridire*
> *nè sa nè può chi di là su discende.*[12]

The deeper the intellect plunges into man's "ultimate desire," says Dante, the further mere imagination and memory must lag behind.

The action of this part of the Poem begins when Beatrice looks directly into the sun (symbol of divine light) and Dante imitates her example. Both begin to move upward by a spiritual gravitation more powerful than that which draws matter downward. Dante felt that he was being "transhumanized." Like St. Paul, he was not sure whether he was ascending solely with his soul or with his body too. All he knew was that a vast lake of light was growing more intense as though another sun had been put into the sky. He became aware of the mysterious music of the heavenly spheres. These unending movements, he felt, were but expressions of the love and longing that draws the whole cosmos to the source of all its being and all its activity. The newness of the music and the great light awakened in him a longing to learn unlike any desire he had ever felt before.

> *Quando la rota che tu sempiterni*
> *desiderato, a sè me fece atteso*
> *con l'armonia che temperi e discerni,*
> *parvemi tanto allor del cielo acceso*
> *de la fiamma del sol, che pioggia o fiume*
> *lago non fece mai tanto disteso.*
> *La novità del suono e 'l grande lume*
> *di lor cagion m'accesero un disio*
> *mai non sentito di cotanto acume.*[13]

Even more than in the "terrestrial paradise," Dante is as bewildered as a child. Beatrice smiles at him and talks to him in tiny words as though he were a baby.[14] Then she explains. It is the first, and in some ways the most remarkable of her theological discourses. There is, she began, a universal order in which all things are one. This order is the "form," the intelligible reality, the idea, the essence that makes it possible for the mind to see in the universe an image of the reality in God.[15] God, the divine Artist, realized, expressed, "actuated" His idea in creation. The cosmos is God's masterpiece. The

[12] *Par.*, i, 5, 6.
[13] *Ibid.*, 76–81.
[14] *Ibid.*, 88–95.
[15] *Ibid.*, 103–105.

beauty of the cosmos, like any other beauty, is the order of its parts, is that which makes it one, is its "form."

As we can see in a work of human art the idea of the artist, so can intelligence see in the cosmos the stamp, the footprint, the image of divine power and wisdom and love. Intelligence can discern the Creator as the cause and the beginning of all things — as well as their purpose or end. The order of the cosmos is not only *from* God but *for* God. And, of course, angelic intelligence can know this even better than human intelligence can.[16] By saying that God is the end, Beatrice means that for all things in the cosmos God is the supreme good, God is that which is ultimately desired by all things, that to which all things tend.

Of the things of which God is both the beginning and the end — the ultimate efficient and the final cause — there are many grades. The likeness to God is close or remote in various degrees. God is a great ocean of being on which ships of different sizes move to ports at various distances. Purely material things are moved by gravity and the force of cohesion; animals move by instinct; men and angels are moved by intelligence and love and, in their special way, they tend toward God as to what is supremely true and perfectly good. Thus instinct, appetite, and rational love are equally the gifts of God. God has created each nature with a specific tendency to Him and to its own perfection. In virtue of the harmony which God has put into creation the spontaneous activity of each creature toward its own perfection is at the same time an actuation of the divine law of love which God has imposed on His creatures.

With this word "love" we reach the center of Dante's theological system. Even Virgil had said: "No Creator nor any creature was ever without love."[17] Love was written on the gates of hell. It is repeated in the last line of the whole Poem.

When Dante thinks of the creation or of the governance of the world, he thinks of divine power as love. In creating the angels, "eternal love diffused itself in new loves, not for the sake of any gain to itself, since that is impossible for the infinitely good, but so that the reflection of the creative rays could say 'I subsist.' "[18] So, too, in the creation of the heavens, it was divine love that gave the first movement to all "lovely things."[19] It is love that governs the skies.[20]

[16] *Ibid.*, 106–108.   [18] *Par.*, xxix, 13–18.   [20] *Par.*, i, 74.
[17] *Purg.*, xvii, 91.   [19] *Inf.*, i, 40.

The ardor of love is the reason why the highest of the nine heavens moves with such rapidity.[21] Divine love is the source of the highest of human inspirations, as when it was the "will of the primal love" that moved Justinian to his task of codifying the Roman law.[22] And, of course, the inspiration of the old and new testaments came from "the abundant shower of the Holy Spirit."[23]

In Dante's conception of the cosmos all creation started as an overflowing of God's infinite love; all creation is held together, moves, and is active in virtue of inherent tendencies or instincts which are reducible to love; the rational part of creation is invited to a final consummation of beatitude in an "intellectual light full of love, and love of supreme truth full of joy, a joy that transcends all other blessedness.[24]

Within this scheme of law and love there is, however, the strange mystery of human liberty. As Dante moves upward as inevitably as an "arrow moving to its mark," Beatrice speaks of this mystery. Just as in art, she says, the artist's idea is not always fully revealed in the form of his creation because the matter with which he has to deal is "deaf to his call," so can human nature be deaf to the call of divine love. Human nature is like an arrow that can deflect itself from the course of its flight; it can turn from its pursuit of God to the pursuit of false pleasure.

Here, for the moment, Beatrice leaves the mystery of human liberty tantalizingly unsolved. She merely states the fact that human liberty is a part of the cosmic scheme of divine law and love. She pursues the matter, however, when she and Dante reach the sphere of the moon and meet Piccarda Donati. Piccarda had been forced against her will to abandon her freely chosen life of consecration to God in a convent. Under duress she had married. What puzzled Dante was why, if Piccarda's will remained attached to her vows, violence could rob her of the merit of being higher up in heaven than, as a fact, she was. Beatrice answered that the will can be effective in two degrees. Piccarda had the choice of accepting the violence while keeping her will interiorly but ineffectively attached to her vows; or she could have sought to escape from the violence and to return to the convent. This would have shown that her will was both affectively and effectively attached to her vows. You can bend by

[21] *Par.*, xxvii, 44–45.
[22] *Par.*, vi, 11, 12.
[23] *Par.*, xxiv, 91–93; 137–138.
[24] *Par.*, xxx, 40.

violence the direction of a flame, but the moment the flame is free
from the violence it will return to its course and soar straight upward. This was the kind of absolute will that kept St. Lawrence on
the gridiron and the hand of Mutius in the fire, but such sound will
is all too rare.[25] What happened to Piccarda was that the direction
in which her will was set was right, and, therefore, she merited
heaven; but her will did not move in the direction in which it was
set because she feared the consequence. St. Thomas Aquinas in the
Summa Theologica[26] had debated this issue. He calls the direction
of the will *voluntarium simpliciter*. The movement of the will
under the impulse of the fear of consequences he calls *voluntarium
secundum quid*. Beatrice calls the former the "absolute will." The
other is a "mixture of violence and will." Beatrice's distinction
seemed to Dante to come from the very "fountain of all truth." It
put his mind at rest. He realized how much more satisfactory in such
matters Beatrice was than Virgil, and he says: "I see that our mind
can never be satisfied unless it is illumined by the truth outside of
which there is no further truth."

> *Io veggio ben che già mai non si sazia*
> *nostro intelletto, se 'l ver non lo illustra*
> *di fuor dal qual nessun vero si spazia.*[27]

However, "doubts grow like shoots on the trunk of truth." Dante
wondered whether there could be any human compensation for
broken vows. This leads Beatrice to speak further on free will. It is,
she says, the greatest gift that God of His goodness gave when He
created the gift that most resembles the character of His own goodness and the gift that He himself ranks highest. It was a gift reserved
for creatures with intelligence. Hence the value of vows. In a vow
one gives back to God the supreme gift of freedom and one gives it
by an act of freedom. There is, therefore, no real equivalent compensation for such a sacrifice. Beatrice, however, makes a distinction.
The essence or "form" of the sacrifice is the promise one makes to
God. The "matter" is that about which the promise is made, as for
example, the renunciation of property or of marriage. The promise
must always be kept. But one can change the matter; not willfully,
of course, but with proper ecclesiastical sanction. Again St. Thomas[28]
had dealt with this subject. On the whole Dante follows him, but

[25] *Par.*, iv, 87.
[26] *Summa Theologica*, I, II, q. vi, aa. 4–6.
[27] *Par.*, iv, 124–126.
[28] *Summa Theologica*, II, II, q. lxxxviii.

with just enough independence to show that he was doing his own thinking. On the point of ecclesiastical authority Beatrice and St. Thomas are at one. In the Poem Beatrice makes this open profession of her Catholicism: "You have the New and Old Testament and the shepherd of the Church to guide you; let this be enough for your salvation."[29]

The question of human liberty is linked with that of divine foreknowledge and that, in turn, with divine justice. On the question of foreknowledge Dante uses his own ancestor as spokesman. Throughout the pilgrimage Dante had heard predictions of his future years on earth, and he had met the grave words with a will that was "foursquare to all the blows of fortune."[30] Before pronouncing his prophecy Cacciaguida explains that merely contingent differences of past, present, and future can relate only to a world of matter. Outside the world of matter there is no time, and hence in the light of God all reality appears in an eternal present. That, however, no more necessitates man's free actions than the vision of one who can see the turnings of a river down to its mouth necessitates the meandering movements of a boat that is being piloted down the river.[31]

To the problem of divine justice Dante devotes cantos XVIII and XIX of the *Paradiso*. In the heaven of Jupiter he finds the souls of those who have exercised justice on earth. They form successively the letters of the Latin words that mean "Love justice ye who rule the earth," *Diligite justitiam qui judicatis terram*. At last the letter *M* at the end of *terram* remains in his vision and this by a gradual transformation takes on the shape of an imperial eagle. The divine Artist, says Dante, was here at work, not the artist that needs a model in nature but the Artist that modeled nature, the Artist whose creative activity is symbolized in the working of the instinct whereby a bird without a model builds a nest.[32] The creative activity of the divine Artist is symbolized, too, in the special inspirations that come to artists here on earth. Dante's vision of the eagle was an inspiration of this sort. What he saw, he says, had never before been put in words nor expressed in ink nor ever conceived by human fantasy.

> *E quel che mi convien ritrar testeso*
> *non portò voce mai, nè scrisse incostro*
> *nè fu per fantasia già mai compreso.*[33]

[29] *Par.*, v, 76–78. [31] *Par.*, xvii, 37–42. [33] *Par.*, xix, 7–9.
[30] *Par.*, xvii, 22–24. [32] *Par.*, xviii, 109–111.

The multitude of the souls spoke in such perfect harmony that when he expected to hear "we" and "our" he heard "I" and "mine." Just as out of many coals comes a single flame, so out of these many loves came a single voice. Here if ever was Dante's chance to learn the unveiled truth about divine justice. The eagle, of course, already knew Dante's question before he uttered it, since souls in bliss know all such things in God. Its answer began with a song in praise of divine goodness, a song "such as only those can hear who taste of heavenly bliss."[34] Then it continued. The power that in creation made the universe a mirror of its mind could not but leave an infinitude of truth unreflected in so small an image.[35] Not even the light in the mind of Lucifer, before he fell, could reflect more than a tiny fragment of the divine wisdom. Lesser minds, like human minds, are still smaller receptacles of light. The most we can do with the ray of divine light in a human intelligence is to understand how far above our comprehension the source of light must be. When, therefore, we strain to catch a clear sight of divine justice we are like a person who tries to see the bottom of the ocean. Near the shore, of course, we can see the sand, but the further we wade the less clear it becomes, until in the depths it is invisible. The bottom is there. Only the ocean is too deep for us to see it.

> Però ne la giustizia sempiterna
> la vista che riceve il vostro mondo,
> com' occhio per lo mare, entro s' interna;
> che, ben che da la proda veggia il fondo,
> in pelago nol vede; e nondimeno
> èli, ma cela lui l'esser profondo.[36]

We ask the direct questions: How can a good man in distant India who never heard of Christ be punished by the loss of the Beatific Vision just because he remained unbaptized? We forget that the very light by which we ask the question is but a ray from the unperturbed infinitude of light. We forget that with a focal distance of a span our eyes strain to see objects that are a thousand miles away. We forget that the divine will could not, by its very essence, be otherwise than just. We forget that the very idea of justice means conformity with that divine will, *cotanto è giusto quanto a lei consuona.*[37]

[34] *Ibid.,* 39.
[35] *Ibid.,* 43–45.
[36] *Ibid.,* 58–63.
[37] *Ibid.,* 88.

We cannot hope, therefore, to understand with human intelligence the mystery of predestination, but this much we can know: wherever there is injustice on earth it will surely meet with retribution in the world to come. In the day of doom many who cry "Lord, Lord," will be far less near to Christ than many who never knew Him.[38]

Heaven loves a just king, and the pagans, Ripheus and Trajan, were found by Dante alongside of David and Constantine. Even where there has been no faith through baptism, Dante realized that "the kingdom of heaven suffers violence from warm love and living hope."[39] The fact is, as Dante expresses it, that Ripheus and Trajan issued from their bodies not, as might be believed, "pagans, but Christians in firm faith." God's gifts of faith, hope, and charity served them in place of baptism. And so it is that predestination works both ways. The best is, therefore, to leave all to God and, like the blessed, to "will what God wills."[40]

III

CREATION

At the root of this mystery, as of so many other mysteries of faith, is the mystery of creation, the fact that the infinite spirit whose very essence it is to be should have given being to contingent realities that in themselves have no reason whatever for existence. This central revelation Dante reserves for St. Thomas Aquinas to explain. The occasion of St. Thomas' speech is not without interest. He had seemed to say that Solomon, for his wisdom, ranked highest among the sons of men. Dante, naturally, wondered what was to be said of Adam and of Christ. St. Thomas answered, first, that these two do not come into comparison since they were made directly by divine action without the play of secondary causes; and, second, that, in any case, he was thinking only of kingly prudence when he ranked Solomon supreme. But the answer of the saint led him to speak of creation in general. Both immortal and mortal substances, he says, are but the splendor or manifestation of that idea which the Eternal Father brings forth by His Love.

[38] *Ibid.*, 106–108.   [39] *Ibid.*, 100–102.   [40] *Ibid.*, 138.

> *Ciò che non more, e ciò che può morire*
> *non è se non splendor di quell' idea*
> *che partorisce, amando, il nostro Sire.*[41]

Thus creation is the work of the Blessed Trinity, of the Father, and Son (or Word or Wisdom of God), and the Holy Spirit (the subsistent, personal breath of eternal Love). The Word, the Wisdom proceeds from the Father like a living ray from a light, save that it remains one with the eternal Flame, one with the Light and the Love. For these three are one.

> *Chè quella viva luce che si mea*
> *dal suo lucente che non si disuna*
> *da lui, nè da l' amor c' a lor s' intrea* . . .[42]

When a person we love smiles back at us we do not merely see the sign of love; we see the very soul of the person in the laugh in the eyes. So did God's love break out into the light and laughter of a created universe. Creation is eternal love expressing the infinite wisdom of almighty power. The light or laughter of love is first mirrored in the nine subsistences of the heavenly choirs. And yet there is no emanation. The light remains eternally unchanged.

> *Per sua bontate il suo raggiare aduna*
> *quasi specchiato, in nove sussistenze*
> *etternalmente rimanendosi una.*[43]

There is thus in creation nothing of the blind necessity involved in Neoplatonic emanations. There is only the free inevitability of urgent love. It is the very nature of the good to spread itself. So did divine love make light issue from an eternal lantern into the darkness of the void. The forms, the ideas of all that was to be created existed in the divine Artist, but unlike the human artist, God had but to think — and the masterpiece was made. In God the very principle of thought, the Word, is also a principle of action. In God thought and will and deed are one. So it is that divine power made the world by wisdom out of love.

But all things are not made directly by God in this way. The plan of creation called for the process of passing from potency to act, and from one generation to another. Creation allows for secondary causes. All causality is ultimately in God and, therefore, the knowledge of all things, of each individual substance and accident

---

[41] *Par.*, xiii, 52–54.   [42] *Par.*, xix, 55–57.   [43] *Ibid.*, 58–60.

and habit is in God and, therefore, nothing escapes His providence. Take the case of human beings. Man is a unity compounded of matter and form, body and soul. Man's body is one of nature's works of art, a product of secondary, natural causes; but the soul in each case, as Statius explains in the *Purgatory*,[44] is a direct creation of God. What made the cases of Adam and of Christ special was that not only their souls but their bodies were direct creations of God. In these two cases, St. Thomas says, the warm love disposed and stamped the clear wisdom of the primal power, so that complete perfection was achieved.

> Però se 'l caldo amor la chiara vista
> de la prima virtù dispone e segna,
> tutta la perfezion quivi s' acquista.
> Così fu fatta già la terra degna
> di tutta l' animal perfezione
> così fu fatta la Vergine pregna.[45]

In the case of Solomon, the wax or matter from which he was made was already in existence; the natural forces involved were those of heredity and the rest. And nature is like an "artist that has the habit of art but a hand that trembles,"

> ma la natura la dà sempre scema
> similemente operando a l'artista
> c' ha l'abito de l'arte e man che trema.[46]

Solomon's human nature could not compete with that of Adam or of Christ. But his prayer for kingly wisdom gave him a gift that made him unique. He was not the first of theologians; he had no special knowledge of the angels that move the heavens; he was not the first of logicians; he had not enquired whether a necessary conclusion can ever be drawn from two premises of which one contains a purely contingent truth; he was not the first of metaphysicians; he had no special answer to the question of the first motion; nor was he an outstanding mathematician with wisdom touching the angles in a triangle. But of kings — and "of these there are many but few good ones" — he was the first in wisdom.

In explaining the mystery of creation, Dante makes St. Thomas imply the doctrine of the Trinity, and especially the attribution to the Father of power, to the Son of wisdom, and to the Holy Spirit of love. No part of Dante's theology is of more frequent occurrence

[44] *Purg.*, xxv, 66–72.　　　[45] *Par.*, xiii, 79–84.　　　[46] *Ibid.*, 76.

in the Poem than this idea of the power, wisdom, and love of God. On the door of hell he found written the words: "I was made by divine power, supreme wisdom, and primal love,"

> *Fecemi la divina potestate,*
> *la somma sapienza e il primo amore.*[47]

And when at last he is granted the vision of the triune divinity he breaks out into the exclamation: "O light eternal, that alone hast being in Thyself, alone understandest Thyself, and understanding and being understood lovest Thyself and hast joy in Thyself."

> *O luce eterna, che sola in te sidi*
> *sola t'intendi, e, da te intelletta*
> *ed intendente, te ami ed arridi.*[48]

Even in such an expression as the "art of that Master who loves it within Himself so much that He never takes his eye from it," one sees in the "master" the Father and in the "eye" the Son and in the "love" the Holy Spirit.[49] Sometimes Dante makes the matter even clearer. Thus: "Looking into His Son with the love that the one and the other eternally breathe, the first and ineffable power, created with order all that is mental and spatial,"

> *Guardando nel suo Figlio con l' Amore*
> *che l' uno e l' altro etternalmente spira*
> *lo primo ed ineffabile Valore*

> *quanto per mente e per loco si gira*
> *con tant' ordine fè, ch' esser non puote*
> *sanza gustar di lui chi ciò rimira.*[50]

The fact that in God power, wisdom, and love are one makes it possible for Dante to speak of God indifferently under any of the three attributes. Thus in the beginning of the *Inferno* he speaks of creation as divine love first giving movement to all lovely things.[51] In the seventh canto he speaks of "Him whose wisdom is above all wisdom" as making the heavens.[52] But most commonly Dante speaks of God as the first cause or the "apex of all being"[53] or the "most universal cause of all things"[54] or the "wonderful and benign sower."[55]

---

[47] *Inf.*, iii, 5, 6.
[48] *Par.*, xxxiii, 124, 12.
[49] *Par.*, x, 10–12.
[50] *Par.*, x, 1–5.
[51] *Inf.*, i, 39–40.
[52] *Inf.*, vii, 73.
[53] *Mon.*, III, xiii, 1.
[54] *Conv.*, III, vi, 5.
[55] *Conv.*, IV, xxi, 12.

IV

INCARNATION, REDEMPTION

One of the most important of Beatrice's lectures is that on the mystery of the Incarnation, of why God became man. Adam, the "man who was not born"[56] in harming himself by his sin harmed all his progeny. He sinned because he "failed to put a bridle, for his own good, on his will." The result was that mankind found itself in a condition of "sickness" in the will and of "great error" in the mind. Because of this sickness and darkness, that is, because the sons of Adam lacked the divine inspirations and illuminations which he once enjoyed, they could be described as fallen. Beatrice does not suppose that man's nature became inherently evil or intrinsically corrupted. Marco Lombardo in the *Purgatory* says that there is no question of a "nature in you that is corrupt."[57] Human nature had fallen from a high tower of supernatural endowment; it had not fallen into a deep well of infranatural depravity. Limping as man was and traveling in the dusk without a supernatural light, he was still on his two feet of intelligence and will, still on the solid ground of human nature. What Adam's sin lost was supernatural grace on earth and the hope of glory — the supernatural vision of God — in the world to come. It was to restore the graces of faith, hope, and charity that "it pleased the Word of God to descend" to earth. He did this in such wise that He united human nature with His divine Person. Dante does not say, as some of the commentators would imply, that the Word was united with a sinful nature. The divine Word was united with human nature as it was created — "pure and good." It was, however, a nature that was "exiled from paradise," deprived of supernatural endowments.

What was monstrous about Adam's sin was the rejection of God's supernatural gifts of grace. No punishment borne by human nature for such a sin could ever be too great. And so, as Beatrice says, if the death on the cross is measured by the human nature assumed by the Word it was perfectly just. However, in the case of the Redeemer the person who was punished was divine. No death, measured by this fact, could be so outrageous.

[56] *Par.*, vii, 26.   [57] *Purg.*, xvi, 105.

So it happened, says Beatrice, that the death, looked at as a redemptive act, was pleasing to God; but looked at as an assault on the God-man it could only have pleased the perpetrators. Because God was satisfied heaven, which had been closed by Adam's sin, was opened, that is to say, supernatural truth and grace became once more available. But because an outrage had been committed by men "the earth trembled."

Dante knew that the real theological problem of redemption was not in such ideas. The real problem is why God, who could have forgiven man by an act of mercy, needed to make the death seem likewise an act of justice. Such a problem can only be debated in the light of faith, by "a mind full grown in the flame of love." Reason can look at the problem, but only faith can see the answer.

What follows is the most beautiful of all Beatrice's theological explanations. She begins with the general idea that love was the cause of all created reality, whether material or spiritual, whether natural or supernatural. What God created directly (like angels and souls) must be immortal — for the divine stamp is indelible. Besides immortality such immediate creations must be free in the sense of not being necessitated by causality involving matter. Such free and immortal spirits are more like God himself than the heavens or the rest of nature can be, and so are more beloved of God. Man in particular is endowed with these gifts of immortality, freedom, and a likeness to God. To fall from man's full nobility it is enough to lose one of the gifts. This is what sin did. It made man unlike the supreme good. Man did not lose the natural "image," but he lost the supernatural "similitude." He did not lose the immortality or the freedom of his soul. He did not lose his reason or his will. He lost the special prerogative of the indwelling in his soul of the Holy Spirit. Man lost this by his own action. A wound had been made in God's established order which, somehow, must be healed. There were two possible ways to heal the wound. God could restore the lost integrity by an act of pure mercy or He could insist on justice, asking man to try to make satisfaction, to try to build his own bridge over the chasm that had been made, to go back along the road on which he had departed. The difficulty was that man by himself could never make adequate satisfaction, he could never build such a bridge, he could never return as far along the road of humility and obedience as he had traveled in the direction of pride and disobedience. There could not be, to use the words of Richard of St. Victor, as full "a humiliation in expiation as there had been presumption in prevarication."[58] Only a descent of the divine to the human, of the highest to the lowest, could remedy the assault of the human on the divine, of the revolt of the lowest from the highest.

The remedy must, therefore, come from God. It was characteristic of divine love, that God should combine mercy with justice. And so God chose the way of the Incarnation, a proceeding so "magnificent that nothing like it has been or ever will be from the morning of Creation to the night" of the day of doom. What God did was to give Himself to human nature to "divinize" human nature, by a hypostatic union, so that human nature could do the work of satisfaction. To use the language of chivalry, God behaved more "magnanimously" than if He had merely forgiven man by an act of mercy.

> Nè tra l'ultima notte e 'l primo die
> sì alto o sì magnifico processo
> o per l'una o per l' altra, fu or fie;
> chè più largo fu Dio a dar sè stesso
> per far l'uom sufficiente a rilevarsi,
> che s' elli avesse sol da sè dimesso.[59]

If God wanted justice to be fulfilled, there was no way but for the Son of God to accept the humiliation of Incarnation.

To this discussion of the Incarnation Beatrice adds a corollary on man's immortality and the resurrection of the human body. The heavens and material and animal nature are not works of direct creation and, therefore, they can have an end. But man's soul is a direct creation, it is breathed into us directly by the supreme benignity, and is so loved by God that He can never cease from loving it.[60] And because the body of Adam was made by direct creation, we may argue that human bodies, too, will be forever a part of our glorified human nature.

One God, then, in Three Persons; Creation, Fall, and Incarnation; Redemption, Grace, and Glory — these are the themes of Dante's theological poetry. The theology is orthodox. But how could dogma like that have been turned into song unless the poet's

---

[58] *De Verbo Incarnato,* 8; cf. *Summa Theologica,* II, II, clxiii, 2; III, i, 2.
[59] *Par.,* vii, 112–117.
[60] *Ibid.,* 142–144.

soul were aflame with religious devotion? This brings us to the question of Dante's Catholicism.

V

DANTE'S CATHOLICISM

It is revealed more intimately and convincingly than anywhere else in the cantos of the *Paradiso* that fall between the pilgrim's two views of the world from the stars. It is a Catholicism that is as clear as philosophy, as passionate as poetry; a Catholicism of the head and heart, radiant with light and warmth in equal measure.

At the end of canto XXII, Beatrice bids Dante prepare his heart for the joyous vision of the Church Triumphant. "Look down," she says, "and see how far below your feet the world now lies."[61] He looked, and saw how "cheap a showing" the fierce "threshing floor" of human passions made. He turned his eyes from earth to the "lovely eyes" of Beatrice. Like a bird covering her young and yearning for the dawn, she was rapt in attention, waiting as though for the sun to rise. "Appeased with hope, yet bursting with desire," the poet looked where Beatrice was looking. "See," she cried, "the ranks of the redeemed and Christ in triumph!"[62] And there before the hungry eyes of faith was a feast for a poet's heart, a vision of the Church in heavenly glory — Christ the "head" of the "mystical body," Mary, His mother, Peter and the Apostles, all the other "members" back to Adam.

Out from the poet's lips gushed a cascade of song, lovelier in music than any lines he ever wrote. Loving to think, as any Catholic would, of the souls of our Lady and all the saints bathed, illumined, made alive, redeemed, "divinized" by the blood of Christ, he sees in a passionate vision of symbolic poetry the "moon" and "stars" in a cloudless sky drawing their "light" from the "Sun." "As when," he sings, "in nights of calm full moon, Diana laughs and all her everlasting nymphs brighten the last recesses of the sky, so did I see, above the innumerable lamps, the Sun that lit them all,"

[61] *Par.*, xxii, 128.
[62] *Par.*, xxiii, 19.

Quale ne' plenilunii sereni
Trivia ride tra le ninfe etterne
che dipingon lo ciel per tutti i seni,
vidi sopra migliaia di lucerne
un sol che tutte quante l' accendea.[63]

The critics and the commentators, great and small, have written endlessly about the beauty of those lines. Their perfection is as high as Catholic art — perhaps, any art — has ever reached. They make the plea for piety without poetry seem as mean and ridiculous as the lie about the "pale Galilean" turning the "world gray" with His breath. The Galilean, "the Sun that lit them all," had, indeed, conquered — in two senses that the pagan Swinburne never dreamed of. Yet in the Poem there is not the slightest shadow of self-consciousness, either religious or artistic. All that a plain Catholic like Dante could do was to cry out with unfinished and unfinishable feeling: "O Beatrice, sweet guide and dear . . . !"[64] She answered — what all who have felt the force of grace will understand — "Against the might that overmasters you there is no defense. Before your eyes is the wisdom and the power that opened to man the longed-for road from earth to heaven." It was an echo of what "Dante" had said, in symbols, when "Beatrice" first appeared: "I feel the mighty power of ancient love."[65] In the light of the triumphant Christ Dante was dazzled into ecstasy. He was wakened by Beatrice who said: "Open your eyes and see what I am."[66]

Dante turned to "the lovely garden enflowered by the rays of Christ." From the "Sun" he turned to the "moon" — from our Lord to our Lady, to the "Rose in whom the Word divine took flesh," the "lovely flower whose name is on my lips every morning and evening of my life." Above her, in a garland of light, danced the angel of the Annunciation. He and the others broke into song to hail the "name of Mary," *Regina coeli* — for so all heaven loved her. From the Rose Dante turned to the "lilies," the Apostles, and, at their head, "the one who holds the keys to all this glory," Peter.[67]

Beatrice pleads with the Apostles as later St. Bernard will plead with our Lady. "Remember his unbounded love," she begs. "You who drink at the fount toward which his longing tends, slake his lips with at least a drop of heavenly dew."[68] Addressing St. Peter, she began: "O eternal light of the great leader to whom our Lord

[63] *Ibid.,* 25-29.
[64] *Par.,* xxiii, 34.
[65] *Purg.,* xxx, 39.
[66] *Purg.,* xxiii, 45.
[67] *Ibid.,* 139.
[68] *Purg.,* xxiv, 8, 9.

entrusted the keys." But, with a laughing and laughable abruptness, dear to the Catholic spirit, she suddenly said: Please examine Dante in the theology of faith!

Thereupon a Scholastic *disputatio* is re-enacted in the court of heaven. Dante, the "bachelor," silently arms himself with reason; St. Peter, the "master," proposes the "questions" for debate. What is the essence, the "quiddity," the "what-it-is," of faith? Promptly the bachelor recalls the definition of Peter's "good brother," Paul: "Faith is that which gives substance to our hopes, which convinces us of things we cannot see."[69] The Vulgate text has the philosophic-looking words, "substance" and "argument." The "master," Scholastic-wise, presses the "bachelor." Why *substance?* Why *argument?* Faith, says Dante, stands below our hope (*substat*). Therefore "substance" is an essential note, a characteristic, a *ratio*, an *intenza*. Faith, too, is the major premise of all our "syllogizing," our "argument," in the supernatural world of things unseen. Therefore, it "convinces" us.

Dante thus demonstrated that, speculatively, his faith was currency of "good alloy and weight." St. Peter presses him. Is this faith in your heart, in your "purse," or only in your head? Dante, with precipitate assurance, answers: "Yes, yes," in my purse, the coin is "bright and round — and no maybe," *nulla mi s'inforsa.*[70] Very well, says St. Peter, but where did you get it? Dante replies: "The immense outpouring of the Holy Spirit over the leaves of the Old and New Testaments is, for me, a syllogism pointing to such sharp conclusion that all other demonstration, in comparison, is obtuse." The master, for the sake of debate, calmly denies the implied major premise. How do you prove that the Spirit inspiring the Bible is divine? Dante answers: A tree is known by its fruits, a "nature" by its "operation," God by the working of miracles; there are miracles recorded in the Bible; there is nothing in the forge of nature to "heat the iron and beat the anvil" for the making of miracles; therefore, a divine Spirit is behind the Bible. "Miracles?" asks the master, coldly. Who said there were any miracles? The Bible itself? But the truth of the Bible is here in question. The bachelor, however, has a dilemma ready. Either there are miracles in the Gospels, or there are not; if there are, divine inspiration is proved; if not, then Christianity conquered the Roman Empire without the mi-

[69] *Heb.*, 11:1.   [70] *Par.*, xxiv, 87.

raculous help of Christ: *that* is a hundred times more of a miracle than all the others. A miracle remains. Divinity is once more saved!

"Praise be to God," the "holy court" of heaven sang. However, the examination was not yet over. "The grace that plays a lover to your mind," St. Peter said, "has so far opened your lips unfailingly; I approve all that has issued forth." It was clear *that* the bachelor believed; it had now to be shown *what* he believed and *why*. "I believe in one God, sole and eternal," Dante began, "the unmoved mover that filled the world with love and longing." For proof he appealed to science, philosophy, and religion. First, God is proved by the law and order that the eyes of the body can discern in visible nature; second, He is proved by the existence of values and virtues that are visible only to eyes of the soul; third, He is revealed by Moses, the prophets, the psalmist, and the Gospels. When Dante adds to his creed the belief that there are three Persons in this one God, St. Peter three times made a garland of light about his head, as though he were declaring him a doctor of divinity — as Virgil had already declared him a doctor of philosophy.

For a moment the poet forgets his Vision. He thinks only of the font in Florence where baptism brought him the beginning of his faith. This in turn made him wonder whether the sacred Poem in "which heaven and earth had taken a hand" would one day win for him the poet's crown. Then the Vision called him back. He heard Beatrice say: "Look, look, there is the great baron for whom men go on pilgrimage to Compostella!" It was St. James, the Apostle of Hope. He proposed three questions: What is hope? How does it flourish in your soul? What is its source? Beatrice took care of question number two. "The Church Militant," she said, "has no son on earth with hope so strong. . . . For that reason it was granted him to escape from Egypt to a vision of Jerusalem before the war of life was over. . . . And may God grant him grace to answer the other questions."[71] Dante had the answers ready. "Hope," he said, quoting Peter Lombard (*Liber Sententiarum*, III, 26: "*Spes est certa expectatio futurae beatitudinis veniens ex Dei gratia et ex meritis precedentibus*"), "is the certain expectation of future glory, the fruit of divine grace and preceding merit."[72] As for texts to prove the definition, the Scriptures are full of them from the psalms to

[71] *Par.*, xxv, 52–67.
[72] *Par.*, xxv, 67–69.

the epistles. What does hope promise? Beatitude — and that in the double life of soul and body.

Last of all came an examination in charity, the theological virtue of love. The "beloved disciple," St. John, danced and sang his way to his brother Apostles like a girl full of joy executing a *pas seul* to honor the bride at a marriage feast. What do we love, he asked, when the grace of charity enflames our hearts? Dante had in mind a famous definition of St. Thomas (*Summa*, I, II, lxv, a. 5, ad 1: *caritas non est qualiscumque amor Dei, sed amor Dei quo diligitur ut beatitudinis obiectum ad quod ordinamur per fidem et spem*), but he uses his own words: The "alpha and omega," the beginning and end, the object of all supernatural charity is "the good that makes this court content."[73] How did he come to aim the arrow of desire at so high a target? Because of reason and revelation. Reason argues thus: When good, as good, is known it kindles love; the better the good the more it is loved; if the good is perfect good — so that all other goods are but rays from its perfection — then it must be loved above all things else. So it was that Aristotle taught that all the heavens yearn for God. And, of course, Holy Scripture from Moses to the Apocalypse is full of the idea that God is supremely good. Hence reason and revelation lead to one conclusion: Of all our loves the sovereign love must be for God.[74] Reason, hope, and living faith had rescued Dante from the "sea of erring love and set him on the shore of charity." He loved all things in God. "I love the leaves on all the eternal Gardener's trees with love proportioned to the goodness He has given them."[75]

The exam was over. The liturgical *Sanctus, sanctus, sanctus* (familiar to Dante from the *Te Deum* and the Preface of the Mass) resounded throughout the court of heaven. Beatrice, of course, joined in the singing.

As for the rest of the members of the mystical body, it was enough for Dante to speak with Adam, "the ancient father." "There," said Beatrice, pointing, "within those rays of light, in love with its Creator, is the first of all the souls that the Prime Power ever made." As "devoutly" as he could, Dante begged Adam to speak with him. He thus learned the date of Adam's creation; the time he spent in Eden; the reason for his fall; the language that he used. When the talk was done, all heaven sang with in-

[73] *Par.*, xxvi, 16.   [74] *Ibid.*, 43.   [75] *Ibid.*, 63–66.

toxicating sweetness the liturgical song, "Glory be to the Father and to the Son and to the Holy Spirit."

Dante sums up his feelings in the exclamation:

> I heard such songs and saw such things, and after
> Was so inebriated with delight,
> The very universe seemed one long laughter.

> O life of love and unperturbèd peace,
> O unimaginable plenitude
> Of blessedness's infinite increase.[76]

In those two words *love* and *laughter* we have, perhaps, the best and briefest expression of Dante's Catholicism. Catholicism was not for him — what the abstractionists have tried to make of it — either a "Johannine" or a "Pauline" or a "Petrine" aspect or view or interpretation of God and Christ and man and nature. It was neither light nor life nor law nor logic, taken alone. It was all these things taken together — and more. It was that most embracing of all experiences, a lover's laughter. Like love, it could never be merely proved; like laughter, never refuted. Like love it could never hate; like laughter, never sneer. Yet, like love, it could be heartbroken, saddened, ashamed; like laughter, it could turn into tears. It is ever demanding reform; never, rebellion. So it was that Peter, who just before had been so "joyful," more "happy" than all the rest,[77] the key-bearer of all "this marvelous mirth,"[78] blushed with shame. "If I turn red," he said, "you need not wonder. For while I speak all heaven will blush with me."[79] Thereupon the first Pope begins to blast Pope Boniface, the reigning Pontiff, "he that usurps my place on earth, my place, my place. . . . Of my cemetery he has made a cesspool of blood and filth." Beatrice blushed, too. And all the others blushed. There was an eclipse in heaven, says Dante, as when Omnipotence had died. Then the saint continued: "The Bride of Christ was not nourished with my blood and Linus' blood and Cletus' blood to be used for gaining gold, but for the gain of this joyous life. . . . It was no part of our plan that Christendom (*il popol cristiano*) should be cut in two, one part on the right and one on the left of our successors; nor that the keys that were given me should become a battle standard in a war on men baptized. . . . O son, who with your mortal body will return once

---

[76] *Par.*, xxvii, 4–9.
[77] *Par.*, xxiv, 10, 20, 21.
[78] *Ibid.*, 36.
[79] *Par.*, xxvii, 19–21.

more down there, open your mouth and hide not what I have not hidden."[80]

With that, St. Peter and all the Church Triumphant disappeared, leaving Dante alone with Beatrice. She told him to look down and take another view of the world below him. After that he was ready for the timeless, spaceless reality of light and love and laughter that exists in the mind of God.

VI

MYSTICAL EXPERIENCE

This brings us to the question of what is sometimes called Dante's "mysticism." The final cantos of the *Paradiso* offer the best evidence we have in regard to this matter. It seems clear that Dante was familiar with the tradition of the mystical theologians. He had made his own what St. Thomas says in the beginning of the fourth book of the *Summa contra gentiles* in regard to three kinds of human knowledge of divine things. "The first of these," St. Thomas says, "is the knowledge that comes by the natural light of reason," when the reason ascends by means of creatures to God; the second "descends to us by way of revelation"; the third is possible only to the human mind "elevated to the perfect intuition of the things that are revealed." Of these kinds of knowledge Dante symbolized the first by Virgil, the second by Beatrice, the third by St. Bernard.

Dante had read St. Bernard's *De consideratione*, Richard of St. Victor's *Benjamin major* and the *De quantitate animae* of St. Augustine. These books are mentioned in the Letter to Can Grande della Scala, in which Dante comments on the lines at the beginning of the *Paradiso*, "he saw such things as no one has the wit or words to tell because the human intellect in drawing close to the end of all desire sinks so deep that memory cannot follow it."[81] This is explained by saying that the human intellect, like the angelic intellect, can be elevated by God to an experience of mystical vision, whereas the memory, which is a part of our animal nature, cannot transcend the measure of humanity. After the intellect in its ascent had gone beyond human reason it could not remember

[80] *Ibid.*, 40–66.   [81] *Par.*, i, 5–9.

what was done outside of itself. This was the case with St. Paul, the three Apostles on the mount of Transfiguration, and Ezechiel. It is no objection, Dante continues, that the recipient of such a mystical grace should be a sinner. Nabuchodonosor was no saint and yet he was able "to see some things divinely."

Is, then, the vision in the last cantos of the *Paradiso* a record of personal mystical experience? Or is it merely the supreme effort of artistic imagination to describe what the mystics have seen and felt? Dante's answer is that the resources of his art were exhausted before the final vision. Even the last beauty of Beatrice was so transcendent that he owns himself more baffled than any other artist by his theme.[82] Up to that last smile, he had followed with his art. But at last he must desist. He has reached the ultimate in human art. Of course, it could be the part of art to speak like this precisely for the purpose of showing how close human art can keep on the heels of mystical experience.

The debate as between Dante's art and his mystical experience must, I think, be left unsettled. There is, no doubt, a point of discontinuity between artistic intuition and mystical insight. It is difficult for the artist himself, let alone the reader, to discern that point.

The difficulty may be illustrated by the account which Dante gives of his entrance into the world of "pure light" beyond the world of time and space. "We have issued," says Beatrice, "beyond the limits of space to the heaven which is pure light." This light is described as "intellectual light full of love, love of true good full of joy, joy that transcends all sweetness."

The effect on Dante was a dazzlement to the point of blindness. Just as lightning can blind the eyes of the body, so the "living light" that shone about him wrapped him in so thick a veil of effulgence that nothing could be seen. This, says Beatrice, is the welcome given to the saints by divine love. In this way the human candle is made ready for the divine flame. All that Dante understood was that he had been lifted beyond the level of human powers.[83]

"I was enkindled with a new kind of vision so that there was no light however bright that my eyes could not sustain." What he saw with this new power of sight was "light in the form of a river of

---

[82] *Par.*, xxx, 22.   [83] *Ibid.*, 56, 7.

running radiance flowing between two banks, covered with the colors of a marvelous spring. And out from the stream shot living sparks that came to rest in the open flowers and looked like rubies set in gold. And then, as though intoxicated with the odors, the sparks replunged into the miracle of surging waters and unendingly as one spark entered another issued forth."[84]

Beatrice, "the sun of Dante's eyes," spoke once more. "The high desire that now burns within you to have some knowledge of what you see pleases me in proportion to your longing. But before you can quench such thirst to know you must drink of the stream itself." She added: "The river and the jewels that enter in and issue forth and the laughing of the flowers are but shadow-bearing prefaces to a reality too lofty for your present vision." Dante drank of the stream. As he did, what had seemed straight before now seemed circular, and the flowers and flames, like dancers at a ball, took off their masks, and, behold, what Dante saw was the two courts of heaven. He calls not upon the muses but on God Himself to aid his song. "O splendor of God by which I saw the high triumph of the realm of truth give me the grace to sing it as I saw it."[85] Who is to say whether this is poetry, prayer, or mystical experience?

The last canto of the *Paradiso* throws little additional light on the question. The opening prayer of St. Bernard is the most perfect tribute that Catholic art has ever paid to the "mother of beautiful love." In what follows Dante brings the ardor of holy desire to its ultimate reach, and he says so unmistakably in the passionate crescendo of the line, *l' ardor del desiderio in me finii.*[86] But when St. Bernard tells him — "with a look and a laugh" — to lift his eyes, we know that our feet are still on the high, but normal, ground of Catholic meditation. The prayer is still not mystical when the poet pleads: "O high light, lifted so far above our mortal thoughts, lend to my mind a little of what I saw, and make my tongue so strong that it may leave to people yet unborn at least a twinkling of thy glory."[87] At last Dante dares to "fix his face on the infinite good." He was blinded by excess of the "eternal light." All he could say was: "In its depth I saw the scattered leaves of all the universe gathered together and bound by love in a single volume." He believed that he saw the "universal form of all this knot of things"

[84] *Par.*, xxx, 61–69.   [86] *Par.*, xxxiii, 48.
[85] *Ibid.*, 97–99.   [87] *Ibid.*, 67–72.

because of the joy he felt in saying so. "But, oh! how short is speech, how weak to utter thought, and thought, to what I saw, how less it is than little!"[88] His clearest vision was of three rainbows with a single center but of equal size and different colors; and, somehow, in the divine effulgence, the human face of Christ, our Lord. As a record of authentic mystical experience it is not convincing. However, he seems to hint at one last storm of light in which his mind and will met God:

> *Ma non eran da ciò le proprie penne:*
> *se non che la mia mente fu percossa*
> *da un fulgore in che sua voglia venne.*[89]

That meeting may have made a mystic of him or, at least, some simpler kind of saint. For myself, I think it left him, what he was before, a laughing citizen of Christendom, loving nature, people, poetry, and prayer, and, above all else, the power, the wisdom, and the love that "moves the sun and all the stars."

[88] *Ibid.,* 121–123.
[89] *Ibid.,* 139–141.